J. G. A. Pocock has taught both history and political science in New Zealand, Britain, and the United States. He graduated from the University of New Zealand in 1946, and completed his Ph.D. at the University of Cambridge in 1952. The greater part of *The Ancient Constitution and the Feudal Law* was written while he was lecturer in history at Otago University, and it was published by the Cambridge University Press while he was Research Fellow of St. John's College. He returned to New Zealand in 1959 and for seven years was engaged in developing the teaching of political science at the University of Canterbury, where he was professor in charge of the department from 1963. He has held visiting appointments at Columbia and Chicago, and is now a Professor of History and Political Science at Washington University, St. Louis. He describes his main interest as the history of political thought, studied as the history of change in the self-conceptualization of political societies.

THE
ANCIENT CONSTITUTION AND
THE FEUDAL LAW

THE
ANCIENT CONSTITUTION AND
THE FEUDAL LAW

A STUDY OF
ENGLISH HISTORICAL THOUGHT
IN THE
SEVENTEENTH CENTURY

BY

J. G. A. POCOCK

The Norton Library
W · W · NORTON & COMPANY · INC ·
NEW YORK

CONTENTS

CONTENTS

PREFACE

I have tried in this book to present a theory of the fundamental nature and problems of constitutional historiography in the seventeenth century. I have not attempted to analyse exhaustively the character of English thought about the past, or to study the way in which constitutional history and theory were used as a source of arguments in contemporary political debate. It has seemed more illuminating instead to oppose to one another what appear to have been the two most important schools of thought: the common lawyers with their belief that the constitution was immemorial, and the few dissentients who sought to upset this theory by pointing out that it had once been informed with the principles of feudal tenure; to show how these interpretations arose; and to consider how they were related to some of the essential ideas in contemporary political theory and how these connexions encouraged or hampered their development. From the whole, it is hoped that there will emerge a picture of one of the most typical and necessary, but by historians one of the most neglected, strands in the thought of the seventeenth-century English: the attempt to understand themselves by understanding their past and their relation to it. This may partly excuse my failure to deal with Elsynge, Selden, Twysden, Somner, and many other good historians of that age, as fully as they deserve.

In trying to carry out this purpose, I have been led to put forward a certain generalization about the history of historiography. This is, in brief, that during the sixteenth and seventeenth centuries one of the most important modes of studying the past was the study of the law; that many European nations obtained knowledge of their history by reflecting, largely under the stimulus of contemporary political developments and theories, upon the character of their law; that the historical outlook which arose in each nation was in part the product of its law, and therefore, in turn, of its history; and that the importance of this aspect of the subject has been too little observed by historians of historiography. I have endeavoured to show, by contrasting English historical thought at one point with French and at another with Scottish thought, that the former's fundamental limitations in this age arose from its having been compelled to contemplate the national past through one system of law alone. The full working-out of the theory would necessitate a history of English historiography far more exhaustive than anything attempted here, and probably also a comparative study designed to show how its character diverged from that of historiography in other western nations, in obedience to the determining forces suggested above. (I may be allowed to express my sense of indebtedness to Sig. Rosario Romeo's study of the development of Sicilian historical thought in his *Il Risorgimento in Sicilia*, from which I have received far more illumination than appears on the surface.) The history of historiography is a branch of study still in process of establishing itself, and it has been said that in England its main problems are not yet even defined; as a contribution to the studies of the future, this work may be allowed some place.

It grows out of a thesis submitted in 1952 for the Ph.D. degree, entitled 'The Controversy over the Origin of the Commons, 1675–88', which was in essence a study of Robert Brady and of the polemic in which he took part. I must express my gratitude to Professor H. Butterfield and Dr J. H. Plumb for their help and encouragement, and it would be improper not to mention two studies of seventeenth-century historiography without which this study would certainly never have been written: Professor Butterfield's *The Englishman and his History* and Professor D. C. Douglas's *English Scholars*. The work has been completed under the auspices of the University of Otago, and it is a pleasure to mention those sources in New Zealand from which I have received help in procuring the books necessary to this investigation: first, the University of New Zealand for two research grants used in making purchases;

Preface

second, the librarian, head of accessions and staff of the Otago University Library; and the Alexander Turnbull Library and General Assembly Library, Wellington, and the Supreme Court Law Library, Dunedin. And both in Cambridge and New Zealand, the friends whose aid and criticism I have enjoyed are too numerous to mention.

J. G. A. POCOCK

DUNEDIN, 1955

NOTE: In quotations from printed books I have followed as far as possible the punctuation, capitalization and italicization of the original; but where contemporary manuscripts are quoted I have expanded the contractions and taken little account of practices differing from modern usage. In translating Latin and French passages quoted I have not attempted to give complete and exact versions; the translations are intended as guides to the sense rather than exact renderings of the often recherché Latin of the scholars of a past time.

FOREWORD

No changes have been made in the text of this edition, but a full bibliography of the sources originally used has been provided and a further selection of books and articles has been added. When this book first appeared ten years ago, the genre to which it belongs was smaller than it has since become. This genre may be described as attempting to unite the study of the political and historical thought of past societies by observing the extent to which both arise from awareness of the society's continuity in time as a legal and institutional structure. Thought of this kind varies with the institutional structure of each society, with its modes of becoming aware of that structure and of time as the dimension of continuity and contingency in which it exists, and with the character of the challenges to which systems of ideas based on this awareness are forced to respond. In an age like our own, of intense and painful consciousness of history, the sources of that consciousness are of importance to humanists and social scientists, and there is growing up a sizeable scholarly literature on those of its roots which lie in the thought of Western European societies during the early modern period.

In order to assist the student, a select bibliography of books and articles in this field has been appended to the present edition.

J. G. A. POCOCK

WASHINGTON UNIVERSITY, ST. LOUIS

NOVEMBER, 1966

CHAPTER I

Introductory: the French Prelude to Modern Historiography

I

THIS book has been written in an attempt to throw light upon one aspect of the rise of modern historiography, a movement whose beginnings in general may with some assurance be dated from the sixteenth century. For it was then that the historian's art took on the characteristic, which has ever since distinguished it, of reconstructing the institutions of society in the past and using them as a context in which, and by means of which, to interpret the actions, words and thoughts of the men who lived at that time. That this is the kernel of what we know as historical method needs no demonstration; that it distinguishes modern from ancient historiography may be seen by means of a comparison with the historical methods of the Greeks and Romans. The ancient historians discovered and brilliantly developed the art of constructing an intelligible narrative of human affairs; they described contemporary societies alien to their own and noted the varieties of human conduct and belief that arose in the context of different climates and traditions; but they did not quite reach the point of postulating that there existed, in the past of their own civilization, tracts of time in which the thoughts and actions of men had been so remote in character from those of the present as to be intelligible only if the entire world in which they had occurred were resurrected, described in detail and used to interpret them. Nor did Greco-Roman historians assert that there existed a distinct and satisfactory method of doing this. The histories that they wrote, therefore, consisted of narratives of military and political affairs, or of comparative political analysis; they did not consist of researches into the past, conducted on the assumption that the past was a special field of study, to be understood only by the discovery of its own laws and the development of an appropriate technique of investigation.[1] Yet this is so much the dominant characteristic of modern historiography as to have taken precedence over the older art of constructing narratives; when (but only when) the historian has completed his researches into a past stage of society, he faces the problem of incorporating his conclusions into a narrative, the theme of which will be not only the actions of men and governments, but the never-ceasing changes in the structure of society—and the interactions between these two aspects of his subject. To discover how the notion of re-constructing the past began to dominate the minds of historians and compete for their attention with the older claims of history conceived as a narrative art is, then, of prime importance to the historian of historiography.

The Greco-Roman historians did not develop a special technique for the exploration of the past because—paradoxical though it may seem in the pioneers of historiography—the past as such was not sur-passingly important to them. This is not the place to discuss the problem of *spatium historicum*, of the boundaries of the historical and the mythical in their vision of the past,[2] but one point can be made which is essential to the present argument. The Greeks and Romans were not conscious, as medieval and modern Europeans have alike been conscious, of an organized civilization existing in their im-mediate past and affecting the whole range of their life through the survival of its institutions, its ideas, its material remains and its documents. There was no past world which they felt the need, or possessed the evidence, to explore; and their historical sense was

[1] The peculiar shrewdness of Thucydides' comments on the past history of Hellas (Book I, ch. I) underline rather than modify the point made here. There is no past civilization for him to reconstruct from its documents; and if, in the absence of written material (other than recorded tradition), he shows a keen sense of the importance of such things as the size and site of towns, the date of their construction, the development of sea power and the fertility of the soil, neither he nor the other Greek historians founded a science of handling this sort of evidence. Modern historiography depends on the survival of a great many documents from a past state of society, and on a deep sense that these are important in the governance of the present.

[2] Some comments on this question are made in an article, 'Spatium His-toricum', by W. von Leyden, in the *Durham University Journal*, XLII, no. 3 (n.s. XI, no. 3), June 1950, p. 89.

developed in the exploration of their own world and its comparison with contemporary alien societies. But the sense that Rome is a past world ever present to us, and the need to understand it and define our own relation to it, have been cardinal facts in the thoughts of Europeans both medieval and modern; and if the desire to conduct researches into the past is a distinguishing mark of modern European historiography, it is surely in Europe's sense of indebtedness to the ancient world that we should look for its rise and origins.

An obvious field in which to make our inquiries is that subtle change in the techniques of classical scholarship—in, that is to say, the method of approach to the ancient world—which we denote by the name of humanism. It has long been a commonplace that phrases like 'the revival of classical antiquity' are meaningless as applied to humanism, unless modified in the light of the fact that medieval thought was fully as obsessed with the importance of classical antiquity as was the thought of the Renaissance, and that the two differed only, if profoundly, in the methods which they adopted in order to understand it better. Medieval and Renaissance men alike sought to model themselves upon antiquity, to accept its teachings and its canons as authoritative so far as they could: but the methods adopted by the synthesizing and allegorizing mind of the Middle Ages were such on the whole as to lead to an imaginative conflation of the life of antiquity with the life of the contemporary world. Hector and Alexander were knights; Christ's trial before Pilate was imagined as taking place according to the forms of feudal law; and, on a more serious and practical level of scholarship, the terminology of Roman law was unhesitatingly applied to the governance of medieval Europe. It lies beyond the present writer's competence to determine how far, if at all, medieval men were conscious of what they were doing in this respect; some sense that Rome was not Christendom there obviously was; but it seems sufficiently clear that no need was felt to distinguish, to point out in what respects the life of the past differed from that of the present, or to found a systematic science of doing so. This came about, however, as a result of the new approach to the past initiated by the humanists; but it came about accidentally, indirectly and paradoxically.

Humanist thought insisted, even more strongly than medieval, on the need to take the ancient world as a model, but it expressed vehement dissatisfaction with the presentation of antiquity by medieval learning. It pointed out that the supposedly authoritative ancient texts had been overlaid with many layers of commentary, allegory and interpretation, and that often it was the commentary and not the text which was being studied. It called for a return to the pure text—such a cry had been raised before—and it claimed continually to understand the text better than the commentators had—a claim which increased source-material and improved techniques often enabled it to make good. At this point, however, we encounter what is at once the paradox and the true importance of the humanist movement, viewed from the standpoint of the history of historiography; for it is not too much to say that in making these claims and demands the humanists were calling for a return to the ancient world 'as it really was'—and we cannot express their programme in these words without realizing that we stand on the threshold of the modern historical consciousness. And the paradox which was to complete the transition was this: the humanists aimed at resurrecting the ancient world in order to copy and imitate it, but the more thoroughly and accurately the process of resurrection was carried out, the more evident it became that copying and imitation were impossible—or could never be anything more than copying and imitation. That which was ancient belonged to the ancient world, was bound up with and dependent upon innumerable things which could not be brought back to life, and consequently it could not be simply incorporated with contemporary society. A recent study[1] has traced anew the way in which the humanist endeavour to return to the language and grammar of classical Latin ended with Latin a dead language, one which could no longer be freely and naturally used as part of every-day European life. It became, says the author, something of merely historical or even antiquarian interest, part of a vanished world important only to those who cared to study it for its own sake. But he also shows how this process was accompanied by the growth of new branches of study aimed at describing the world

[1] R. R. Bolgar, *The Classical Heritage and its Beneficiaries* (Cambridge, 1954).

in which Latin authors had lived, sometimes even at seeing it through their own eyes, and at interpreting their writings as part of that world.[1] In short, the humanists, going far beyond their original purpose, relegated Greco-Roman wisdom inescapably to the past and robbed it, in the end, of all claim to be applied immediately and directly to modern life; but at the same time they called attention to the problem of the past as an independent field of study and began vigorously to perfect techniques for its exploration. If research into the past conceived as a distinct science is the mark of the modern historian, it was the humanists who laid its foundations.[2] Nor was this all. They showed that Greco-Roman civilization formed an independent world, a world of the past, but they did not, indeed could not, rob the European mind of its sense of being deeply and vitally affected by the fact that the past, in some way, still survived. Thus their work raised the whole question of the relation between past and present. Was the past relevant to the present? was there any point in studying it? what was the status of its survivals in the present? and, perhaps above all, how had it become the present? The problem of historical change, conceived as more complex and universal than ever before as new researches into the character of ancient civilization were undertaken, was affecting European thought well before the end of the sixteenth century. It is, then, to the paradox of humanism that we should look for the beginnings of modern historiography.

The humanist contribution was to institute a historical outlook and the rudiments of a historical technique in many branches of European scholarship. But the importance of this movement does not seem to have received the attention it deserves in our histories of

[1] Bolgar, *op. cit.* pp. 376–7. The auxiliary studies he mentions are geography, botany, literary criticism, archaeology and chronology, all in application to classical antiquity.

[2] A similar process is described by some students of the revolutionary changes that have come about in Confucian scholarship in China during the last half-century—see e.g. Ku Chieh-kang, *The Autobiography of a Chinese Historian* (Leiden, 1931), translator's preface by A. W. Hummel. It would be interesting to have some comparative studies of the effects which the transmission and scrutiny of authoritative texts have produced upon historical thought in different civilizations.

historiography. Many causes may be assigned for this apparent neglect. The movement was extremely slow—its full effects were not felt before the early eighteenth century—and it was often helped on its way by scholars unaware of the full import of what they were doing, who continued to believe that the past should be studied for the sake of moral instruction, as a storehouse of examples to be imitated or avoided. This cardinal principle of humanism, as is often pointed out, hindered, or at least did not favour, the development of historical thought; yet it is not the whole story about the history of historiography in the sixteenth and seventeenth centuries, and the mistake should not be made of writing as if it were. The development of historical thought can be shown to have continued, in a multitude of diverse ways, in spite of the humanist bent for moralizing. But the neglect of historians can be further accounted for by the fact that this development was so various and diffuse. Its history is not a simple question of one or two distinct and easily recognizable sciences evolving rapidly and carrying others along with them—as mathematics, physics and astronomy provide the central theme in the history of the scientific revolution—but of a historical approach developing accidentally and perhaps marginally upon the fringes of innumerable departments of scholarship, and evolving in each case a historical technique appropriate to that branch of study. The history of historiography cannot therefore be written as the study of a single evolution; all that can be done, at least for the present, is to trace the growth of the historical outlook in some of the fields where it most plainly manifests itself.

But it is one of the great facts about the history of historiography that the critical techniques evolved during the sixteenth and seventeenth centuries were only very slowly and very late combined with the writing of history as a form of literary narrative; that there was a great divorce between the scholars and antiquarians on the one hand, and the literary historians on the other; that history as a literary form went serenely on its way, neither taking account of the critical techniques evolved by the scholars nor evolving similar techniques of its own, until there was a kind of pyrrhonist revolt, a widespread movement of scepticism as to whether the story of the past could be reliably told at all. The character of this revolt has been

6

studied by Paul Hazard;[1] the eyes of its leaders were plainly fixed
upon history in the sense of literary narrative, to the exclusion of the
critical methods of determining the reliability of facts about the past
which were being rapidly developed by scholars such as Mabillon. If
they had paid closer attention to such men, the intensity of their
pyrrhonist despair might have been less.[2] But a rather similar error
seems to have been made by modern historians. The history of
historiography has been studied as if it could be identified with the
history of those literary works which bear the title of histories, and
in consequence a one-sided view has arisen which ascribes not
nearly enough importance to the work of scholars who did not
write narrative histories. The late Johan Huizinga, for example,
wrote on one occasion that of all the modern sciences history owed
least to the medieval university.[3] With this one exception, he said,
the modern sciences had evolved by a process of budding-off from
one or other of the three great faculties of theology, medicine or
law, or from one of the lesser arts of the trivium or quadrivium;
but if history figured in the medieval curriculum at all, it was as a
sub-department of rhetoric, as a mere form of declamation without
critical purpose or method, and consequently its evolution into a
critical science had occurred outside the university altogether.

Now this is a judgment which can be maintained only if we are
resolved to identify history with the literary form bearing that name.
Once we are rid of that obsession, we shall remember the fact—
perfectly well known from a variety of standard works[4]—that non-

[1] In ch. 2 of *La Crise de la conscience européenne* (Paris, 1935), 'De l'ancien
au moderne'. See also A. Momigliano, *Contributo alla storia degli studi
classici* (Rome, 1955), pp. 79–94.

[2] Marc Bloch's *Métier d'historien* brings out most clearly the contrast
between Mabillon's critical method and any sort of pyrrhonism.

[3] In *Sobre el estado actual de la ciencia histórica* (Madrid, 1934), pp. 12 ff.;
quoted in F. Rosenthal's *A History of Muslim Historiography* (Leiden, 1952),
p. 29 n.

[4] E.g. F. W. Maitland's *English Law and the Renaissance*; Holdsworth's
History of English Law, vol. IV; H. D. Hazeltine, 'The Renaissance', in *Cambridge Legal Essays* (1926); W. F. Church, *Constitutional Thought in Sixteenth-
century France* (Cambridge, Mass., 1941); M. P. Gilmore, *Argument from Roman
Law* (Cambridge, Mass., 1941); J. Declareuil, *Histoire générale du droit
français* (Paris, 1925); R. Dareste, *Essai sur François Hotman* (Paris, 1850).

narrative historical work of the highest originality and complexity was being carried on in the French universities of the sixteenth century—a time when their organization and curriculum were certainly still medieval—and that this historical thought had developed in the faculty of law. The historical school of Renaissance jurists furnishes the subject of the remainder of this chapter, but one further point remains to be made. Text-book accounts of the history of historiography tend to produce the impression that, when the contribution of the sixteenth- and seventeenth-century scholars came to be reunited with narrative history to produce major historical writings recognizably like those of the present day, it amounted to little more than a vast accumulation of more or less verified facts, of which giants like Robertson or Gibbon could make use. This is not altogether so, as will be seen. The earlier scholars were more or less consciously engaged in returning facts to their historical context and interpreting them there, and it has already been suggested that this was bound to present complex problems for historical reflexion; problems concerning the relation of the past to the present, and its survival in the present. With the lawyers this was peculiarly the case, because the data they were assigning to a past context were simultaneously the principles on which present society was endeavouring to govern itself. The historical problems with which a sixteenth-century scholar found himself concerned could therefore be adult, practical to the point of urgency, and even philosophically profound. His thought about them might be of great importance to himself and his generation, and might permanently affect the historical understanding of his civilization. Thought of this kind therefore forms a real and significant part of the history of historiography.

II

The historical approach to the study of Roman law was a product of humanism and shared in the characteristics, already traced, of that movement. It arose, primarily in French universities but under some Italian influence, in the form of a reaction against the methods of legal study associated with the name of Bartolus. The principal humanist criticism of the Bartolist school was that they had overlaid the original Justinianean text with an unmanageable wealth of glosses and commentaries, and that a return should be made to the purity of the original. But it had also been Bartolus's constant endeavour to adapt the Roman text to the world he himself lived in by applying Roman principles and definitions to contemporary phenomena—the degree of his historical awareness does not form part of the present inquiry—and this lent a peculiar importance to the legal humanists' endeavour to return, not only to the pure text of the Roman original, but to the meaning which these laws had possessed in the minds of the Romans who penned them. In the first place, it may be imagined, many of the humanists set about their task in the belief that the true principles of Roman jurisprudence, when found, would prove of such surpassing wisdom that they need only be directly imitated and applied in the present day; but they ended by achieving something much more than even a complete undoing of the work of Bartolus. They set out to establish the exact meaning of the Roman texts, and this, as they rightly saw, involved a detailed exegesis of the exact meaning of all technical or doubtful words which the texts contained. Therefore they set about comparing and establishing the various meanings which all such words bore, first in the separate legal texts which employed them, and secondly, in any other works of ancient provenance in which they might be found; and thus it was that detailed and conscious historical criticism made its appearance in the schools of jurisprudence under the name of 'grammar', the science of the meaning and use of words.[1] It is the peculiar characteristic of a comprehensive system of law like the Roman that it provides a close and extensive description of the principal institutions and many of the ideas of the society for which it was formed; and the historical school—as the humanist lawyers soon became—could not translate the language of Roman law back into its original meanings without reconstructing just such a picture of the society of imperial

---

[1] The best study of a jurist of this school at work seems to be P. E. Viard's *André Alciat* (Paris, 1926, for the University of Nancy). See also L. Delaruelle, *Guillaume Budé (1468–1540): les origines, les débuts, les idées maîtresses* (Bibliothèque de l'Ecole des Hautes Etudes; Sciences Historiques et Philologiques, 162e fascicule, Paris, 1907).

Rome. They gathered much of their evidence for this picture from the text of the law itself, but much more important was the fact that they sought to interpret the law according to the context of a reconstructed society. Inadequate, piecemeal and *ad hoc* their work may have been, but the essentials of the historical method were there and were known to be there. In this way the legal humanists came to be historians, and the full impact of their work on European thought has never yet been measured.

They had begun to study the past on principles which assumed its unlikeness to the present, and this soon brought them into contact with profound educational and practical problems. The society they were reconstructing was one which differed in all its structure from their own, and one, furthermore, which no longer existed. The law which they were studying belonged to that past world, and all its language and all its thoughts had reference to social institutions which were no longer anywhere to be found. Yet this same law was still in force over a wide, indeed an increasing area of Europe, and the world stood deeply committed to an endeavour to rule itself according to Roman principles. Were not the historical school making nonsense of that endeavour, for how should a law be obeyed which had been framed for utterly different conditions and no longer bore its original meaning? And if this question were satisfactorily answered, why then should young men spend years of their lives reducing the law to its original meanings? What was the status of ancient law in a changed world; why should it any longer be studied? The lawyers here touched unexpectedly on the problem of time, encountering it in a new and urgently practical form. There are signs of mounting discontent with the historians soon after 1560; for as France moved into an era of administrative breakdown and devastating civil war, it became more than ever necessary for her intellectuals to lay down clear principles of right and obligation, which might guide her back to order and peace. The whole medieval attitude to questions of legal and secular wisdom, the whole tradition of French governmental and political thought, predisposed her to seek such principles in Roman law. But the very possibility of this the professors of Bourges and Toulouse seemed to deny. Cujas (the story may be apocryphal), when asked to apply

his learning to contemporary problems, would reply merely:
'Quid hoc ad edictum praetoris?' It was a heroic answer, for in the
name of pure scholarship he was in effect denying European civilization the use of one of the principal canons by which she was accustomed to guide herself. That civilization had been shaped, in large
measure, by the traditional interpretation of certain authoritative
documents. In the name of a more accurate interpretation, a
historical interpretation had been formulated; and in the name of
historical interpretation, the relevance of the past to the present was
apparently being denied. The moment was revolutionary and the
tension could not be allowed to endure. A remedy was indeed
found, but one which took account of the new learning. Though
the attempt to draw fundamental political principles from Roman
law continued, it had suffered a radical criticism which could not
but modify its character.[1]

In the first decade of the French religious wars three books at
least were written—each of them addressed, in whole or in part, to
the Chancellor, Michel de l'Hôpital—in the endeavour to solve the
problem, bring history and jurisprudence back into concord, and
restore the past to some sort of relevance to the present. These were
François Baudouin's *De institutione historiae universae et ejus cum
jurisprudentia conjunctione* (1561), Jean Bodin's *Methodus ad facilem
historiarum cognitionem* (1566), and François Hotman's *Anti-Tribonian*
(1567). Of the three, Hotman's book is probably not the greatest;
that title must be granted to the strange semi-ruinous mass of Bodin's
Methodus; but *Anti-Tribonian* tells us much about the directions in
which historical thought in the field of law was moving, and reveals
to what lengths the new method of criticism might be carried by an
impudent and restless mind. With the promptness of the *enfant
terrible* (admittedly he was forty-three and about to take up Cujas's
chair at Bourges) Hotman announces that the Roman law is the
most useless of all studies to the modern Frenchman, be he practising
lawyer or cultivated amateur. He bases this declaration on the
ground that Roman law is the law of a past society, radically differ-

---

[1] Gilmore's *Argument from Roman Law*, just cited, traces the successive
interpretations of the Roman concept of *merum imperium* and shows how they
were affected by the methods of Cujas and by the reaction against them.

ent in structure from that of contemporary France, so that when he reproaches the 'grammarians' like Cujas with devoting themselves to useless antiquarianism, it is actually their own discovery that he is using to make them ridiculous. In all that he wrote, Hotman was standing on the shoulders of the historical school and endeavouring to carry their method beyond anything they had envisaged and indeed to reduce it to absurdity. They had shown that Justinian's code was the law of a past society; he would show that it was not even that. His two-edged criticism of Roman law as a subject worth studying is expressed in the heading of his third chapter: 'Que l'estat de la Republique Romaine est fort different de celuy de France, & neantmoins ne se peut apprendre par les liures de Iustinian.'[1]

The Codes and Digests are useless to the lawyer because they bear no relation to modern society; they are useless to the historian because they are not the law that was practised at Rome at any time in its history. Justinian's codifiers preserved no connected body of earlier law; they altered much and what they did not alter they scattered and rearranged; what they did not retain they destroyed; and, in short, there is nothing in their work which gives us any picture worth having of Roman law under either the republic or the empire—as is clear from the work of those scholars who have attempted to reconstruct Roman methods of government and have been compelled to do so from sources outside the law.[2] Nor are the Codes of much assistance even to the historian of Byzantium:

Quant au Constantinopolitain (qui fut blasonné le nouueau Romain) ie confesse que l'on en void à la trauerse quelques traces & enseignes, principalement aux trois derniers liures du Code, mais si petites & si escartees par-cy par-là, que par le iugement d'vn chacun il en faut deuiner les deux tiers: & qui plus est, tant s'en faut que des trois liures du Code on cognoisse l'estat du dernier Empire Romain, qu'au contraire il est impossible d'entendre lesdits liures sans preallablement auoir acquis la cognoissance dudit estat par la lecture des historiens: comme (apres les sus-nommez) d'vn Iulius Capitolinus, d'vn Vopiscus, d'vn Ammianus, Procopius, Zonaras et

---

[1] All quotations are from the 1603 edition of *Anti-Tribonian*, published at Paris.
[2] *Anti-Tribonian*, pp. 13–15, 18, 35–6, 86–7.

leurs semblables: tellement que c'est vne pure mocquerie de dire qu'il faille lire les liures de Iustinian pour cognoitre l'histoire. Car tout à rebours il est force de sçauoir l'histoire pour les entendre, & encores auec fort grande difficulté; & mesmes vsant souuentesfois plutost de coniecture que de fondement certain & asseuré.[1]

The criticism is in some respects shallow, in others profound. In its virtues and its vices, it is dominated by the idea of carrying historical criticism to the point where it destroys itself. The school of Cujas had shown that it was possible to describe law in terms of the society from which it came; but Hotman believed he could prove that the law of Justinian was not the law of Roman society at any time before Justinian's own. This in his eyes robbed it of nearly all its value. Law must be appropriate to the state it was designed to govern—Cujas's researches had underlined that truth—but the fact that Roman law could not be used as a guide to the historical interpretation of republic or empire showed that it was appropriate to none, and was therefore hardly a law at all. In *Anti-Tribonian*, Hotman would not even allow that it was appropriate to the conditions of Justinian's own time, although in a later work[2] he admitted that the Byzantine lawyers, 'qui non Rempub. ad Leges, sed has ad illam accommodandas esse intelligebant', did right to alter most of the Roman law in favour of 'nouas suas leges ad suae Graeciae rationem accommodatas'. But in the earlier book Justinian's law is nothing but a mass of 'inconstances et mutabilitez', neither a clear statement of Rome's traditional law nor an exposition

[1] 'As for the law of Constantinople (which proclaimed itself that of new Rome) I confess that we can dimly perceive a few hints and traces of it, mostly in the last three books of the Code, but so small and so scattered are those that by common consent we must attempt to divine two thirds of it; and what is more, so far from true is it that from these three books of the Code we can understand the condition of the late Roman Empire, that on the contrary it is impossible to understand these books of law without having previously acquired some knowledge of that state by reading the historians: such as (in addition to those mentioned earlier) Julius Capitolinus, Vopiscus, Ammianus, Procopius, Zonaras and their fellows; so that it is complete nonsense to say that we must read the books of Justinian in order to understand history. Quite the reverse; we are compelled to learn history in order to understand them, and even then it is extremely difficult, and we must often rely on conjecture rather than certain and assured knowledge.' *Anti-Tribonian*, pp. 20–1.   [2] *De feudis commentatio tripertita* (Lyons, 1573), dedication.

of the principles of jurisprudence. Of the controversy between Bartolists and humanists Hotman observes that it is not the method of either which is at fault.

Nous parlons du vice naturel & du deffaut interieur qui est en la matiere et substance de la discipline: lequel est bien plus difficile à corriger que les corruptions qui y sont arriuées par accidens exterieurs.[1]

In order to emphasize further the unreality and unsatisfactoriness of Roman law, Hotman contrasts it with the customary and feudal law prevailing in other parts of France; and it is here that the argument of *Anti-Tribonian* leads us into a new field, of wide significance. The writer rolls out the gnarled terminology of customary law, and points out with relish that if a man came into a French court knowing only the Roman code, though he knew it 'aussi parfaittement...comme fait vn Caton, vn Sceuola, ou vn Manlius', he might as well be among American savages.

Car là il n'orra jergonner que d'heritages cottiers ou surcottiers, des droits seigneuriaux, de iustice directe, censiue, recognoissance, de retraits lignagers ou feodaux, de rente fonciere ou volage, vest, deuest, saisine, dessaisine, droit de quart ou de requart, quint ou requint, droit d'afeurage ou chambellage, droit de champart, de frarenseté ou escleiches, de douaire coustumier ou prefix, de communauté de biens, & autres semblables propos qui lui s̄eront aussi nouueaux & estranges, comme s'il n'auoit en iour de sa vie ouy parler ny de loy ny de police.[2]

Now it is clear that these uncouth vocables, 'barbarous' according to all humanist standards, are being contrasted favourably with the classical clarity of Roman law, and that this is being done on the ground that they are custom and therefore appropriate to the state of France in a way that the written law of Constantinople can never be. Hotman's appeal from written to customary law is part of a fairly widespread reaction that was going on in sixteenth-century juristic thought; and one of the attractions of custom was precisely that it offered a means of escape from the divorce of past and present threatened by the criticisms of the historical school. Because Roman

---

[1] 'We are talking of the vices and faults which are inherent in the substance of this discipline, and are much harder to correct than the corruptions which have arrived by accident from outside.' *Anti-Tribonian*, p. 130.

[2] *Anti-Tribonian*, pp. 36–7.

law was written and unchangeable, it could be subjected to grammatical analysis and proved to belong to a past state of society, but because custom was by its nature unwritten law, the usages of the folk interpreted through the mouths of judges, it could be argued with some plausibility that it could never become obsolete. If this custom no longer suited the needs of the people, it was said, they would by now have thrown it away; that they have not done so proves that, however ancient it may be, it cannot be out of date. Conversely, the essence of custom was that it was immemorial, and the argument could with equal facility be used that, since the people had retained a given custom through many centuries, it had proved itself apt to meet all the emergencies which had arisen during that period. Custom was *tam antiqua et tam nova*, always immemorial and always perfectly up-to-date. We shall see both arguments developed, and the idealization of custom carried to an extraordinary height, by the English common lawyers of James I's reign. Hotman does not adopt such extreme views, but there can be little doubt that it is as custom that he is praising French native law in the passage quoted. He emphasizes that France is a feudal society of non-Roman origin; that the purity of Frankish custom was preserved for five hundred years untrammelled by Roman influences;[1] and that it is legal dogma that the authority of Roman law is never so great as that of use and custom.[2] There were good reasons, as we shall see, why Hotman's juristic theory could never be founded exclusively on custom, but we are safe in seeing in *Anti-Tribonian* one sign of that reaction towards the customary, the native, the feudal and the barbarous, which was discernible in contemporary thought and may have furnished one of the roots of European romanticism:[3] for it constantly opposed the folk to the legislator, the primitive, the inarticulate and the mutable to the rigidities of ordered reason.[4]

But with the reaction in favour of customary and native codes of

---

[1] *Anti-Tribonian*, pp. 137–8.   [2] *Anti-Tribonian*, pp. 101–2.

[3] H. D. Hazeltine, *loc. cit.*, termed this reaction that of the 'national jurists'.

[4] 'We were having a little Renaissance of our own; or a Gothic revival, if you please'; Maitland (in *English Law and the Renaissance*) on the renewal of common-law studies, which took the form of an idealization of custom.

law we enter the field of contemporary political thought. If it is no longer as certain as it once was that the extension of monarchical authority and the reception of Roman law went everywhere hand in hand, the fact remains that the sixteenth and seventeenth centuries were throughout western Europe a time of collision between the authority of kings and local or national privileges, liberties and constitutions. Many of these latter were rooted in feudal custom, some could even be dimly traced back to the customs of the Germanic invaders of the empire, and all were more or less permeated by the essential medieval idea of law as a thing ancient, immanent and unmade, proof against invasion by human wills because no will had made it. Since there was an increasing tendency to claim sovereignty in the full sense for the king, it was natural that those who sought to defend threatened privileges or liberties should emphasize in return that their rights were rooted in a law which no king could invade. Theologians and philosophers might try to equate these rights with reason and nature, which should be above all wills; but another and no less telling argument was to demonstrate that they partook of the nature of immemorial, sacred custom. In this way there grew up—or rather, there was intensified and renewed—a habit in many countries of appealing to 'the ancient constitution', of seeking to prove that the rights it was desired to defend were immemorial and therefore beyond the king's power to alter or annul. Hotman in *Francogallia* asserted the antiquity of the assembly of the nation; Coke in England that of parliament and the common law; Pietro de Gregorio in Sicily that of baronial privilege and the *parlamento*; François Vranck in the Netherlands that of the sovereign and independent Dutch towns; Erik Sparre in Sweden that of the nobles in their *riksrad*.[1] By 1600 or there-

---

[1] *Francogallia* was first printed in 1573. Coke began to publish his *Reports* in 1600. De Gregorio's chief works were published in 1596; there is a full study of the evolution of Sicilian historical opinion down to 1848 in R. Romeo, *Il Risorgimento in Sicilia* (Bari, 1950), *passim*. Vranck's *Corte Vertooninghe* appeared in 1587; see G. N. Clark, 'The Rise of the Dutch Republic', *Proc. Brit. Acad.* (1946), pp. 196–7. Sparre was executed at Linköping in 1600; Michael Roberts in *Gustavus Adolphus: a History of Sweden, 1611–32*, vol. 1 (London, 1953), pp. 16–17, says his 'legal antiquarianism, his appeal to the *landslag*, recall Coke's brandishing of Magna Carta'.

abouts there was hardly any constitutional movement without its accompanying historical myth. No man granted us this liberty, it was said; it has been ours from beyond the memory of man; and consequently none can take it from us. In reply, the kings and their partisans tried to show that, in the words of James VI (and I), 'kings were the authors and makers of the laws and not the laws of the kings'.[1] If the constitutionalists could show that the laws were as old as, or older than, the kings, they might go on to assert a contractual or elective basis for kingship; but if the laws had come into being at a time when there was already a king, then nothing but the king's authority could have sanctioned them or made them law, and the king might assert a sovereign right to revoke what his predecessors had granted. The constitutionalists were therefore always being driven to argue that the laws were of a practically infinite antiquity, immemorial in the sense of earlier than the earliest king known. It could happen in this way that historical criticism became one of the sharpest weapons of monarchy, while the constitutionalists were forced into a kind of historical obscurantism—compelled to attribute their liberties to more and more remote and mythical periods in the effort to prove them independent of the will of the king. There were thus great dangers to the clarity of historical thought in the multiplication of these constitutional myths; but their importance in the history of historiography is nevertheless great.

There existed, therefore, in a number of European nations a kind of political thought which cannot satisfactorily be termed 'constitutionalism', since it involved a more intensive use of historical and antiquarian thinking than the use of that term normally implies. It may be provisionally defined as the attempt to settle fundamental political questions, notably those involving law, right and sovereignty, by appeal not directly to abstract political concepts, but to the existing 'municipal' laws of the country concerned and to the concepts of custom, prescription and authority that underlay them, as well as to the reverence which they enjoyed by reason of their antiquity—an attempt which necessarily involved the study, critical or otherwise, of their origins and history. One may reasonably

[1] *Political Works of James I*, ed. C. H. McIlwain (Cambridge, Mass., 1918), p. 62.

claim that the history of European political thinking, at any rate in the sixteenth to eighteenth centuries, will be incomplete until we know more about this branch of thought than we now do; but relatively little work has been done upon it and we still lack a compendious term with which to describe it. To call it 'constitutional antiquarianism' would perhaps do less than justice to the quality of the historical thought which its practitioners sometimes displayed; and the South Italian scholars, who appear to be the only historians who have studied its evolution as naturally forming part of the history of their states, use such terms as 'cultura storico-giuridica' and 'tradizione giuridica', which do not go well into English.[1] This form of thought is found in many countries besides Italy and, until Cartesian and Lockean techniques of political argument in part overcame it about 1700, it placed no small part in the history of political thinking. It is a thread which leads to Montesquieu, and to Burke. But its importance is not less in the history of historiography. It was largely through these attempts to determine the antiquity of their institutions that the nations of Europe embarked on the study of their medieval past and barbaric origins; and just as the Roman law had provided a highway to the historical study of Roman society, so now antiquarian-minded lawyers began to study the medieval past through the interpretation and analysis of those medieval systems of law which concerned them by surviving in their midst. But these forms of law differed so greatly, in their character and basic ideas, from the law of Justinian that it was inevitable that the historical thought engendered in their study should differ as greatly from that of Alciati and Cujas; and it is easy to see that in this way the idea of custom exerted a wide influence upon European historiography. Roman law, for instance, laid stress upon the concepts of will, command and the legislator, and tended therefore to encourage the already existing idea that each institution had originated at a particular time in the will of a particular individual who had established it in substantially its present form. This was the period in which Polydore Vergil wrote his *De inventoribus rerum* on the assumption that every invention

[1] Both terms are employed by Romeo, *op. cit.*; e.g. pp. 49, 81. See also L. Marini, *Pietro Giannone e il Giannonismo a Napoli nel Settecento* (Bari, 1950).

could be traced to an individual discoverer;[1] and in the field of legal history, Machiavelli could write with what seems singular naïveté of the man 'chi ordinó' so complex a creation of history as the monarchy of France.[2] To thought of this kind the idea of custom offered a salutary corrective; all its emphasis was on gradual process, imperceptible change, the origin and slow growth of institutions in usage, tacit consent, prescription and adaptation. We may never know how much of our sense of history is due to the presence in Europe of systems of customary law, and to the idealization of the concept of custom which took place towards the end of the sixteenth century. To it our awareness of process in history is largely owing.

But this freedom was bought at a great price, and the concept of custom undoubtedly did much to impede the growth of a critical approach to medieval and barbarian history. As we have seen, it was because Roman law was written that it could be reduced to the context of a past society and its relevance to the present day questioned; and custom owed much of its popularity to its unwritten character, which enabled it to elude such drastic criticism and present the dangerously attractive spectacle of a form of law which was ever-changing yet ever the same, immemorial yet perfectly adapted to present needs. Custom therefore escaped the fate of being relegated to form part of a vanished society, while conversely medieval society was not reconstructed around the framework of a reinterpreted custom; and a critical spirit in medieval historiography was consequently slow to develop. The concept of the immemorial encouraged the fabrication of myths about immensely remote times, and the fact that the appeal to early national history took the form of partisan controversy between sovereign and constitution enhanced this tendency in the way already outlined. In minds preoccupied with the idea of custom there arose a species of sixteenth-century romanticism: their myths derived the national laws not only from legendary and heroic times, but also from the primitive and inarticulate wisdom of the folk, expressed in age-old custom which

---

[1] See Denys Hay, *Polydore Vergil* (Oxford, 1952), ch. III.

[2] *Discorsi*, I, xvi; discussed by Pierre Mesnard, *L'Essor de la philosophie politique au XVIme siècle* (Paris, 1951), p. 83, who quotes de Maistre's comment, 'Je voudrais bien le connaître.'

was often contrasted favourably with the mere conscious ratio-
cination of individual legislators. Since their pursuit of ancient
laws and liberties often led them to seek these things in the customs
of the barbarian invaders, whom they identified with the Germans
described by Caesar and Tacitus, they made many contributions
to the legend of primitive Teutonic freedom and virtue, which was
growing up so rapidly in the sixteenth century and can expect so
little sympathy in the twentieth. There was a constant temptation to
deny that the law's history could be known, to wrap its origins in
mystery and assert that it had always, since time out of mind, been
as it was now. The study of the past through the medium of customary law was a dangerous business, and the enthusiast for custom
too often ended by alleging that his people had changed their laws
not at all since their heroic German ancestors had brought their free
institutions, already ancient, out of the forest to overthrow a
Roman Empire corrupted by tyranny.

Hotman's *Francogallia* may seem a book of this kind. The original
freedom of the Gauls, it says, virtually destroyed by the Romans,
was restored by the life-giving incursions of the Franks, and for
centuries thereafter, until the successful usurpations of Louis XI,
the assembly of the nation was supreme if not sovereign. By writing
in this way, Maitland thought, Hotman 'made himself in some sort
the ancestor of the Germanists',[1] and his pursuit of liberty into
barbaric times does indeed suggest that he idealized both ancient
custom and primitive Teutonic liberty. But the truth, it appears,
is less simple. To André Lemaire, the publication of *Francogallia*
in 1572 marked precisely the moment at which French publicists
ceased to represent their liberties as founded in ancient custom and
derived them instead from an original act of the sovereign people—a
very different idea, scholastic and civilian in its origin and not rooted
in the study of customary law. The medieval belief in custom,
according to this interpretation, was decaying in French thought,
assailed by partisans of royal absolutism on one hand and popular
sovereignty on the other.[2] There is the further difficulty that any

[1] *English Law and the Renaissance*, n. 28.
[2] Lemaire, *Les Lois fondamentales de la monarchie française d'après les
théoriciens de l'ancien régime* (Paris, 1907), pp. 92–102.

theory of sovereignty, rigorously interpreted, renders the appeal to the past unnecessary or of only emotional weight. If Hotman thought the people were sovereign, he added little to his argument by declaring that they had been so always; and J. W. Allen characteristically concluded that Hotman could not have given a satisfactory explanation of why he wrote in the form of an interpretation of history at all.[1] But on Lemaire's own showing, the older idea that French fundamental law derives its force from ancient custom is never far below the surface of Hotman's thought and he is prepared to revert to it at need. We should not think, therefore, that his political ideas were uninfluenced by his preference for customary over Roman law. But, as we shall see, it is not certain that he was in the habit of exalting the primitive liberty of the Germans. Neither idealization of custom nor idealization of German freedom appears to account satisfactorily for the thought of *Francogallia*, and it seems necessary to modify the account of constitutional antiquarianism so far given. If we now make a fresh approach to the question which Allen thought unanswerable, it may not solve the riddle of *Francogallia*, but it may further the objects of the present inquiry.

III

It has been assumed so far that the purpose of alleging an 'ancient constitution' was always to prove that the existing constitution, or some part of it, was immemorial custom and derived legally binding force in the present from that alone. But this is not altogether true: the sanctity of immemorial custom was only one reason why a law proved to be ancient should be immune from the sovereign's interference at the present day. It might instead be argued that the people were originally (and had remained) free and sovereign, and could be discerned in the deeps of time arranging their constitution to suit their convenience; or it might merely be held that the ancient constitution had kept the people happy for centuries and should accordingly be retained, or restored, as the case might be. There were a great many reasons why the ancient

[1] *Political Thought in the Sixteenth Century* (London, 3rd ed. 1951), pp. 309–10.

should be authoritative, and a great many influences at work to determine which of those reasons a polemicist would adopt. One of the most important of these determining factors must have been the character of the system of law prevailing in the country where the appeal to antiquity was being made. The various concepts of what is essential to law—custom, command, reason—were differently blended in different structures of legal thought, and as the blend varied so would the reasons for appealing to the past and thinking it authoritative in the present. A people accustomed to thinking in terms of customary law would naturally emphasize the idea that what was ancient and unmade was binding for that reason alone; a people accustomed to Roman law and the *lex regia* would go to the past in search of the original transfer of sovereignty and the character of that transaction. In countries where both systems of law obtained, thinking of this kind would be more complicated still. If a country was governed wholly by customary law, then it would be easy and natural to believe that everything in the constitution was rooted in immemorial usage and binding even on kings for that reason alone. But if the country was divided between a system of customary law and a system of law deriving its authority from the commands of named emperors living at stated times, then the appeal to the merely immemorial could not be made with at all the same degree of confidence; we should expect to find that if there was an appeal to antiquity, it was being made for much more complex and perhaps indeterminate reasons, and that the concept of custom itself was being subjected to criticism by those whose profession disposed them to think of law in terms of command. In this so far hypothetical comparison it would be possible to see that where there were different systems of law, the appeal to antiquity would be made for different reasons, and radically different attitudes to the history of institutions might arise.

France was a country of this kind, with Roman law in some of her provinces and various systems of customary law in others; and if we now return to the argument of *Anti-Tribonian*, we shall find that, though Hotman uses the naturalness and flexibility of custom as a stick with which to beat Roman law, his programme of legal reform by no means involved the wholesale abandonment of *droit écrit* in favour of *coutume*. Instead he proposes a plan of legal training in which the pupils undertake a comparative study of all known and valuable systems of law with the aim of distilling the essential principles of juristic reason which are common to all, until at the end all systems are swallowed up in the developed thought of the perfect judge, who (like St Louis under the oak at Vincennes) can dispense pure equity with no need of a law-book.[1] Hotman thus enunciates the principle known as neo-Bartolism, which came to dominate French juristic thought towards the end of the century, its central concept being that of discovering the fundamental principles of all systems of law. Since neo-Bartolism arose as a reaction against the rigidly historical approach of Cujas, its place in the history of historiography ought to be considered. Its primary aim was to restore the unity of past and present and deliver Roman law from the reproach of being irrelevant to the present day. The means it adopted strongly recall the humanist doctrine that the utility of history in general was that it could provide moral and practical examples to be imitated or avoided in the present; yet neo-Bartolist thought is somewhat more subtle than that. In the first place, like the destructive criticism of *Anti-Tribonian*, it virtually admits the validity of the theory it intends to displace. It tacitly agrees that Roman law belongs to the vanished world of Rome and cannot uncritically be taken over and used today; what is asserted is that Roman law contains certain principles of universal value, which may be isolated and universally applied. But this process must logically follow the process of historical criticism, and to that extent the validity of Cujacian procedure is not denied. 'I regret none of the time I have spent in expounding the law,' said Baudouin, 'but something more is needed.'[2] In the second place it ought to be noted that the neo-Bartolist, like any other lawyer, was not regarding the past as something dead and finished and merely to be imitated—a reproach which may sometimes be justly brought against the literary humanist. He started from the incontestable

[1] *Anti-Tribonian*, p. 140.
[2] Quoted in R. Dareste, *Essai sur F. Hotman*, p. 20. Baudouin's words were 'in jure docendo', and he appears to have meant the Cujacian technique of establishing the text and its meaning.

fact that laws belonging to a vanished past survived in the present and were playing an active part in shaping his own world, and he wanted to know how this was possible. If the explanations he put forward were sometimes unhistorical, this could not altogether change the fact that to the lawyer the past is alive in the present and history is contemporary history. There again is the peculiar importance of law in the history of historiography.

But Hotman's version of neo-Bartolism is not simply a means of bringing the study of Roman law back into relevance to the present —indeed, his criticisms had carried him past the point where he could admit that Roman law would be of much use in his scheme of legal education. It also affects the relations, within France, of written law and custom. Hotman does not make it perfectly clear in *Anti-Tribonian* whether the student will also study the *coutumes* and distil essential principles from them, though qualified judges have thought it safe to assume that this was his meaning.[1] But it seems just possible that custom was to be immune from this process of digestion. The end of Hotman's plan was to fill the pupil's mind with unwritten principles of equity, which he could apply to all circumstances and cases without need of a law-book—as St Louis did at Vincennes. But the law dispensed by St Louis might very well be termed the custom of his people, and it would not be impossible to claim that the collective wisdom of the folk achieved in custom an unwritten law applicable to all cases and capable of being identified with the unwritten equity to be evolved in Hotman's scheme of training. Custom might be idealized and described as perfect equity; the English common lawyers virtually reached this point. However, it is true that Hotman alludes to the possibility of codifying the customs,[2] and French historians have not found it possible to think of his proposals without relating them to the great labours of codification carried out in and after his time. In this process custom was subjected to the neo-Bartolist techniques of criticism, conflation and digestion; Du Moulin, the master of codi-

[1] E.g. Dareste.
[2] *Anti-Tribonian*, pp. 154–5; however, the reference here is to a plan of Louis XI's, who appears in *Francogallia* as the subverter of the ancient constitution.

fication, rather than Hotman, Bodin or Baudouin, is the great figure of the neo-Bartolist tradition. Let us take it, then, that the thought of *Anti-Tribonian* leads to the digestion of custom into more developed systems of law or equity.

But in this process custom lost much of its essential character. It has been shown at length in an American study[1] how in sixteenth-century France custom ceased to be regarded as something almost aboriginal, law merely in virtue of its antiquity, and was increasingly interpreted as subject to the authority of the king, until it was denied any legitimacy unless formally recognized and registered by a royal court. Now this did not come about merely because the king drew upon Roman ideas which found the origin of all law in *quod principi placuit*; it could only occur because the French king was ruler alike over *pays de droit écrit* and over *pays de coutumes*, and therefore imposed his authority alike upon both forms of law. Codification was an act of sovereignty, an assertion that the ruler's will and reason were superior even to ancient custom, and consequently it gave rise to the historical claim that custom had never had force but by the king's permission. And when replies were attempted, French constitutionalists could not very well assert that the laws of all the land at large were immemorial custom, because those of the *pays de droit écrit* manifestly were not. Some more universal reason must be found for the sanctity of ancient law. The reply usually made to the claim that custom was subject to the king, therefore, was, as the century went on, less and less that custom was simply immemorial usage, and more and more that it was derived from the people's right to provide for their own needs; and so a doctrine of popular sovereignty—itself perhaps of Roman origin—came to replace the older, purely medieval appeal to ancient unmade law.[2] Where custom co-existed with Roman law, thinkers could not simply allege that the laws of the land were immemorial; nor could the very doctrine that custom was immemorial escape

[1] W. F. Church, *Constitutional Thought in Sixteenth-century France*, pp. 100–20.

[2] Church, pp. 86–7, associates this doctrine with the name of Simon Marion (1570); it 'had rarely been expressed in France earlier in the century'. Of course the doctrine of popular sovereignty was itself medieval; the difference is that the doctrine of pure custom did not survive the transition to modern times.

criticism in the light of the competing idea that law originated in command. There would be a tendency for historians—whether party men or impartial scholars—to search for the act of will that had set up custom, and this would, in the first place, help to correct the obscurantist tendencies latent in the idea of custom; but in the second place, it would tend to dissolve the concept altogether and replace it by some doctrine of sovereignty, whether popular or royal. The simultaneous existence of systems of law that could be compared had a complex but stimulating effect upon both historical and political thought.

We are now perhaps better placed to understand the nature of the thought in *Francogallia*. Hotman is putting forward a doctrine of ancient liberty; yet its antiquity is not that of pure custom. Perhaps those scholars are right who take him to mean that popular sovereignty originally lay with the Gauls, was restored by the Franks and remained binding until his own day;[1] perhaps Allen had the truth of the matter, and Hotman fell between two stools and did not know what he meant. What is more, he is still writing as a neo-Bartolist who would like to see a conflation of all laws into some form of enlightened equity—a programme which could hardly be carried out without the assertion of some species of sovereignty; but though we hear once more of St Louis and the ideal unwritten justice which he dispensed at Vincennes, the saint's judgments, as quoted in *Francogallia*,[2] prove to have been commands that disputes between himself and his vassals should be heard in courts of vassals, and not in assemblages of learned lawyers such as the *parlements*, so that St Louis's justice would seem to have been essentially an injunction to observe feudal custom. It is not necessary to the present argument to determine exactly what Hotman meant in *Francogallia*; all that is necessary is to show why his appeal to ancient liberty cannot be reduced to the simple statement that the existing constitution of France is rooted in immemorial custom. It cannot be so, because there is no single system of customary law in France; because only parts of the constitution can be attributed to immemorial custom; and because the existence of laws with a

[1] Church, *op. cit.* p. 87, following Lemaire, *op. cit.* pp. 101–2.
[2] See pp. 143–5 of Robert Molesworth's translation (2nd ed., London, 1721).

known origin in command makes it harder than it would otherwise be to think of custom itself as immemorial. The thought of *Francogallia* is (it seems possible) incoherent, but if we turn to a work which its author published in the same year we can observe that, on the whole, these conditions stimulated rather than hampered a critical approach to the history of non-Roman systems of law, and that Hotman, for all his appeals to the *francsgaulois*, was far from idealizing Teutonic law as such.

De feudis commentatio tripertita, a study of the history of the feudal law, was written before the St Bartholomew massacres drove Hotman to flee from his chair at Bourges and was published in 1573; it is dedicated to Caspar Seydlitz, one of the German students who had urged him to lecture on the feudal law at Bourges.[1] Here if anywhere Hotman might have given rein to the 'Germanizing' tendencies so often attributed to him, and expressed the view, not uncommon in his day, that freedom was ancient Germany's gift to Europe. But after summarizing the attacks first made in *Anti-Tribonian* on the study of Roman law, he turns in his epistle dedicatory to the laws of the conquering barbarians.[2] 'Dici vix potest, quam absurdae atque inconditae leges'; the early Germans excelled beyond doubt as men of war, but as legislators they can only be compared to men teaching the Cimmerians to distinguish colours in the dark, while those who solemnly study and annotate their attempts to draw up codes are like the philosophers in Lucian, of whom some milked the he-goat while others held the sieve. In 'Francogallia nostra' there are as many laws and customs as there are cities and provinces, and a man might think there was no one form of justice or equity. Very little can be said about the written *coutumes* which was not said by the sophists who collected them. The Neapolitan Constitutions are a joke even to their editors; the law of England, as Polydore Vergil has shown, is dangerous, incomprehensible and written in a barbarous dialect; the authors of

[1] E. Blocaille, *Etude sur François Hotman* (Dijon, 1902), p. 40. Seydlitz seems to have been a Silesian; 'hic apud nos esses, de magno Germanorum adolescentum numero'.

[2] The rest of this paragraph is from the epistle dedicatory to Seydlitz, which is not paginated in the edition of 1573.

the *Sachsenspiegel* were probably fine fighting men. As for the feudal law, to which the sizable volume prefaced by this diatribe is entirely devoted, Hotman seems to regard it as worth studying principally for the light it sheds on the history of titles, honours and posts of government throughout all the states of Europe.

In the rather heavy facetiousness of this dedication, it may be felt that we have the humanist at his petulant worst; but that is in a sense its importance. Hotman remained a humanist, trained in the school of Bourges, and his attitude to all systems of law remained that of a historian, modified in the direction of neo-Bartolism. Because he thought it necessary to study all systems of law for the essential principles that were in them, he regarded none of them as more than relatively important or valuable. He regarded neither custom nor Germanic law as containing anything essential, original or fundamental that any other system of law might not contain. Each must be studied critically, which implied a readiness to reduce it to the context of the society from which it had sprung. We shall meet him in a later chapter performing this operation in a search for the origins of feudal custom, and there too it will be apparent that he was less disposed to emphasize the Germanic element in European law than is sometimes suggested. But the point of immediate importance is that Hotman's historical thought, even in its confusions, reflects the duality of custom and written law that marked the French legal structure. It was reaction against the Cujacian school that made him a neo-Bartolist in his attitude to Roman law, and gave him some traces of a tendency to idealize custom; but in the last analysis it would appear that he extended the neo-Bartolist critical approach to custom as well. Because custom in France existed side by side with Roman law it was possible to envisage the two growing up together in a single historical process, and this powerfully checked any tendency to exaggerate the purity and antiquity of custom. There were myths of constitutional antiquity in French thought, but they were formed in other ways.[1]

[1] See Jacques Barzun, *The French Race* (Columbia, New York, 1932); and Franklin L. Ford, *Robe and Sword* (Cambridge, Mass., 1953), ch. 12, 'The Restatement of the *Thèse Nobiliaire*'. But see also Lemaire, *op. cit.*, for a fuller study of the concepts of an 'ancient constitution' prevailing in France.

Introductory: the French Prelude to Modern Historiography

It could not be maintained that the whole of French law was custom, and it was hard to maintain that custom was immemorial in any too literal sense of the word. But where nothing but custom existed, there might be no such checks on the development of its myths.

It is suggested therefore that law did much to determine the character of sixteenth-century historical thought in the various countries of Europe: that the historical thinking encouraged by the study of Roman law, for instance, was of a different character from that bred in the study of customary law, and that each nation's thought about its past—it might be said, each nation's relationship with its past—was deeply affected by the character of its law and the ideas underlying it. That is the case for the importance of jurists and constitutional antiquarians and controversialists in the history of historiography.[1] The remainder of this book is concerned with the legal historiography of England—with the sort of historical thought that developed in a country where only one system of law, and that essentially customary, seemed ever to have prevailed.

[1] Readers of Professor Momigliano's paper 'Ancient History and the Antiquarian' (in his book cited above, pp. 67-106) may like to consider whether the legal historians of this epoch did not occupy a place midway between the historian and the antiquarian as defined by him. They were not narrative historians, but neither were they collectors of facts about the past like the antiquarians. The nature of their subject forced them to consider questions of the relevance of past to present and even (if in a rudimentary form) of historical development. Nevertheless, the present writer suspects that Professor Momigliano exaggerates a little (pp. 77-8) the extent of the rapprochement between historians and antiquarians in the field of post-classical history, with which, of course, the lawyers and constitutionalists were mostly concerned. His book, it must be added, is of the greatest value to the history of historiography.

CHAPTER II

The Common-law Mind: Custom and the Immemorial

I

AS a key to their past the English knew of one law alone. It was possible for them to believe that, as far back as their history extended, the common law of the king's courts was the only system of law which had grown up and been of force within the realm; for the records and histories of England did not reveal that any other law had been of comparable importance. The common law was and had been the only law by which land was held and criminals deprived of life by their country, and by which consequently the greater part of men's secular rights and obligations were determined. Civil and canon law and law merchant could be regarded, especially after the Reformation, as systems borrowed from abroad and confined within limits by the common law; and, most significant of all, there were no *pays de droit écrit* in which civil law governed the main fabric of social life. Except in Ireland, Celtic law was forgotten, and local customs, like those of Kent, survived only because the king's courts recognized them. The English need not think, as the French must, that a different system of law existed alongside their ancient native custom, one which had a different origin, had been introduced into the land at a different time and had grown up along different lines. Once the French began to think historically of their written law, they were bound to make some extension of this way of thinking to their customary law as well, and this acted as a check to any tendency they may have had to represent the whole of their law as immemorial custom. But in England it was precisely this tendency which ran riot. The English supposed that the common law was the only law their land had ever known, and this by itself encouraged them to interpret the past as if it had been governed by the law of their own day; but in addition the fact that the common law was a customary law, and that lawyers defined custom in a way which heavily emphasized its immemorial character, made even more radical the English tendency to read existing law into the remote past. An inclination to do this, to interpret the past according to the ideas and institutions of the present, is probably common to all societies aware of their history; it can never be absolutely expunged from historical thought, and there have been times in the history of historiography when it has been altogether dominant. But the historical thought of seventeenth-century England is not merely an example of a universal tendency; it acquired much of its special character and its power over the English mind from the presence and nature of that uniquely English institution, the common law.

The interpretation which the English of this period made of their legal, constitutional and, consequently, national history was accordingly one which arose within the schools of the common law, spreading from them to become the general belief of the gentry they did so much to educate. As we shall see, some of its assumptions are also the basic assumptions of the common law, and there is a sense in which it is as old as that law or older. But deeply rooted though it was in medieval thought, for its formulation in the version which was to dominate the seventeenth century we should no doubt look to that recrudescence of inns-of-court and parliamentary activity, intellectual as well as practical, which marks the later Tudor period. It received its classic formulation soon after 1600 from Sir Edward Coke, who was born in 1552; but a common lawyer who was a mature man at the time of Coke's birth would not have thought quite as Coke was to do half a century later. He would have been far more aware of the civil law as a part of the English fabric, and far more open to the medieval concept of law as a thing universal, more important in its universal characteristics than in its local and municipal manifestations. His mind would probably have been less insular than Coke's, less massively convinced that English law was purely English and that the only purely English law was the common law; and his interpretation of English history would have differed accordingly. Between 1550 and 1600 there occurred a great hardening and consolidation of common-law thought, whether this arose as the common law sought to defend itself against aggressive conciliar rivals, or whether the effect of Tudor centralization was to deliver it from more rivals than it created and actually make it easier for it to regard itself as the sole and supreme system of law in England. Coke's thought does not read like that of a man on the defensive; he does not insist or argue that the common law is the only system that has ever prevailed in England, but takes it as much for granted as the air he breathes; and the assumption seems to be made no less instinctively by the other lawyers of his generation and by most of the royalists and parliamentarians of the mid-century. It is hard to believe that the common-law interpretation of history was consciously and polemically constructed; it is much easier to see it as the result of deep-seated and unconscious habits of mind; but a detailed study of Tudor common-law thought would be necessary to show how and when it came into being. All that will be attempted here is an analysis of the assumptions on which it was founded and built up in the reign of James I.

In the first decade of the new century, then, English lawyers were prepared to define common law as custom and to defend custom against written law in language which recalls certain French ideas of an earlier generation. Whether this was done as a direct reaction to the humanist and civilian criticisms described by Maitland, neither he nor Holdsworth has perhaps made absolutely clear;[1] but whatever the cause, Sir John Davies, then Attorney-General for Ireland, in dedicating his *Irish Reports* to Lord Chancellor Ellesmere in the year 1612, stated the case for common law and custom in prose of admirable clarity, which reveals some degree of unconscious kinship with the ideas of *Anti-Tribonian*.[2]

For the *Common Law* of *England* is nothing else but the *Common Custome* of the Realm: and a Custome which hath obtained the force of a Law is always said to be *Jus non scriptum*: for it cannot be made or created either by

[1] Maitland, *English Law and the Renaissance*; Holdsworth, *History of English Law*, vol. IV, pp. 252–93.

[2] All quotations from Davies in this chapter are from the unpaginated preface dedicatory to *Irish Reports* (*Les Reports des Cases & Matters en Ley, Resolves & Adjudges en les Courts del Roy en Ireland. Collect & digest per Sir John Davis Chivaler, Atturney Generall del Roy en cest Realm*), London edition of 1674. 'Davies' is the spelling favoured by *D.N.B.*

Charter, or by Parliament, which are Acts reduced to writing, and are alwaies matter of Record; but being onely matter of fact, and consisting in use and practice, it can be recorded and registered no-where but in the memory of the people.

For a Custome taketh beginning and groweth to perfection in this manner: When a reasonable act once done is found to be good and beneficiall to the people, and agreeable to their nature and disposition, then do they use it and practise it again and again, and so by often iteration and multiplication of the act it becometh a *Custome*; and being continued without interruption time out of mind, it obtaineth the force of a *Law*.

And this *Customary Law* is the most perfect and most excellent, and without comparison the best, to make and preserve a Commonwealth. For the *written Laws* which are made either by the Edicts of Princes, or by Councils of Estates, are imposed upon the Subject before any Triall or Probation made, whether the same be fit and agreeable to the nature and disposition of the people, or whether they will breed any inconvenience or no. But a *Custome* doth never become a Law to bind the people, untill it hath been tried and approved time out of mind, during all which time there did thereby arise no inconvenience: for if it had been found inconvenient at any time, it had been used no longer, but had been interrupted, and consequently it had lost the virtue and force of a Law.

Fortescue had long ago written that the laws of England must be the best in the world, because they were certainly the most ancient—older than those of Rome or Venice—and from the Romans to the Normans the rulers of the land had had ample opportunity to change them if they had not seen that they were good.[1] But his words, important as they are in the English cult of the law's antiquity, do not of themselves imply Davies's elaborate argument from the nature of custom, which has much in common with the sixteenth-century revolt against written law. Hotman had laid it down that law must be appropriate to the nature and circumstances of the people, and had hinted that the essential character of custom was such that it must satisfy this requirement. Davies made this explicit and proceeded to praise English customary law:

so framed and fitted to the nature and disposition of this people, as we may properly say it is connatural to the Nation, so as it cannot possibly be ruled by any other Law. This Law therefore doth demonstrate the strength of wit and reason and self-sufficiency which hath been always in the People

---

[1] *De laudibus legum Angliae*, ch. XVII.

of this Land, which have made their own Laws out of their wisedome and experience, (like a silk-worm that formeth all her web out of her self onely) not begging or borrowing a form of a Commonweal, either from *Rome* or from *Greece*, as all other Nations of *Europe* have done; but having sufficient provision of law & justice within the Land, have no need *Justitiam & judicium ab alienigenis emendicare*, as King *John* wrote most nobly to Pope *Innocent* the Third....

And—just as Hotman had revealed his pleasure in the unclassical terminology of French customary law—Davies wrote a defence of law French, admitting that it was a wholly artificial language which had never been spoken outside the English courts, but arguing that centuries of use had invested its words with meanings so exactly appropriate to the legal terms and ideas they were expected to convey that it could not possibly be replaced by any other language without serious loss to the law's intelligibility. The implication was that usage had made it more perfect than any mode of expression which the individual intelligence could devise. An idealization of custom was developing which would exalt its wisdom above that of the individual. The laws enacted by prince or parliament may grow obsolete, but custom must always be perfectly up-to-date, since if it had proved inadequate to the problems of the present age the people would simply have abandoned it. On the other hand, the fact that they have retained it shows that it has confronted and solved more problems over the centuries than the present age can hope to imagine. Written laws contain no more than the wisdom of one man or one generation, whereas custom in its infinite complexity contains the wisdom of many generations, who have tested it by experience, submitting it to a multitude of demands, and by retaining it have shown that it has proved equal to them all. Custom therefore embodies a wisdom greater even than the wisdom of parliament, for, says Davies, it has often happened that a statute has altered some fundamental rule of the common law and bred thereby such a multitude of inconveniences that it has had to be repealed. Last of all, custom is purely native: that the people are ruled by customary law is proof that they have evolved their own law 'out of their wisedome and experience' and disdained foreign borrowings, which—as well as being open to the reproaches which may be directed against any merely enacted law—would be derogatory to the people's glory and self-sufficiency.

All these arguments, including the defence of law French, are to be met with in Coke; the preface to his *Fourth Reports*, for instance, lists many statutes which have injudiciously altered the common law and been repealed in consequence. Coke's emphasis is less upon custom, in the pure sense in which Davies uses the word, than upon the activity of the judges in constantly refining the law, declaring its principles with even greater precision and renewing it by application to the matter in hand. But the idea of judge-made law is only a sophistication and extension of the idea of custom. The law which the judges declare is unwritten and immemorial, and Coke praises it for precisely the same reasons as Davies. It embodies the wisdom of generations, as a result not of philosophical reflexion but of the accumulations and refinements of experience. This is Coke's famous concept of 'artificial reason'; what speaks through the judge is the distilled knowledge of many generations of men, each decision based on the experience of those before and tested by the experience of those after, and it is wiser than any individual—even James I—can possibly be. In his much quoted burst of eloquence upon *Calvin's Case*, Coke declared:

we are but of yesterday, (and therefore had need of the wisdom of those that were before us) and had been ignorant (if we had not received light and knowledge from our forefathers) and our days upon the earth are but as a shadow in respect of the old ancient days and times past, wherein the laws have been by the wisdom of the most excellent men, in many successions of ages, by long and continual experience, (the trial of light and truth) fined and refined, which no one man, (being of so short a time) albeit he had in his head the wisdom of all the men in the world, in any one age could ever have effected or attained unto. And therefore it is *optima regula, qua nulla est verior aut firmior in jure, neminem oportet esse sapientiorem legibus*: no man ought to take it on himself to be wiser than the laws.[1]

As will appear further when we study the thought of Sir Matthew Hale, this concept of law is essentially Burkean.[2] There is a process by which society constantly adapts its institutions to the dictates of

[1] Coke, *Seventh Reports, Calvin's Case*; here from the edition of the *Reports* by Thomas and Fraser (London, 1826), vol. IV, p. 6. Subsequent references to the *Reports* (T.F.) are all to this edition.   [2] Ch. VII, section III, below.

new situations. Institutions which have survived this process for a long time must be presumed to have solved innumerably more problems than the men of the present age can imagine, and experience indeed shows that the efforts of the living, even mustering their best wisdom for the purpose, to alter such institutions in the way that seems best to their own intelligence, have usually done more harm than good. The wisdom which they embody has accumulated to such a degree that no reflecting individual can in his lifetime come to the end of it, no matter how he calls philosophy and theoretical reason to his aid. These propositions may all be found in the writings of Coke, Davies and Hale, as well as in those of Burke. In the three former they depend unmistakably on the notion of custom, and if Burke owed any debt at all to preceding generations, the foundations of his thought were laid at the end of the sixteenth century, when the common lawyers learned to define their law as custom in opposition to written law.

But in saying this we come upon a paradox. If the idea that law is custom implies anything, it is that law is in constant change and adaptation, altered to meet each new experience in the life of the people; and it might seem that there was no theory more likely to lead to a historical conception of the nature of law. Yet the fact is that the common lawyers, holding that law was custom, came to believe that the common law, and with it the constitution, had always been exactly what they were now, that they were immemorial: not merely that they were very old, or that they were the work of remote and mythical legislators, but that they were immemorial in the precise legal sense of dating from time beyond memory—beyond, in this case, the earliest historical record that could be found. This is the doctrine or myth of the ancient constitution, which bulked so large in the political thought of the seventeenth century and furnishes this book with half its title. The present chapter and the next are devoted to studying the assumptions and the limitations of thought on which it was based.

The clue to the paradox lies in the fact that the concept of custom is ambiguous; Selden was never more suggestive than when he called the common law the English Janus. We may regard it as that which is in constant adaptation, and to do so will give rise to

The Common-law Mind: Custom and the Immemorial

ideas that are unmistakably historical. But it is equally possible to regard it as that which has been retained throughout the centuries and derives its authority from its having survived unchanged all changes of circumstances; and once we begin to think of custom as unchanging, we must remember that it is also immemorial, for if it were known to be the work of some founder it would be written or statute law and not custom at all. The political thought of the age underlined this point heavily. The Middle Ages, often seeing no essential difference between written law and custom, had spoken quite happily of kings who ordained new customs and of the two or three lifetimes which qualified a law to be considered immemorial.[1] But by Coke's time the increasing activity of a nearly sovereign monarchy had made it seem to most common lawyers that if a right was to be rooted in custom and rendered independent of the sovereign's interference it must be shown to be immemorial in the full sense of 'traceable to no original act of foundation'. The idea of the immemorial therefore took on an absolute colouring, which is one of the key facts in Stuart historico-political thought. It ceased to be a convenient fiction and was heatedly asserted as literal historical truth; and the more that came to be known about remote ages, the more vigorously it was insisted that the law was before Abraham.

The common law was by definition immemorial custom. For hundreds of years before Coke and Davies it had been accepted, by an assumption common in medieval thought, that English law was *jus non scriptum* and that the function of the courts was to declare the ancient custom of the realm. Even statutes could be so interpreted, and Coke eagerly takes at least the earliest of them to be declaratory judgments. Innumerable decisions were consequently on record as declaring that everything which they contained, down to the most minute and complex technicality, had formed part of the custom of England from time out of mind; or at least so the common lawyers read them to mean, and this fact is at the root of their interpretation of history. They took everything in the records of the common law to be immemorial, and they treated every piece of evidence in those records as a declaration of what was already

[1] The classic discussion of the medieval ideas of custom and ancient law is in Kern, *Kingship and Law in the Middle Ages* (ed. Chrimes), Cambridge, 1939.

immemorial; so that the beginning of the records of the king's courts in the twelfth century was proof, not that those courts began at that time, but of their great antiquity, and it was usual and—given the presumptions—logical to add that if the earlier records had not been lost or stolen, they would prove the existence of the courts in times earlier still. But at however remote a date the series of records had begun, the common-law mind would still have taken their beginning as proof that at that time the laws were already immemorial; since *jus non scriptum* must by definition be older than the oldest written records.

The belief in the ancient constitution therefore rested on assumptions which were fundamental to the practice of the common law, and it had very great influence in a society whose political and social thinking were so largely dominated by this one law. It cannot therefore be regarded as the creation of any single mind. But Coke did more than any other man to summarize it and make it authoritative; at the same time he reveals the patterns of thought on which it was based with the clarity of truly representative genius. His historical thought could be described as founded on the presumption that any legal judgment declaring a right immemorial is perfectly valid as a statement of history. Thus in the preface to the *Third Reports*—his first published exposition of the view that the law was immemorial and the *locus classicus* of his methods of historical reconstruction—he selects a case from the books of assize of 26 Edw. III:

it appeareth that in a writ of assise the Abbot of B[ury] claimed to have conusance of pleas and writs of assise, and other original writs out of the King's courts by prescription, time out of mind of man, in the times of St Edmund, and St Edward the Confessor, Kings of this realm before the Conquest, and shewed divers allowances thereof, and that King H.I. confirmed their usages, and that they should have conusance of pleas, so that the Justices of the one bench, or the other should not intermeddle; out of which record (being now above three hundred years past) it appeareth that the predecessors of that Abbot had time out of mind of man in those Kings' reigns, (that is whereof no man knew the contrary either out of his own memory, or by any record or other proof,) writs of assise, and other original writs out of the King's Courts.[1]

[1] Preface to *Third Reports* (T.F. vol. II), pp. ix–x. Cf. *First Institutes* (8th ed. 1670), fol. 71b, and *Second Institutes* (4th ed. 1671), pp. 22–5.

The Common-law Mind: Custom and the Immemorial

The fact—often paralleled—that a fourteenth-century abbot had alleged that he had precedents from pre-Conquest times, should remind us of the extreme antiquity and universality of this way of pleading and thinking in English society. Coke and his contemporaries were indeed only continuing and developing a habit of mind as old as the common law itself; but now he goes on,[1] in a way too full of antiquarian learning to be simply a continuation of medieval thought, to argue that since writs of assize have been proved immemorial and older than the Conquest, so too must be sheriffs, because the writs are directed to them; trials by the oaths of twelve men, since the writs instruct the sheriff to conduct them; the king's courts, since the writs are returnable into them; the court of chancery, since it issues the writs; and the entire science and practice of the common law, since, as Fitzherbert points out, the procedure to be followed when writs are issued provides the fundamental rules about which it is built up. Thus a judgment that one part of the law is immemorial is first taken with historical literalness that might have surprised some of the judges, and then made the basis of an argument that the whole of the law must be of equal antiquity. Coke uses a similar technique in the preface to the *Ninth Reports*, when, having proved to his satisfaction that there were parliaments before the Conquest, he proceeds to argue that there were representatives of the commons in them.

It is evident that there were tenants in ancient demesne before the Conquest; and for a certainty therein, and to know of what manors such tenants did hold, it appears by the book of Domesday, that all the tenants that did hold of any of those manors that were in the hands of King Edward, the son of King Ethelred, or of King William the Conqueror, were tenants in ancient demesne. And these tenants then had, and yet have these privileges amongst others, for that they were bound by their tenure to plow and husband, etc. the King's demesnes before and in the Conqueror's time, and therefore they were not to be returned Burgesses to serve in Parliament, to the end they might attend the King's husbandry the better.

2. They were not to be contributory to the fees to the Knights of Shires that served in Parliament: which privileges (though the cause ceaseth,)

[1] *Third Reports* (T.F. vol. II), pp. x–xii.

39

continue to this day: therefore there were Parliaments unto which the
Knights and Burgesses were summoned both before and in the reign of the
Conqueror.[1]

Here it is matter of record, rather than an actual judgment, on
which the case is built up; but the procedure is exactly the same.
The presence of tenants in ancient demesne in Domesday Book is
taken to mean that they existed before the Conquest (and therefore
from time out of mind); and their exemption from parliamentary
attendance at a later date still is taken to prove the existence of a
parliament with commons, both at the time of Domesday and
before. The fact that Coke allows the unwary reader to assume that
the parliamentary exemption is in Domesday is probably not proof
of disingenuousness; he would simply take it for granted that what
was mentioned at a later date must have been present at an earlier.

In the preface to the *Third Reports* Coke follows up the passage
already cited with further proof of the law's antiquity, drawn from
early British history as it was then understood.[2] Brutus of Troy,
he said, the first king of Britain, was reputed to have drawn up a
book of laws; so had King Dunwallo Molmutius, Mercia the
queen of King Gwintelin, Sigebert of East Anglia, Alfred, Edward
the Elder and reputedly many others, so that there had been at
least seven books of the law (two of them Dunwallo's) before the
Conquest. It is of importance to the understanding of this subject
to note that it was not Coke's belief in fabulous kings out of
Geoffrey of Monmouth which was primarily responsible for his
belief in the antiquity of the law. He had his doubts about Brutus—
'I will not examine these things in a quo warranto; the ground
thereof I think was best known to the authors and writers of them'
—and his interpretation of the past was soon to survive unscathed
the disappearance of the legendary Trojan and British kings from
the stage of serious history. His references to Brutus and Dunwallo
occupy second place after the proof of the law's antiquity founded
on legal, not historical sources. Coke not only accepts a legal
judgment dating a law from time out of mind as historically valid,

[1] Preface to *Ninth Reports* (T.F. vol. v), pp. xxi–xxiii.
[2] Preface to *Third Reports* (T.F. vol. ɪɪ), pp. xiv–xx.

but he regards such statements as better historical evidence than those made by chroniclers. Where the courts have adjudged an institution immemorial and a historian alleges that it was set up in such a king's reign, Coke leaves little doubt that we are to think the historian wrong, and he urges the historiographers of his own day to consult a lawyer before making any statement about the history of the law.[1] He was not relying upon legendary histories, but using them to illustrate a proof that the law was immemorial which he drew from the thought of the law courts; and conversely, he was not seeking to derive the law from any mythical founder. When, with the aid of the *Mirror of Justices*, he had traced parliament back to the reign of King Arthur, he added: 'Not that this court and the rest were instituted then, but that the reach of his [Horn's] treatise extendeth no higher than to write of the laws and usages of this realm continued since the reign of that king.'[2] In the same way Davies had written:

Neither could any one man ever vaunt, that, like *Minos*, *Solon*, or *Lycurgus*, he was the first *Lawgiver* to our Nation: for neither did the King make his own *Prerogative*, nor the Judges make the *Rules* or *Maximes* of the Law, nor the common subject prescribe and limit the *Liberties* which he injoyeth by the Law. But, as it is said of every Art or Science which is brought to perfection, *Per varios usus Artem experientia fecit*; so may it properly be said of our Law, *Per varios usus Legem experientia fecit*. Long experience, and many trials of what was best for the common good, did make the *Common Law*.[3]

The law was immemorial and there had been no legislator. In this respect at least common-law thought was independent of fashionable classical models. Its eyes were turned inward, upon the past of its own nation which it saw as making its own laws, untouched by foreign influences, in a process without a beginning.

[1] Preface to *Third Reports* (T.F. vol. II), p. xxiii; *Second Institutes*, p. 499. See Sir Roger Twysden, *Certain Considerations upon the Government of England* (Camden Society Publications, XLV, 1849, p. 23).

[2] Preface to *Ninth Reports* (T.F. vol. v), p. xi.

[3] Davies, preface to *Irish Reports*.

II

But if neither a putative Trojan nor a putative Arthurian origin was of much importance in this interpretation of legal history, there was one event in the English past over which the common lawyers expended floods of ink and burned much midnight oil. This was the Norman Conquest, the one great apparent breach in the continuity of the nation's history. The motives which spurred them to their unending denials that this event had caused any change in the essential character of the law were various: sheer patriotism furnished one, and Polydore Vergil, that gadfly of the older English historiography, another with his gibes at a law derived from the semi-barbarous Normans and still uttered in their jargon; while, as we shall see, once the interpretation of history became involved in the struggle of king and parliament, a powerful political motive was added to the others. But from whatever point of view it was regarded, the idea that William I had carried out a systematic importation of new law cut right across the belief in custom and the immemorial that was coming to be an integral part of English political thought, and the common lawyers set out to deny it with all the resources of their learning and ingenuity. With Coke the argument that the courts, parliament or the law are immemorial often seems to be identical with the argument that they are pre-Conquest. Once over that stumbling-block, the rest may be taken for granted; and all the subtleties of the common-law technique of reading history backwards are called into play.

But Coke's endeavours were powerfully abetted by the conduct of the Normans themselves. While the main features of common-law historiography must be deduced from habits of mind peculiar to that profession, it remains true that the feeling that all rule must be by ancient law was one of the deepest-seated preconceptions of the medieval mind. It had seemed of scarcely less importance to the Normans than it did to Coke himself to maintain that they governed England according to the *laga Eadwardi*, and throughout the twelfth and thirteenth centuries a succession of political programmes had been expressed, by claimants to the throne or dissident barons, in the form of promises or demands to restore the good old law of Edward the Confessor. The story that among the Conqueror's first acts had been to codify and confirm the Confessor's law had found its way into most of the chroniclers; and not only this, but several ingenious and quite possibly sincere men had in and after the twelfth century sat down to supply the absence of any text of this law or the Conqueror's by composing the apocryphal *leges Edwardi Confessoris, Willielmi, Henrici Primi*, the chronicle of 'Ingulf of Croyland' (supposed to be an eye-witness of the confirmation), and so on. The edifice had been completed by the insertion in the coronation oath—where it remained until 1688—of a promise to observe the laws of St Edward. When the common lawyers began to write their histories, therefore, the belief that the laws of the last Anglo-Saxon king had been confirmed by the Conqueror and his Norman and Angevin successors had long been orthodox history, though the reprehensible Polydore had as usual expressed some doubts. Furthermore, William Lambarde had in his *Archaionomia* (1568)— one of the key books of the common-law interpretation—published the apocryphal *leges* in unbroken series with such genuine texts of Anglo-Saxon law as he had been able to collect. Coke, and nearly all other historians, accepted them at their own valuation; and as the authors of the *leges Confessoris* and the *leges Willielmi* (which were supposed to represent the Anglo-Saxon laws as amended by the Conqueror) had not unnaturally attributed to pre-Conquest times the feudal institutions, described in the Norman terminology of their own day and age, there was no sign in these apparently authoritative texts of any radical breach with the past at the Conquest. Coke indeed was able to make very extensive use of Lambarde's book to prove that institutions which had in fact been introduced by the Normans formed part of the immemorial law; and he employed with no less faith and frequency two other medieval apocrypha, the fourteenth-century *Modus Tenendi Parliamentum* and (with far less excuse) the lavishly fantastic *Mirror of Justices*, to attribute to the times of Alfred and Arthur the characteristic machinery of Angevin and Plantagenet monarchy. There are few pages of his *First* or *Second Institutes* on which one of these works is not cited.

The picture thus constructed of the early history of the law is summarized by Coke—speaking in this for nearly every Englishman of the seventeenth century—in the preface to the *Eighth Reports*.[1] Explaining that he has been asked whether the chroniclers agree with him that the law is immemorial, and first carefully reminding us that the proofs drawn from the law itself stand in no need of their corroboration, Coke proceeds to narrate that William I swore to observe the ancient laws, ordered twelve men in each shire to state what they were, and summarized them, with a few emendations of his own, into a Magna Carta, the first of its kind, under the name of the 'laws of King Edward'. Henry I, promising at his accession to take away all evil customs, restored King Edward's laws in a purer form, and thereafter both Stephen and Henry II confirmed them anew in coronation charters. Matthew Paris says that John's charters contain little that is not in Henry II's charter or in those laws which are called King Edward's, not because the latter enacted them but because he reduced them to writing. All this, as Coke proudly points out, is extracted from medieval chroniclers; but to get its seventeenth-century flavour we have to read it in the belief that the whole apparatus of common law was immemorial. But the apocryphal *leges* and Lambarde's Anglo-Saxon dooms are not of course the common law; Coke describes them as statutes, but succeeds in some peculiar way in regarding their existence as proof of the antiquity of the unwritten law which they do not contain:

...by all which it is manifest, that in effect, the very body of the common laws before the Conquest are omitted out of the fragments of such acts and ordinances as are published under the title of the Laws of King Alfred, Edward the First, Edward the Second, Ethelstane, Edward, Edgar, Etheldred, Canutus, Edward the Confessor, or of other Kings of England before the Conquest. And those few chapters of laws yet remaining, are for the most part certain acts and ordinances established by the said several Kings by assent of the Common Council of their kingdom.[2]

The myth of the confirmations, as it may be called, culminates with Magna Carta (which Coke liked to say had been confirmed by more than thirty parliaments), and his treatment of it, both in the posthumously printed *Second Institutes* (1641) and in the Commons

[1] T.F. vol. IV, pp. iii–xi.
[2] *Ibid.* p. xi.

debates leading up to the Petition of Right, has received most attention of all his historical interpretations.[1] It has two aspects. In the first place he links the Charter, through Stephen Langton and Henry II, with the successive confirmations of the Confessor's law; and in the second he studies it clause by clause to prove that it enacts the main principles of common law and parliamentary liberty in his own day, so that the men of 1628 could believe that they were not only repeating the solemn act of 1215, but taking part in a recurrent drama of English history at least as old as the Conquest. This second process, by which Coke discovers the rights of parliament and property in a feudal document of the thirteenth century, was at bottom one with the greatest work of his life, the revitalization of the common law so that precedents and principles laid down by the king's courts in the attempt to govern a feudal society could be used and found apt in the freeholding and mercantile England of James I. Coke, as we shall see further in the next chapter, had no conception that in the early common law he was dealing with the law of a society organized upon feudal principles. Therefore—still on the presumption that the law declared what had been law always —he was able to identify the law of his own day with the law of the earliest records, just as he had established the doctrine that the latter contained what had been law since time out of mind before the Conquest. At this point the identification of past and present was complete, and the possibility that the idea of custom might give rise to ideas of law being in continuous development was altogether suppressed.

Such then—assuming that Coke, whose vast influence was after all partly posthumous,[2] may be taken as a safe guide to the thought

[1] *First Institutes*, fols. 80 b–81 b; *Second Institutes*, pp. 1–78; Faith Thompson, *Magna Carta: its Role in the Making of the English Constitution, 1300–1629* (Minnesota, 1948), part III in general and ch. XII in particular; H. Butterfield, *The Englishman and his History* (Cambridge, 1944), pp. 54–68.

[2] The first eleven books of the *Reports* were published between 1600 and 1615; the *First Institutes* in 1628 and revised in 1629. Coke died in 1634. The *Second Institutes* were published in 1642, the *Third* and *Fourth* in 1644 and the *Twelfth* and *Thirteenth Reports* in 1655 and 1658. But of those writings which reveal most of his historical mind only the *Second Institutes* are posthumous, and the writer's views on Magna Carta, which form perhaps their most

of his profession—seem to have been the main features of what may be termed the common-law interpretation of English history, the predecessor and to a large extent the parent of the more famous 'Whig interpretation'. It arose essentially from latent assumptions governing historical thinking, which had been planted deep in the English mind by centuries of practice of a particular form of law; but it possessed also a political aspect, the need to make a case for an 'ancient constitution' against the king; and though this book is designed primarily as a study, not of the uses which were made of it in political argument, but of the historiographical conditions which made its existence possible, the former question is an inseparable part of the latter. Only a very detailed study of seventeenth-century thought could fully reveal the variety of uses to which it was put, or enable us to estimate accurately its importance as compared with other forms of political discussion. But the greatness of that importance cannot be denied. Put very briefly, what occurred was that belief in the antiquity of the common law encouraged belief in the existence of an ancient constitution, reference to which was constantly made, precedents, maxims and principles from which were constantly alleged, and which was constantly asserted to be in some way immune from the king's prerogative action; and discussion in these terms formed one of the century's chief modes of political argument. Parliamentary debates and pamphlet controversies involving the law or the constitution were almost invariably carried on either wholly or partially in terms of an appeal to the past made in this way; famous antiquaries were treated as authorities of recognized political wisdom; and nearly every thinker noted for his contribution to political theory in its usual sense—Hunton, Milton, Lilburne, Hobbes, Harrington, Filmer, Nevile, Sidney: only Locke appears to be an exception among notable writers—devoted part of his pages to discussing the antiquity of the constitution. It would be possible to construct both a history of the

---

prominent feature, would already be well known from the parliamentary debates culminating in 1628. (See Thompson, *Magna Carta, passim.*) These facts would suggest that all Coke's historical opinions could have been well known while he lived, even if we do not suppose that he was giving voice to ideas already widely accepted.

ways in which historical thought was used in political argument, and a study of the ways in which historical and political theory were related in the minds of the men who wrote and thought in both modes. To the typical educated Englishman of this age, it seems certain, a vitally important characteristic of the constitution was its antiquity, and to trace it in a very remote past was essential in order to establish it securely in the present. We may therefore maintain that the historical thought which lay behind this belief helped to shape the mind of the century and will consequently help us to understand it.

It must be evident in the first place that historical thinking of the kind we have seen in Coke would make it possible to claim, with sincere and entire conviction, that many of the privileges or rights which parliament, or the courts of common law under a vigorous chief justice, desired to possess in the present had been theirs in the remote past. Thought of this kind encouraged the production, from legal or chronicle sources, of evidence of action taken in very distant times, which could then be identified with contemporary conditions and claimed as a precedent. This must very largely explain the intense interest taken in the production of remote precedents during every controversy of the period before the Civil War—as for instance during the *Ship-money Case*, when evidence from the reign of Egbert was produced and examined with perfect seriousness by both sides. But it would be insufficient to explain the seventeenth-century's habit of recourse to the past merely as a search for precedents, as an eager legal antiquarianism; it was plainly much more. To claim that a precedent exists is to claim that a system of law as old as that precedent is still in force, and the arguments used in the *Ship-money Case* implied Coke's principle that the law of England was of pre-Conquest antiquity. When it was claimed that a remote precedent existed for such a right, it might very well be claimed in addition that the right was of immemorial antiquity. When Elizabeth I's parliaments began to claim rights that were in fact new, they indeed produced precedents, but they did much more. They made their claim in the form that what they desired was theirs by already existing law—the content of English law being undefined and unwritten—and it could always be claimed, in the way that we have seen, that anything which was in the existing law was immemorial. The common lawyers began to rewrite English history on parliamentary lines in the Elizabethan House of Commons—Sir John Neale comments on the process[1]—and by the time of the Apology of 1604 the Commons were already insisting that the whole body of their privileges should be recognized as theirs by right of time immemorial. The search for precedents resulted in the building-up of a body of alleged rights and privileges that were supposed to be immemorial, and this, coupled with the general and vigorous belief that England was ruled by law and that this law was itself immemorial, resulted in turn in that most important and elusive of seventeenth-century concepts, the fundamental law. Much has been written about fundamental law by modern scholars in the light of the contrary theories of judicial review and parliamentary sovereignty,[2] but it does not seem to have been stated in so many words that if you had asked the representative seventeenth-century Englishman the question 'What is it that makes the fundamental law fundamental?' he might indeed have been embarrassed for an answer,[3] but would probably in the

[1] *Elizabeth I and her Parliaments, 1558–81* (London, 1953), pp. 155–6, 305–6, 407–10, 420. The case of Arthur Hall is the best-known example of controversy on this question; see H. G. Wright, *Life and Writings of Arthur Hall of Grantham* (Manchester University Press, 1919).

[2] The latest study is that of J. W. Gough, *Fundamental Law in English Constitutional History* (Oxford, 1955). It does not appear that the seventeenth-century habit of appealing to the past gives us much help in deciding how far it was believed that parliament declared law, or how far that it made new law. Plainly, the whole weight of the appeal to ancient custom would tend to make parliament think it was declaring law; but that does not mean that parliament was incapable of knowing when it was making new law, only that it could believe itself to be declaring old whenever it chose to do so. The preamble to the Act in Restraint of Appeals reminds us that there were no limits to its power to believe this, and that in fact the distinction is often meaningless.

[3] An interesting instance is that of 1641, when Edmund Waller asked what the fundamental laws might be, and was told by Maynard that if he did not know, he had no business to sit in the house. This incident reads as if Waller had succeeded in exploding the whole concept, but we should remember that Maynard probably identified the fundamental law with no single set of enactments, but with the entire body of unwritten customary law; to him, therefore, Waller's question would practically amount to a demand to be told what the laws of England were, and his retort may have been more of a

end have replied: 'Its antiquity, its character as the immemorial custom of England.' The adjective 'ancient' was used little less often than 'fundamental', was frequently coupled with it and (it may be suggested) could in the majority of cases have been substituted for it without serious loss of meaning. The fundamental law or constitution was an ancient law or constitution; the concept had been built up by the search for precedents coupled with the common-law habit of mind that made it fatally easy to presume that anything which was in the common law, and which it was desired to emphasize, was immemorial.

The content of the concept differed from time to time (as also from man to man): as parliament laid claim to new powers these were represented as immemorial and included in the fundamental law, and close study would probably also reveal that as later controversies, particularly those of the mid-century, gave rise to new political ideas and principles, these also were included. It would certainly reveal that as the century progressed assertions that the law was immemorial tended to be replaced by assertions that parliament, and especially a house of commons representing the property-owners, was immemorial. One of the underlying themes in the history of seventeenth-century political thought is the trend from the claim that there is a fundamental law, with parliament as its guardian, to the claim that parliament is sovereign. Books are still being written in the attempt to decide how far this transition was carried and at what times; but it seems to be fairly well agreed that it was both incomplete and largely unrealized. Parliament claimed its increasing powers in virtue of the fundamental law; when in 1642 its claims reached such a height as to become a claim to arbitrary sovereignty, it still alleged that these were substantiated by fundamental law. The lower house's claim to be sole sovereign often took the form of a claim that it was immemorial and therefore subject to no checks. The attempt at single-chamber despotism failed, and both the Restoration and the Revolution of 1688 could be represented as efforts to restore the fundamental law, rather than to

sincere explosion and less of a debater's trick than one at first supposes. But the occasion was the attainder of Strafford, and what was said is not to be scrutinized too closely. Gardiner, *History of England, 1603–1642*, vol. IX, p. 336.

establish the sovereignty of king in parliament. The concept of fundamental law therefore did much both to cloak and to delay the transition to a full assertion of parliamentary sovereignty. Granted the importance of fundamental law, and granted also that the concept rested on Coke's concept of ancient law, we have here perhaps the true importance of common-law historical thought in the seventeenth century.

To what ultimate political principle were men appealing when they made the claim that their rights formed part of a pre-Conquest constitution? Why did they think a law's antiquity made it binding in the present? Taking Coke as representative, we have analysed the assumptions and arguments on which that claim was based, and they have been shown to rest on the basic assumption that the law declared the immemorial custom of England. It was the idea of custom which convinced men that the law was ancient; the conclusion is a tempting one that it was as custom that they thought it was still binding. Coke and still more Davies do indeed seem to have thought at bottom in just this fashion; but does it follow that the average parliament man, barrister or pamphleteer, who made his appeal to 'our ancient and fundamental laws, our ancient constitution', was knowingly and deliberately appealing to the binding force of immemorial custom, and was clear in his mind what those words meant? It seems unlikely, yet it is hard to imagine what other ultimate basis his appeal could have had. No doubt for many it was enough to declare that the laws were ancient and fundamental, without troubling to inquire why that should make them binding. Some research, it seems, might profitably be done on the place which the concept of custom occupied in seventeenth-century thought. It appears to have been far less prominent and familiar in the scholastic and academic tradition of political discourse—the political theory of the text-books—even in the schools of natural law, than it was among common lawyers. If this impression is upheld, what are we to make of it? Was there some unifying body of assumptions, or were there more ways than one to approach political problems, arising in different intellectual milieux and stressing different basic concepts? and if this was so, which was the more representative and effective in seventeenth-century England?

The Common-law Mind: Custom and the Immemorial

To ask such questions, or suggest that they might be asked, is to raise in a new form the problem of the relations between historical thought of Coke's kind and academic political theory. Was the chief justice a political thinker and, if so, in what sense? But, however such a line of inquiry might turn out, it could probably be agreed that, even if a clearly thought-out concept of custom were proved to be not specially prevalent in the seventeenth-century mind, still the concept of an ancient constitution, very prevalent indeed, rested ultimately upon the idea of custom; and that, in this sense, common-law historical thought represented a most vigorous survival of the medieval concept of custom in English political thinking. As for the men who said 'this is the ancient law' without troubling to inquire on what juridical principle that law rested, they too were carrying on the tradition of many medieval minds, who lived so much surrounded by the notion of 'law' that they did not find it necessary to say very clearly from what authority—other than God or nature—the law in question derived.[1] In the common-law interpretation of history, it seems, we have a powerful stream of medieval thought flowing into the seventeenth and eighteenth centuries, its strength surviving at least until the coming of philosophical radicalism.

But the attraction which the concept of the ancient constitution possessed for lawyers and parliamentarians probably resided less in whatever ultimate principle provided its base, than in its value as a purely negative argument. For a truly immemorial constitution could not be subject to a sovereign: since a king could not be known to have founded it originally, the king now reigning could not claim to revoke rights rooted in some ancestor's will. In an age when people's minds were becoming deeply, if dimly, imbued with the fear of some sort of sovereignty or absolutism, it must have satisfied many men's minds to be able to argue that the laws of the land were so ancient as to be the product of no one's will, and to appeal to the almost universally respected doctrine that law should be above will. A later generation, we shall see, having witnessed

[1] This observation does not of course apply to most of the systematic political thinkers of the Middle Ages, but there must have been many who thought in the way here described.

with alarm the spectacle of a revolutionary sovereignty styling itself that of the people, and by no means anxious in consequence to derive the laws from the act of some original popular assembly, found in the ancient constitution the perfect argument for pre-Lockean Whigs; as when the Lords were told in 1688 that 'the original contract between king and people' consisted in the king's undertaking to maintain laws which he certainly had not made.[1] Once more we see how the concept of antiquity satisfied the need, still widely felt, for a rule of law which, like Magna Carta, 'would have no sovereign'. But it was an argument which fell far short of logical perfection. By the very vehemence with which they insisted that the laws were immemorial and not of the king's making, its champions tacitly conceded that if the laws were not immemorial they were of the king's making—since few were prepared to go to the quasi-republican length of asserting that the laws had preceded the kingly office and brought it into being[2]—and that if they were of the king's making the reigning king was sovereign over them. These conditional propositions appear to have been accepted more or less on all sides; some few tried to find a way round them but hardly any succeeded. The notion of historical relativity—the suggestion that the law still in force might indeed have been made by a king in some high and far-off time, but in conditions so remote that neither 'king' nor 'law' meant what they meant at the present day, and that consequently no conclusions could be drawn as to current rights and liberties—was after all still virtually unknown. Consequently, to prove that the laws of England had originated at a time within the memory of man was to suggest the existence at that time of some human sovereign possessing the right to make law; and the heirs of that sovereign could not be denied the right to unmake all that he had made. Once men had appealed to the immemorial, the laws must be either absolutely immemorial or subject to an absolute sovereign—there seems to have been no idea of a middle way. A polemical situation could therefore arise, in which to put forward any theory as to the origin of English law at a time

[1] See ch. IX, below.
[2] For the most part this argument belongs to the Civil War period and after.

within recorded human history could be interpreted, and even intended, as an argument in favour of absolute monarchy. We shall see this happening in 1681.[1] For their part, those who saw in the immemorial constitution a good argument for limiting the prerogative would sooner or later be compelled by the same logic to attribute to it an altogether fabulous antiquity, insisting that it could be traced in and before the remotest events known to contemporary historical thought, and denying, in essence, that its origins could ever be discovered by the historian.

The doctrine of antiquity was therefore most vulnerable to criticism, and some awareness of this must explain why those who believed in it were so tirelessly and monotonously insistent that the establishment of the Normans in England did not constitute a conquest. In theory, one can easily see why this should have been so. If the monarchy of England had ever been sovereign, it had been at that moment; and if Duke William, even for a single instant, had been an absolute ruler—if he had been king by *jus conquestus*—then it did not matter if he had maintained English law instead of introducing French, and it did not matter what charters and grants of liberties he had subsequently made to his new subjects; all that had been done—even to increase the sphere of freedom and law—had been done by virtue of his unfettered will, on which his grants depended and on which (transmitted to his descendants) the laws and liberties of England for ever afterwards must depend likewise. To admit a conquest was to admit an indelible stain of sovereignty upon the English constitution. A conquest was therefore not admitted in the age of Blackstone any more than in the age of Coke. William was no conqueror, said the lawyers and the antiquaries and the parliamentarians in chorus; he was a claimant to the crown under ancient law who had vindicated his claim by trial of battle with Harold, a victory which brought him no title whatever to change the laws of England. If he had done so, it was a lawless act without validity, put right within a few generations of his death by the coronation charters of his successors and by Magna Carta, which had restored and confirmed the immemorial law of the Confessor's time.

[1] Ch. VIII, below.

The Common-law Mind: Custom and the Immemorial

But the remarkable fact is that the contrary argument was very seldom put forward—certainly with insufficient frequency to justify the incessant refutations which appeared. A writer of 1680, William Petyt, casting about for names with which to substantiate his allegation that a conspiracy existed to establish absolute monarchy on the theoretical basis of a conqueror's right, was able to name none who had argued in this sense except 'one Blackwood, a Scotchman'—and, he might have added, a good deal of a Frenchman as well[1]—and Mr Christopher Hill, who believes that the conquest theory was a staple argument of pre-Civil War monarchism, can add to the mention of Blackwood only some half-hearted remarks by James I[2] and a few sentences of Laud's which appear to bear a rather different meaning.[3] The fact seems to be that the conquest theory was no more an essential part of pro-Stuart reasoning before the Civil Wars (or indeed after them) than was absolute sovereignty.[4] Those who supported what the Stuart kings were doing did not normally regard their ruler as a sovereign maker of law—however vigorously they might assert his prerogative—and consequently did not argue that the laws flowed from his will or that he ruled above the law as a conqueror—the two doctrines to which a theory based on historical criticism would have led. This conclusion makes it hard to explain why the opposition constantly thought it necessary to refute an argument which nobody was putting forward; but it reminds us that the belief in an immemorial law was not a party argument put forward by some clever lawyer as a means of limiting the king's prerogative: it was the nearly universal belief of Englishmen. The case for the crown was not that the king ruled as a

[1] W. Petyt, *Miscellanea Parliamentaria* (1680) and *The Antient Right of the Commons of England Asserted* (1680).

[2] Christopher Hill, *Puritanism and Revolution* (London, 1958), "The Norman Yoke," pp. 50-122.

[3] What Laud says, as quoted by Hill (*ibid.*), is that the Conqueror's following insisted on being governed by his will and would not accept the laws of St Edward; but in a generation or two 'they became English' and appealed to the ancient law to protect them against King John. This is hardly a claim to *jus conquestus* on behalf of the king.

[4] It will be argued later (chs. VII and VIII) that there is no serious attempt to derive the royal power from William's conquest until 1680-8.

sovereign and that there was no fundamental law, but that there was a fundamental law and that the king's prerogative formed part of it. The antiquity of the law and the denial of the Conquest are arguments scarcely less frequently or vigorously employed by crown lawyers, or at a later date by royalist pamphleteers, than by their opponents. It is too easily forgotten that there was a common-law case for the crown as well as against it, and the former case was expressed in the same language and based on the same assumptions as the latter. Consequently, the king's side was late, slow and half-hearted in developing any historical criticism of the doctrine of immemorial law. Later chapters of this book attempt to explain how they came to do so in the end; but the conclusion seems inescapable that English historical ideas—those, that is, on the constitution and its antiquity—were not created primarily by party polemics. They were, before all else, the result of assumptions latent in the common-law mind, themselves the result of centuries of practice and experience of a purely insular form of law: the product, in short, of English history itself, reflected in the character of the country's legal structure and shaping and limiting the way in which her lawyers thought. Those who wished to change them must do more than put forward a theory of sovereignty, founded on a doctrine of conquest or on the idea that kings were older than laws; they must destroy the limitations under which English historical thinking was carried on. What these limitations were is further explored in the following chapter.

CHAPTER III

The Common-law Mind: the Absence of a Basis of Comparison

COKE'S mind, it is clear, was as nearly insular as a human being's could be. He saw the law he idolized as the immemorial custom of England, and he imagined it as being immemorial purely within the island. For this reason his doctrine of ancient law should be sharply distinguished from another contemporary belief, at this time spreading in popularity: that the liberties of western Europe, including the English law and parliament, were derived from the 'Goths', as the early Germans were then termed. An American scholar, S. L. Kliger, has lately shown[1] that this belief was held in England, and in common-law circles, from a time as early as 1567, when Rastell seems to have adopted it; but it is not to be found in Coke. When the latter quotes from Tacitus' *Germania*, ever a favourite work with believers in early Teutonic liberty, it is 'concerning the Antiquity of descents which the Germanes had agreeable with the ancient Laws of the Britons, continued in England to this day'.[2] The purely insular character of his ideas could hardly appear more clearly; the law is immemorial in Britain and ancient Continental law merely happens to agree with it. Moreover, as we have seen, when he has traced a law back to the time of some ancient king, whether Alfred or Arthur, he never fails to add that this king was merely confirming what was already immemorial, a habit scarcely reconcilable with the theory that the law was imported by Hengist. Contemporary Saxon scholarship, the work of Nowell, Verstegan and Camden, with its tendency to idealize the Saxons as beneficent conquerors and derive many things from them, seems to have made little impact on Coke; he shows no special interest in the Saxons as a people, and if they

[1] *The Goths in England* (Cambridge, Mass., 1952); for Rastell see pp. 24–5.
[2] Coke, *Second Institutes*, p. 7.

figure prominently in his writings this is because the need to prove the law older than the Conquest renders it important to show that every feature of later law can be discovered in their time. But Coke would never have been content to stop with the Saxons; for him the law was immemorial and the Saxons only one stage on the journey into its ever-receding past. He plunged into British and Trojan antiquities, in which probably even he only half believed, rather than admit that the law had a beginning. Contemporary Saxonists could criticize him for this; we shall see how Spelman used the similarities between Anglo-Saxon and early Germanic law to argue that the laws of England were less ancient and less native than sometimes supposed.[1] To be a Teutonist was to think differently from Coke, to derive English law from a Continental instead of a purely insular source. His thought owed little or nothing to the Gothic school, and was built entirely on the single assumption that the common law was the immemorial custom of England.

Mr Kliger is constrained to remark in a footnote that though Coke was 'strong for the common law', he does not figure importantly as a 'Gothicist'.[2] This is certainly true; but if so overpowering a figure as the chief justice was no 'Gothicist', that fact alone would seem sufficient ground for supposing that common-law and 'Gothic' thought were two different, if intermingled, lines of intellectual development. But Mr Kliger sometimes appears to be treating every seventeenth-century reference to the existence of law and parliament among the Anglo-Saxons as evidence of 'Gothicism'; and the agreed fact that Coke stressed Anglo-Saxon possession of these things without being a 'Gothicist' should show that the distinction exists and ought to be maintained. To work it out fully would be difficult, because it would involve deciding and proving whether insular 'Cokean' thought or 'Gothic' thought was more important and characteristic in seventeenth-century England, as well as keeping track of what were doubtless many occasions on which the two were blithely combined and confused by persons unaware of the different foundations on which each rested. But the distinction exists: there can be no reconciling a view which insisted on the antiquity of the law within the island and which

[1] Below, pp. 96-7.   [2] *The Goths in England*, p. 122 n. 19.

could not have survived in minds aware of the similarities between early English and early Continental law, with one which based itself on these similarities to argue that English law had once formed part of a body of barbarian institutions common to all western Europe. Contemporaries intent only on asserting the antiquity of the law might combine the two; the historian of ideas must keep them, initially at least, distinct.

This book is concerned with a series of writers who followed and argued with one another throughout the century, in a continual debate which appears to possess a fair degree of logical unity; but it so happens that in their writings the Gothic idea does not figure at all prominently.[1] All can be explained on the assumption that the common-law writers took their law to represent the immemorial custom of their country and did not derive it from any source outside their own coasts. Without, therefore, any necessary implication that 'Gothic' thought was unimportant in seventeenth-century England, it is henceforth neglected; and a pattern of ideas—asserted to have been at least of no less importance and to have existed on a basis relatively untouched by 'Gothicism'—is worked out as a contribution to some larger history of English thought.

Maitland, on more than one occasion,[2] observed that the principal defect of the common lawyers' historical and legal thought was their ignorance of any law but their own, and added that some degree of comparative knowledge was an essential prerequisite of historical understanding where the law was concerned. Like many of Maitland's remarks in this field, this is a highly compressed judgment in which several meanings are hidden. It will help the progress of this study to distinguish some of them and place them in order.

In the first place, it must already be evident that the presumption that the law declared what was already immemorial would have been quite impossible if more than one system of law had obtained in England in the way in which they did in France. If it had been known that two laws had existed side by side and that they had

---

[1] Harrington is an exception (see ch. VI), but he is not engaged in the controversy for or against the ancient constitution.

[2] *Constitutional History of England*, pp. 142–3; *Collected Works*, I, p. 489.

competed and conflicted with, and borrowed from, one another, it would have been an inescapable conclusion that each law had reached its present state as a result of a complicated process whose stages could be dated and character known. If, for example, the civil law had been more than an importation and had taken territorial hold and competed with the common law as an alternative means of judging the same range of matters, it might have been evident three centuries before Maitland that civilian principles were embedded in the common law and had been used to build it up in its early stages. As it was, neither Fulbecke nor Cowell succeeded in bringing out this truth—perhaps because the *mos Italicus* prevailed among English civilians and they seem to have known little of the historical method of the Frenchmen—and Selden and the whole common-law school expressly denied it. No system of law was so constantly before the eyes of the English as to compel the realization that its principles had played a part in the creation of their own law.

But for the seventeenth-century mind, to be compelled to study the history of two laws in contact gave rise to historical ideas more far-ranging than this; and that stimulus too the English were denied. A partial exception which nevertheless illustrates this rule is to be found in the works of that Sir John Davies whose eulogy of custom we have already studied. In 1612, two years before the *Irish Reports*, he published *A Discoverie of the True Causes why Ireland was never entirely Subdued, nor brought under Obedience of the Crowne of England, untill the Beginning of His Maiesties happie Raigne,*[1] and in it he analysed the shortcomings of English policy since Henry II under two principal heads. The first is the failure to achieve a complete military conquest, and this Davies explores in some detail: though he knows little about medieval military organization, he utilizes the Tower, Westminster and Dublin Castle records in an attempt to estimate the number of soldiers on various expeditions from the arrangements made for their pay.[2] But the second aspect of his theme is the failure to bring Ireland at an early time under the rule of English law. Davies quotes Bodin for the view that a prince

---

[1] All quotations are from Davies, *Discoverie etc.* (London, 1747); reprinted from the edition of 1612.

[2] *Discoverie*, pp. 12, 23–6, 39, 45, 70.

is not sovereign where others (in this case the Irish chiefs) give law without reference to him;[1] but he carries the consequences of failure to impose the common law much further. He recognizes that the Irish are a historical paradox: they are far from an uncivilized people, yet their social life is barbarous.

> For, though the Irishry be a Nation of great Antiquity, and wanted neither wit nor valour; and though they had received the Christian Faith, above 1200 yeares since; and were Lovers of Musicke, Poetry and all kinde of learning; and possessed a Land abounding with all thinges necessary for the Ciuill life of man; yet (which is strange to bee related) they did never builde any houses of Bricke or stone (some few poor Religious Houses excepted) before the raigne of King *Henrie* the second, though they wer Lords of this Island for many hundred yeares before and since the Conquest attempted by the English.... Neither did any of them in all this time, plant any Gardens or Orchards, Inclose or improve their Lands, live together in setled Villages or Townes, nor made any provision for posterity....[2]

Davies finds the explanation of this in the 'unreasonable' inheritance customs which prevail under Irish brehon law, particularly in that of tanistry and the division of the inheritance among the heirs, legitimate and illegitimate, which he calls by the Kentish name of gavelkind. These have given rise to constant civil war over the succession to chiefdoms, and a state of things in which no man's inheritance is safe and no material progress possible. Now that Ireland is conquered and the king's writ runs everywhere, the brehon law of tenure and inheritance must be replaced by common-law tenures which the royal courts will protect and which will guarantee a sensible system of primogeniture (for gavelkind 'must needs in the end make a poore Gentility'[3]); and the Irish will learn husbandry and swiftly become as peaceable and prosperous as the Welsh have done in similar circumstances.[4]

In Ireland Davies had before his eyes two laws and two incompatible social systems. He was therefore able to observe, first, that each law consisted essentially of a particular way of holding, inheriting and doing service for land; and second, that from

[1] *Discoverie*, pp. 17–18. [2] *Discoverie*, pp. 170–1 *et seq.*
[3] *Discoverie*, p. 172.
[4] *Discoverie*, pp. 120–2, 131–3. Davies himself was of Welsh descent.

observance of one or other system of law there followed consequences in every department of economic and social life. He can
be seen applying these two ideas to the history of the Anglo-Irish,
whom (rather than the 'mere' Irish) he rightly saw to be the key to
the medieval story of Ireland; and it is in his treatment of them
that his historical thought is most highly developed. Because the
medieval kings failed to keep sufficient forces in Ireland, it fell
to the Anglo-Irish lords to raise and maintain men. Unable to
pay or equip them out of their own resources, they had recourse to
the Irish custom of 'coign and livery' and simply quartered them
on their tenants. English yeomen settlers refused to endure this
and returned to England in large numbers, but the Irish expected
nothing better, and it became to the lords' interest to stock their
lands with Irish tenants whose tenure and services were those prescribed by brehon law. The lords thus came to stand in exactly the
same relation to their tenants as an Irish chief, and by natural
consequence they adopted Irish customs, dress and language.[1] Even
if they did not join the ranks of the *Hibernis ipsis Hiberniores*, they
became a class neither enemies to nor servants of the crown. The
conquest of the island, originally held up because the king had not
sent forces sufficient to carry it out, was now much further delayed.
The lords discovered an interest in excluding the Irish from the
benefits of English law[2] and keeping up a constant state of border
warfare, because these conditions brought them franchises and
delegations of royal authority from a king whose power they had
ceased to advance; but they were equally interested in discouraging
further royal conquests, because if all Ireland were brought under
the king's writ the courts of common law would give their tenants
justice even against themselves.[3] If their power were threatened by
royal activity they did not hesitate to rebel and even to Hibernicize.[4]
Thus the mere Irish, the Hibernicized English and the Anglo-Irish
maintained a semi-chaotic balance of forces from which the chief
sufferers were the populace and the royal power. It was for these
reasons that no solution existed short of the systematic conquest of

[1] *Discoverie*, pp. 29-32, 56.   [2] *Discoverie*, pp. 99-120, 133-4.
[3] *Discoverie*, pp. 144-6.
[4] *Discoverie*, pp. 147-55 *et seq.*, 183-227.

the whole country, carried out by forces organized, maintained and commanded from England and aimed at making the king's writ run everywhere and ultimately at replacing brehon land law with common-law tenures which the king's courts would recognize and protect. The glory of Mountjoy and James I was to have achieved the former and prepared the way for the latter—work in which Davies was himself engaged.

Specialists in Irish history will no doubt find faults in Davies's analysis—though it may still be read with profit—but it remains perhaps the most outstanding piece of historical writing achieved by an Englishman in James I's reign. Davies describes men's actions in terms of the social system of which they form part, and shows how the Anglo-Irish were caught between two such systems and reacted by creating a border world of their own, which possessed the strength of neither but kept an uneasy balance between them. They were compelled to do this by the military weakness of the English government, and when this deficiency was remedied their world was at an end. Davies writes like this only because he views Ireland, in his own day and for long past, as the battleground of two laws, and is aware that each law can be reduced to a particular manner of holding land and doing military service for it, but on the other hand has the widest consequences in every department of life —so wide that the whole history of the Anglo-Irish, of their agriculture, speech and habits as well as of their political conduct, can be written in terms of their adherence to one or other law. Such were the effects which contemplation of a nation's history as comprising more than one system of law could have on historical thought.[1]

But Irish history was remote and alien, and brehon law had come into contact with common law only when the latter was already well developed. It presented no striking points of resemblance, no principles of its own which might be found embedded in the com-

---

[1] It might be observed here that Davies's ideas represent a definite tradition among English officials (and especially lawyers) in Ireland; many of his points are taken from a manuscript treatise on the 'Decay of Ireland' written by Baron Finglas in Henry VIII's reign, and he seems to have used other similar works. (For Finglas, see *D.N.B.*; his treatise was published in 1770.)

mon law and suggest new ideas as to how the latter had been built up; for in that process brehon law had of course played no part. Davies's Irish researches therefore had no effect whatever upon his thought about English legal history; as we have seen, two years after the *Discoverie* he was able to repeat unhesitatingly the theory of immemorial law and give almost classical expression to its underlying assumptions. His English and his Irish writings compared, therefore, underline the point that was made at the beginning of this chapter: there was nowhere within the dominions of the English crown or within the four seas of Britain a rival system of law which might be seen to have radically influenced the growth of the common law and thus compel Englishmen to think that their law had grown up under varying influences and at varying times. Until they were thus brought to think of the law as a product of history they would go on accepting its assumption that every record, judgment and statute was a declaration of immemorial custom. But no such basis of comparison was to be found within the British Isles. Civil law was an exotic; Scots law too little unified and articulate for the purpose;[1] Irish law the product of a wild and uncomprehended society. None had played a discernible part in English legal history, which, since the records began, revealed nothing but the self-perpetuation of the common law of the king's courts.

It was the kernel of Maitland's contention, therefore, that a basis of comparison must be found outside Britain. Until English law was viewed as part of the law of western Europe, none of the influences which had shaped its development could be discerned, and consequently no historical analysis of its growth was thinkable. The root of Coke's thought was his firm belief that the law was a purely insular product, and as far back as the records extended he was right; during all that period English law had received no important access of ideas from outside. The first comparative attack on common-law history, consequently, was unlikely to be made by the common lawyers themselves, engrossed in the study of their own records; and it must be made at a point in time belonging to the prehistory of the common law, when England could be shown

[1] However, the works of Sir John Skene were useful to Spelman; see ch. v, below.

to have received from Europe some at least of those institutions and ideas out of which the common law was afterwards built up. The most recent obvious example of such an occasion—and the most important of all—was the Norman Conquest. The common law was above all a law regulating the tenure of land, and the rules of tenure it contained in fact presupposed the existence of those military and feudal tenures which had been imported by the Normans; but this fact had been forgotten and could only be rediscovered by comparing English law with those continental laws which were avowedly feudal—since even the meaning of the word had been largely forgotten in England. When this was done, it became evident that a large part of English law could be identified as based upon a form of tenure no older than the Conquest and distinguished from those elements in the law which were older; and by a secondary operation, that since many of the obligations and ideas which had once flowed from feudal tenure no longer obtained in England, some kind of distinction must be drawn between the law of the twelfth century and the law of the seventeenth. These consequences were far greater in importance than those of the near-contemporary discovery that Anglo-Saxon law was so like that of the continental barbarians that it could be no older in England than the fifth century A.D. This discovery abolished Brutus and Arthur as lawgivers for all time, but the Anglo-Saxons remained a people of the dawn about whom legends clustered; and by a blending of the myth of immemorial law with that of Gothic liberty, it was possible as it were to transfer 'time beyond memory' to the primitive German forest. On the whole, therefore, the discovery of a Germanic element in early English history encouraged the spread of myths rather than checking them. But with the introduction of Norman feudalism, brought in when highly developed and imposed on an already articulate society by a single catastrophic act of conquest, no such devices were possible; and English historiography has oriented itself about that conquest ever since. The rediscovery of feudalism—which Maitland has permanently associated with the name of Sir Henry Spelman[1]—had other consequences, which must be considered in their place; but the next few chapters are concerned

[1] *Constitutional History, loc. cit.*

with the conditions under which it was made. First, then, we must examine the thought of the common lawyers on the subject.

Coke had administered one of his more resounding rebukes to the memory of Hotman, who had in his *De feudis commentatio tripertita* spoken disrespectfully of Littleton's *Tenures*; and Maitland pointed out that this was probably connected with Littleton's definition of what Hotman saw to be the *feudum*:

> Feodum idem est quod haereditas, et simplex idem est quod legitimum vel purum, et sic feodum simplex idem est quod haereditas legitima vel haereditas pura.[1]

As late, then, as the opening years of the seventeenth century no alternative to this definition was accepted by the chiefs of the common law. Sir Thomas Smith had indeed attempted to suggest that the word was current in continental law-schools in a very different sense, to which English jurists ought to pay some attention; but the rejoinder had instantly been made that Littleton's definition was the only one valid in English law.[2] This as far as it went was perfectly correct, but to accept it unquestioningly was the sign of a radical deficiency in the historical knowledge of English lawyers; one, however, which was a natural product of English history. Over the centuries, the courts of common law had operated to rob English custom and its language of any meaning except that which they themselves recognized, so that *feudum*, in the present case, had come to mean nothing more than a piece of land held in a tenure which the courts recognized as heritable according to certain fixed rules—the subject of most of Littleton's *Tenures*. It was no longer thought of as a piece of land given and received in a special way between lord and vassal, a consequence of the relationship expressed in homage, involving the vassal in the performance of certain express or implied services and radically affecting the way in which justice was done between the two men. Yet tenure *in capite*, homage,

---

[1] Hotman, *Opera*, ed. 1599, vol. II, p. 913; Coke, *First Institutes*, lib. I, cap. I, sect. I, and preface to *Tenth Reports*; Maitland, *English Law and the Renaissance*, pp. 12–14 and n. 29.

[2] See L. Alston's edition of Smith's *De republica Anglorum* (Cambridge, 1906), pp. xlvi, li, 133–7.

knight service, a multitude of usages incidental to the *feudum*, survived in England to a greater or lesser extent and were known to the common law and commented on by its learned men, even while the meaning of the relationship upon which all had been founded was now quite forgotten. Coke and Littleton, therefore, treated these things not as consequences of the vassal's homage and the lord's grant, but simply as part of the immemorial custom of England, known to be such because recognized by the courts. It is usual, and quite correct, to say that Coke knew nothing of feudal law; but he knew that doing homage was distinct from taking an oath of allegiance, though the two commonly went together.[1] He knew that it was legal dogma that all the land in England was held of some lord by some service, and ultimately of the crown, so that the tenant might have a hierarchy of lords above him.[2] He knew that the tenant could not alienate parcel of his fee to the prejudice of the lord's right to distrain in any part of it for the services due him.[3] He knew that knight-service was a thing common to many nations, and that in every language but English the word for knight reflected the fact that he was bound to serve on horseback.[4] He knew all these things and a great deal besides; in fact, it could well be maintained that he knew all there was to know about feudal law in England, except the single fact that it was feudal. Since his definition of the *feudum* was also Littleton's, he could not deduce all these things from its nature, and therefore saw very little connexion between them. He knew that they were all linked in a general way with lordship and tenure, but did not know that the characteristics of the *feudum* explained them all and that they formed a distinct class of legal phenomena, to which some such adjective as 'feudal' could properly be applied. To him their only essential characteristic was that the courts of England recognized them as custom; they were in no way distinguished from any other part of the law so recognized.

He could not therefore think historically of this element in the common law. It is true that when he writes of the law that we

---

[1] *First Institutes*, 8th ed., fol. 65.
[2] *Ibid.*
[3] *Ibid.* fols. 43a–43b.
[4] *Ibid.* fol. 74b.

should call feudal he shows some signs of knowing that he is dealing with a state of things now past. He is aware that lords no longer exact homage from their tenants—though he deplores this and thinks that they could still do so if they chose[1]—or lead them to battle in the king's wars.[2] He recognizes that tenure *in capite* was once an indispensable adjunct to territorial titles and baronies, but now is so no longer;[3] and he knows that the legislation of Edward I brought about important departures from the law of tenure described by Bracton.[4] But this awareness of change rests upon general impressions and is quite unsystematized. Coke never comes near to saying that these things were based on the *feudum* and that with the *feudum* they declined. What is more serious, since he does not regard these institutions as feudal, but merely as part of immemorial custom, he takes them too to be immemorial and dilates upon their antiquity. On the authority of the *Mirror of Justices* he states that the first kings of the realm, notably King Alfred, enfeoffed the barons with their lands and gave them the right to hold courts baron;[5] and as we have already seen, with the aid of the apocryphal *leges* printed by Lambarde, there is something like a wholesale attribution of Norman feudal usages to the times before the Conquest.[6] It is likely that no other shortcoming in their historical knowledge did more to make the common lawyers' interpretation of history possible than their ignorance of the *feudum* and feudalism, and here a word should perhaps be spoken about Coke's alleged credulity. Certainly he was a credulous man, in the sense that he had always far too passionate and extreme a conviction of the truth of the case he was pleading,[7] and beyond doubt that affected his treatment of history; he ought, for example, to have smelt one

[1] *Ibid.* fol. 68 a.
[2] *Ibid.* fol. 71 a. Note that Coke is here talking of the indenture system.
[3] *Ibid.* fol. 83 b; *Second Institutes*, 4th ed., pp. 5–6.
[4] See the treatment of these statutes in *Second Institutes* generally.
[5] *First Institutes*, fols. 58a–58b.
[6] See both *First* and *Second Institutes*, *passim*. A partial exception is to be found in *Fourth Institutes*, *sub* 'Court of Wards and Liveries' (ed. London, 1889, pp. 190–3), where Coke admits that wardship and marriage were imposed by the Conqueror, though knight service was already ancient.
[7] His conduct in the *causes célèbres* of Raleigh and Overbury would seem to bear this out.

or two of the horde of rats which populate the pages of the *Mirror*. But if the interpretation of his historical thought put forward in this chapter and the last is correct, it must follow that he was largely the prisoner of intellectual conditions imposed upon his age by the whole course of English law and history. There was an enormous weight of tradition and evidence supporting the view that the law was immemorial; while as long as Littleton's definition of the *feudum* was accepted, the feudal element in English law could not be identified, much less treated historically. The whole power of the 'Edward the Confessor' myth supported the belief that there was nothing in Anglo-Norman law which had not been in Anglo-Saxon, and until a new definition of the *feudum* was adopted, and its implications pressed home in defiance of all orthodoxy, this belief must remain. Such a new definition would never be found by study of the common law alone. Littleton's authority was too great and 'idem quod haereditas' appeared a perfectly satisfactory account of *feudum* as the common law had always used the term. The stimulus to new thought must come from outside.

We have now almost arrived at the full inner meaning of Maitland's remarks on this question. English lawyers would never attain to a historical view of their own law by study of its records alone, since these revealed no important changes in the course of their history and nothing interfered with the presumption that the record declared the immemorial custom. But, as Maitland pointed out in the *Constitutional History*, comparison of English with continental law would reveal that the former contained certain principles, institutions and usages common to nearly every law of western Europe, and that many of them were those known outside England as 'feudal' and related to a definition of *feudum* very unlike Littleton's. This discovery must lead to the realization that the myth of the immemorial must be abandoned, since an important element of English law was of foreign origin and had been brought in by some European people among whom it had grown up. Moreover, said Maitland in another context,[1] what was needed was 'a theory of feudalism': as the common law's definition of *feudum* could not be employed as a basis on which to explain the whole range of

[1] *Collected Works*, vol. I, p. 489.

feudal phenomena, another definition, drawn from continental law, must be put in its place, so that an entire sector of the common law would be interpreted by a principle which it did not itself contain. When English law was compared with continental law, the thought of English lawyers would be stimulated by a graft from abroad. Of the resistance which this process would meet in England Maitland said nothing; but we must now investigate the way in which it was set going.

CHAPTER IV

The Discovery of Feudalism: French and Scottish Historians

IT is one of the paradoxes of European historiography that the most recent authority on the character of feudalism, Professor F. L. Ganshof, should have laid it down that the feudalism of Lombardy can no longer be regarded as typical of that form of society as we see it in European life as a whole.[1] A paradox because it was through the study of Lombard feudal law that the Renaissance historians first became aware of the existence of feudalism—though so abstract a term lay beyond their vocabularies[2]—as a complex and variable set of institutions, whose place in the general pattern of European law (and, therefore, in history) required to be explained. The historians of law in western Europe, as we have seen, were students of written law before they turned to the unwritten customs and the archival deposits of particular regions; and Lombard feudalism possessed, in the *Libri Feudorum*, the only written systematization of feudal law which had become part of the general legal heritage of Europe. To the original Milanese studies of the law of the *feudum*, compiled in the twelfth century, had been added a number of imperial constitutions, chiefly Salian and Hohenstaufen, bearing upon the feudal law of descent and forfeiture; and the *Libri Feudorum* had thus a peculiar authority for any European lawyer concerned with the interpretation of these matters. Though they were hardly working or enforce-

[1] F. L. Ganshof, *Feudalism* (*Qu'est-ce que la féodalité?*), Eng. trans. by P. Grierson (London, 1952), p. 60.
[2] Terms such as 'feudalism', 'féodalité', seem not to occur in any of the writers discussed in the present volume. They speak only of 'the feudal law', 'jus feudale', which is thought of as a single set of institutions arising in Lombardy and disseminated throughout the West. The word 'feudalism' has, however, been used on occasion in the following attempt to convey their thought to the modern reader.

able law anywhere, they had doctrinal authority in most lands where there was feudalism; it was recognized that the *feudum* was a universal institution, and that the Lombard books, in virtue both of the clarity of the original expositions and of the authority of the imperial decrees which they contained, possessed the status of universal law. They were, in effect if not formally, part of the *Corpus Juris Civilis*, and as such were glossed by Bulgarus in the thirteenth century and were the subject of *Summae* by Hugolinus and Odofredus and *Commentarii* by Baldus, Jason and others.[1]

In the southern and south-eastern provinces of the kingdom of France they were cited and studied with particular attention—less because these lands were strongly feudal in their law and character than because, formerly associated with the empire, these were *pays du droit écrit*. When therefore the French humanist school of legal scholars in the sixteenth century set about their work of textual criticism and historical interpretation, the *Libri Feudorum* received their attention. Both Cujas and Hotman produced critical editions —Cujas adding new texts to the compilation in 1567—and Hotman was able to quote the opinions (with which he disagreed) of a formidable array of European scholars, including Budé, Zasi, Connan, Torelli and Du Moulin. It is characteristic of both Hotman and his age that the context in which he quoted them was a debate on the origins of the *feudum*, and this contention arose at a most fruitful time. Legal scholarship, as we have seen, was willing and able as never before to turn aside from the history of the Roman texts to explore the customary and barbaric elements in European law, and the legal foundations of French society and monarchy were being investigated, alike by civil and by customary lawyers, with close attention to the diverse and multiracial origins of the rights of monarch and people. The study of the *Libri Feudorum*, therefore, swiftly passed the limits of merely textual clarification. It was recognized as presenting the problems of explaining exhaustively the social arrangements which arose when a fee was given and received, and of ascertaining the place occupied by this phenomenon in the tangled Roman and Germanic history of Europe. The

[1] Declareuil, *Histoire du droit français à 1789* (Paris, 1925), pp. 858–9.

systematic thoroughness of the medieval Lombard lawyers made it possible to arrive at a definition of the *feudum* whereby it could be recognized in any part of Europe, and the new interest in Germanic philology made it possible to open the question of the fee's barbaric origins. Both discoveries were to be of the utmost importance in the belated development of English historiography; but first it will be necessary to study that phase of continental scholarship in which it seemed uncertain whether feudalism and the fee were to be thought of as Roman or Germanic in origin, and to see how this problem and the definition of the fee were treated in the works of Cujas and of Hotman.

Cujas's edition of the *Libri Feudorum* was dedicated from Bourges in June 1566.[1] Earlier humanist commentators—Budé, Torelli, Zasi—had not unnaturally tended to seek for an explanation of feudal law in the Roman world.[2] They had followed medieval etymologists (among whom one of the original Milanese compilers, Obertus de Orto, must be counted) in deriving *feudum* from *foedus* or *fides*; and out of their encyclopaedic knowledge of Roman law and classical historical sources, they remembered a wide variety of patron–client relationships and of land-tenancies of a precarious or conditional kind, involving various degrees of dependence, clientage, service or actual loss of rights or liberty. Among all these it was natural that a large number of 'Roman' theories of feudal origins should be put forward, and in the third quarter of the century an alternative 'Germanic' interpretation was only beginning to gain ground, chiefly among the students or the partisans of French customary law, whose paths (in the nature of their work) lay largely among the Frankish and Teutonic materials for early French history. Cujas, a man of the south, might be pardoned for leaning to the Roman side, but in actual fact he displays a respectable knowledge of the possible German derivations of several characteristic terms in feudal law. Saying that the derivation of *feudum* from *fides* is to be preferred to that from *foedus*, he points out that the recipient of benefices among the Franks were known as *leudes*, the French *loyaux*: 'unde puto Germanos feudum appellare Leudum, sive

[1] In Cujas (*Iacobi Cuiacii operum quae de iure fecit*, t. 2, Paris, 1637).
[2] Cf. R. Dareste, *Essai sur François Hotman* (Paris, 1850), pp. 27–8.

Lehnen'.[1] Whatever may be thought of his etymology in these instances, Cujas was at least not unconscious of the need to explore barbaric and Germanic sources (though it will be observed that his argument would support the idea that the Franks and Goths translated a pre-existing term *fideles* by *leudes*); a number of lines lower he observes:

> Sed et Vassi, et Vassali nomen, quod eisdem competit, servitium significat, sive comitatum, cum deducatur non ex eo quod sint quasi in vasario nobilium, et vasa eorum instrumentaque censeantur, sed a Germanica, et veteri Gallica voce *Gessel*, qua significatur comes, qui nobis servit mercede certa....[2]

Throughout his lengthy preface, however, Cujas is concerned rather to define the *feudum* and its accompanying relationships than to seek for its origins, and it is on these grounds that he repudiates the identification of *vassus/vassalus* with *cliens*. The clients owed no military service, which was the essence of vassalage; they 'praedia sua pleno iure possident', while the vassals had only the temporary or perpetual usufruct; the clients received *sportulae* or dined at the patron's table, whereas the vassal abandoned property in his own land to receive a grant from his lord. 'Clienti respondet patronus.... Vassalo autem respondet dominus, qui et senior dicitur....'[3] But having gone thus far on the road towards describing the feudal relationship as one in which a man gives himself to a lord while remaining free, performing military service in return for a usufruct in a piece of land, Cujas turns back to the question of origins. Gerardus, he says—Gerardus Niger, traditionally supposed the author of the first of the *Libri Feudorum*—describes feudal law as 'antiquissimum'; and since Gerardus was himself a Lombard:

[1] Cujas, p. 791.
[2] 'But the term "vassus" (or "vassalus", which is applied to the same people) implies service or companionship, for it is derived not from the fact that the vassals are as it were part of the nobleman's equipage (*vasarium*) or are regarded as his utensils (*vasa*) or tools, but from the old German and Gaulish word "gessel", which means a companion serving for a fixed reward.' Cujas, p. 791.
[3] 'The client has a patron.... But the vassal has a lord, also known as a seigneur....'

inepte id repetieris ex Langobardis ipsis sive Gothis, quorum leges nihil de feudis habent palam, nec antiquissimum esse nobis unquam persuaseris, nisi id liquido deduxeris ex moribus P. Romani, quod siet ita commodissime.[1]

The argument is very much less dogmatic than it seems. Not the least of Gerardus's services to posterity—and in it he displayed a historical sense not too common at the beginning of the twelfth century—was his clear statement that the *feudum* had within human memory passed through an evolution of several distinct stages, from tenure at will or for a limited period, through tenure for one life, to tenure which was perpetual and heritable with few or no limitations.[2]

Antiquissimo tempore sic erat in dominorum potestate connexum, ut quando vellent possent auferre rem in feudum a se datam. Postea vero

---

[1] 'It would be a mistake to seek its origin among the Lombards themselves or the Goths, whose laws contain no clear reference to "feuda"; nor are we to be persuaded that it was "antiquissimum", unless it can be convincingly derived from the institutions of the Roman people, which would be very suitable.'

[2] 'In the very earliest times the benefice was so far subject to the lord's authority that he might take away at will what he had granted in fee. But afterwards it came about that the vassal had security of tenure for a year only; and then it was ordained that this should be extended to the length of his life. But still his sons had no right of succession; so the next stage was that the benefice should pass to the sons, that is to whichever of them the lord chose to grant it, which today is agreed to mean that it belongs to all of them equally. When, however, Conrad journeyed to Rome, the vassals in his service petitioned him to enact a law extending the succession to the sons of a son, and granting that the brother of a man who died without legitimate heirs would succeed him in their father's benefice. But if one of a number of brothers accepted a fief from a lord and died without legitimate heirs, his brother should not succeed him; if, on the other hand, the brothers received the fief jointly, one should not succeed the other unless this were expressly provided: with the condition, that if one died without legitimate heirs his brother should succeed him, but that the survival of an heir removed the brother from the succession. It should also be noticed that though daughters as well as sons may succeed their father, they are by law excluded from succeeding to a fief; and so are their sons likewise, unless it is specially stated that the daughters may succeed. It must in addition be observed that a benefice does not descend to collaterals, other than the sons of a father's brother, in the usage established by the lawyers of antiquity; but in the modern epoch the succession has been extended even to the seventh degree. So that in contemporary law a benefice passes to the male descendants *ad infinitum*.' Cujas, *Libri Feudorum*, lib. I, tit. I. Spelman's transcript of the passage (*Archaeologus*, 1626, p. 257) contains one or two interpolations and transpositions. The page is wrongly numbered 158.

eo ventum est ut per annum tantum firmitatem haberent: deinde statutum est ut usque ad vitam fidelis produceretur. Sed cum hoc iure successionis ad filios non pertineret: sic progressum est ut ad filios deveniret, in quem scilicet, dominus hoc vellet beneficium confirmare, quod hodie ita stabilitum est, ut ad omnes aequaliter filios pertineat. Cum vero Conradus Romam proficisceretur petitum est a fidelibus qui in eius erant servitio, ut lege ab eo promulgata, hoc etiam ad nepotes ex filio producere dignaretur, et ut frater fratri sine legitimo herede defuncto, in beneficio quod eorum patris fuit succedat. Sin autem unus ex fratribus a domino feudum acceperit, eo defuncto sine legitimo herede, frater eius in feudum non succedit: quod etsi communiter acceperint, unus alteri non succedit, nisi hoc nominatim dictum sit: scilicet, ut uno defuncto sine legitimo herede, alter succedat: herede vero relicto alter frater removebitur. Hoc autem notandum est, quod licet filiae et masculi patribus succedant: legibus tamen a successione feudi removentur: similiter et earum filii, nisi specialiter dictum fuerit ut ad eas pertineat. Hoc quoque sciendum est quod beneficium ad venientes ex latere, ultra fratres patrueles, non progreditur successione, secundum usum ab antiquis sapientibus constitutum: licet moderno tempore usque ad septimum geniculum sit usurpatum. Quod in masculis descendentibus novo iure usque in infinitum extenditur.

Round this invaluable statement all legist thought on the history of feudalism was to organize itself. What Cujas is saying above is that feudal law cannot as a whole be *antiquissimum*, because its significant characteristics were formed in a process of development after the intrusion of the Lombards into the Roman empire. He declares that he finds nothing feudal in the first written laws of the Lombards or the Goths, and leans to the opinion that the essential features of feudal tenure (i.e. all that is truly *antiquissimum*) were drawn by the invaders from late Roman law. Nor can he be accused of uncritical Romanism even in this judgment. He thinks he detects in the feudal tenant the lineaments of various types of usufructuary and temporary tenant whom he knows from the Roman law, and suggests that under the Lombards these became hereditary and at the same time militarized, assuming the character and the nomenclature of members of the barbarian *comitatus*. The whole passage should perhaps be quoted:

Fit saepe in libris nostris hominum mentio, qua appellatione frequentius servi significantur. Sed et liberi, puta actores, procuratores, custodes praediorum insularii, conductores emphiteuctarii [*sic*], chartularii, precarii possessores. His possessio conceditur ad tempus. Quae actori, feudum est gastaldiae. Quae custodi, feudum gardiae. Iisdem postea coepit concedi in perpetuum, quod est verum et proprium feudum, atque ita...paulatim qui erant actores, custodesque praediorum nostrorum temporarii, perpetui esse coeperunt. Latinumque Hominum nomen retinuerunt, novum et exterum Vasallorum sive Leodum et Feudatariorum acceperunt a principibus et nobilioribus, qui eis sua praedia in perpetuum concedere maluerunt, si militiae oneribus se obligarent, invecta in Italiam nomina a principibus Germanis, quibus fuere semper multi Comites (sic Cor. Tacitus vasallos vocat. Glossae συστρατιώτας interpretantur) et principum aemulatio magna, cui plurimi et accerrimi.[1]

He proceeds to give further Tacitean characteristics of the *comites*, and without interruption to quote Constantine Porphyrogenitus for the existence of lands held 'eadem fere hominum conditione', and under the obligation of military service, in the Eastern Empire.

Cujas, it is plain, must not be accused of a 'Roman' bias in his account of the history of the *feudum* without one all-important qualification: he knew that it was a problem of the development of barbarian institutions within the Roman world. Subject to that statement of the question, he thought the *feudum* could be explained by a conflation of the Roman law regarding the tenure of land with the *mores* and vocabulary of the barbarian war-band; but he knew, as all students of the *Libri Feudorum* knew, that he was not merely looking for the origin of the *feudum*, but tracing its evolution towards

[1] 'Our books make frequent mention of "homines", a term generally employed to designate slaves. But it can also refer to free tenants, such as "actores", "procuratores", "custodes praediorum insularii", "conductores emphiteuticarii", "chartularii", and "precarii possessores". Possession was granted to such tenants for a time only. The grant to an "actor" corresponds to "feudum gastaldiae", that to a "custos" to "feudum gardiae". At a later time these grants began to be perpetual, which constitutes the true *feudum*, and so...by degrees those who had been temporary "actores" and "custodes" of estates began to be so in perpetuity. They kept the Latin name of "homines", but adopted also the new foreign names "vassals", "leudes", "feudataries" from their chieftains and nobles, who preferred to grant them perpetual estates if they would bind themselves to do military service. These names were brought into Italy by the German chieftains, who always had many "comites" (so Tacitus designates the vassals; the glosses call them συστρατιωταί) and competed keenly to see who could acquire the largest and most daring following.' For this and the preceding passage, Cujas, p. 793. See also pp. 799-800.

the full heritability guaranteed by the constitutions of Conrad II. Within the idea that feudalism is at once Roman and Germanic, there was and is room for an infinite variation of emphasis and definition, and subsequent developments of thought have taken us away from Lombardy altogether; but the fact that Cujas struck a balance, recognized that he faced a complex evolution, and gave no crude or one-sided interpretation of the problem, is very largely due to the historical perspective of the medieval Milanese whom he knew as Gerardus Niger.

As for François Hotman, though it is true that he stressed the Germanic aspects of the *feudum*, very much the same must be said of his treatment of the problem. In the 'Disputatio de feudis', which forms part of his *De feudis commentatio tripertita* (published in 1573), he begins by emphasizing the essentially military character of the *feudum*. The word is old Lombard, he says, and concerns the horse-soldier—'atque ad praedia equitibus alendis assignata pertinet'.[1] The fact that the *feudum* is a military grant did more than any other consideration to convince Hotman that the word is to be derived, not from *foedus* or *fides*, 'sed a Germanica voce Feed', which the barbarian laws use in the sense of 'blood-feud' or private, as well as public, war. He emphasized that the *Libri Feudorum* are predominantly concerned with fees granted by lords to their followers in their private contentions. Lastly, he challenges the world to show him any mention 'aut verbi huius, aut iuris, hoc est clientelae feudalis,' before the Gothic and Germanic invasions.[2]

It will be observed that Hotman's argument for the Germanic character of the *feudum* is based rather on a conviction of its military purpose than on any subtleties of philological science. In all that follows, he seems to be concerned much more to distinguish the military vassal-relationship from other forms of subordinate tenure than to argue for its 'Germanism'; and he is scarcely whole-hearted, much less dogmatic, in the attempt to ascribe the *feudum* to German prehistory. Thus, he remarks that it does seem reasonable ('mihi non inconcinnum videtur') to seek for the origins of vassalage ('Vasallicarum clientelarum') among the ancient Germans, and

[1] Hotman, *op. cit.* 'Disputatio de feudis', p. 6.
[2] Hotman, p. 7.

proceeds to quote, *in extenso*, Tacitus' account of the *comitatus*.[1] But he adds instantly that in the *Germania* 'nulla prorsus beneficiorum, aut feudorum, aut militarium praediorum mentio fit'. Moreover, two pages later[2] we find him controverting François Connan's attempt to derive vassalage from the Gallic *comitatus* described by Caesar, and urging in the forefront of his argument that the express obligation of the *comites* to die with their fallen chief is unknown among feudal vassals—and he can hardly have failed to recall that the selfsame custom occurs in the passage of Tacitus quoted, two pages earlier, by himself. Hotman's case against the claim of all forms of *comitatus* to figure as the prototype of feudal vassalage is the same: 'non certos et proprios agros ei rei attributos fuisse: qua tamen in re magnam feudorum partem constare, deinceps pro locis intelligetur.'[3] Was it in his mind that some point in time must be found at which the *comites* began to acquire grants of land held in virtue of their military service? Cujas had attempted, as we have seen, to provide just such a theory; but Hotman—without naming Cujas—dissents expressly from the view that the origin of the *feudum* may be found in the precarious tenures of the *actores*, *custodes*, and the rest, grown perpetual. We know what became of these tenants, he says: they became *coloni* and lost their freedom; their tenure became perpetual only in the sense that they were bound to the soil; and they were expressly debarred from the practice of arms. Nothing less like the feudal vassal—'conditio ...non modo liberalis, atque ingenua, verum etiam plane militaris' —could very well be imagined.[4] But Hotman's conclusions are ultimately no more than negative; he has singled out the *comitatus* for special emphasis, urged against it that its members were not feudally endowed with land, refuted Cujas's attempt to show how this came about and offered no alternative explanation.

[1] Hotman, pp. 7–8.

[2] Hotman, p. 9. This is part of the chapter: 'Variae doctorum hominum sententiae de Feudorum origine et instituto' (ch. II).

[3] 'that there was no assignation of definite and individual grants of land in connexion with it; but that the great majority of *feuda* rested on this basis will be constantly evident from the sources.'

[4] 'a condition not only free and freeborn, but actually military.' Hotman, pp. 10–11.

It would appear that Hotman's real purpose was not to argue for either a 'Roman' or a 'Germanic' origin for the feudal relationship, but, by refuting all theories of its origin which he thought obscured its true nature, to keep its full complex character clearly before the minds of his readers. Thus he repudiates Budé and Zasi, who would identify it with Roman clientage, because this obscures the fact that it was military in character; Connan, who would identify it with the *comitatus*, because it was founded on grants of land; Torelli, who wanted to connect it with the Roman *limitanei*, because the vassal is not a veteran being rewarded for his services to the republic, but a warrior endowed by a lord out of the lord's own land. The multitude of arguments in the opening chapters of the 'Disputatio' describe exhaustively what the giving and receiving of *feuda* was like, and what it was unlike. From the whole emerges the picture of a unique and many-sided relationship, which must be regarded as having been born at or after the irruption of the Germans (notably the Lombards) into the empire, and matured at the time when the fee became fully inheritable under Conrad II.[1] That this work of definition, presenting as it did a picture of the fee universally recognizable and easily related to a single process of development, was what European historiography chiefly needed, is demonstrated by the subsequent work of English and Scottish historians, and first of all the Scot Sir Thomas Craig.

Craig was born in 1538 and studied law in Paris from 1555 to 1561. It is stated that his master in the civil law was François Baudouin.[2] He was therefore in direct contact with French thought at a time which antedates by some years the work of Cujas and Hotman on the feudal law; but the historical chapters of his *Jus Feudale* (published in 1603 and dedicated to King James) reveal the influence of Hotman at every turn, notably in the chapter designed to refute the theory that feudal tenures derive from the Roman law, and the work must certainly be taken as displaying the effects of French thought concerning feudal history on the mind of a highly intelligent foreigner who carried on his studies throughout the second half of the century. The peculiar significance which his book derives from its Scottish authorship must be considered later.

[1] See Hotman, ch. II, *passim*.   [2] *D.N.B.*, *sub* 'Craig, Thomas'.

For Craig, feudal law is a European fact of the first importance; it is a universal law and the law of his own country:

in eo subjecto circa quod versatur, juris sibi principatum in potentissimis totius Europae regnis occupav[it], et adhuc retin[et]. Hoc jus Feudale, hujus nostri regni proprium et peculiare jus esse, et ad quod in rebus dubiis decidendis sit recurrendum, quoties de rebus immobilibus, id est, de hereditatis acquisitione vel amissione agitur, contendo....[1]

and its history therefore needs to be traced from the beginning. In carrying this out he has no documents more authoritative than those contained in the *Libri Feudorum*, and these in the view he has received from his teachers prove the *feudum* to be primarily a Lombard institution. He is aware of the necessity to pursue its origins at least as far back as the Germanic invasions; but it soon becomes apparent that no more than Hotman can he document the gap between the *comitatus* and the *feudum*. He begins, therefore, by explaining that, for reasons of climatic influence which recall Bodin, servitude among the northern peoples was more just and clement than among the southern, and took in fact the form of the voluntary devotion displayed by the Tacitean *comites*. We next behold the war-bands invading and partitioning the Roman empire, and here the origin of the *feudum* is explained by a subtle and remarkable piece of reconstruction. The Germanic chief, keeping the better land for himself, left the worse to be cultivated by *coloni*, exacting from them various rents, principally in kind since the use of money was then nearly unknown. But 'robustiores in comites assumebat, eis, unde alerentur, praestabat';[2] he maintained his retainers out of the dues paid him. In time, however, the *comites* preferred to settle in person upon the estates out of which they

[1] 'in that branch of jurisprudence with which it is concerned, it has occupied and holds to this day the chief place among forms of law in all the greatest realms of Europe. That this feudal law is the true and unique law of this kingdom of ours and should be referred to in the deciding of all doubtful matters, whenever it is a question of immovable property, that is, of the acquisition or loss of an inheritance: such is my contention.' Craig (*D. Thomae Craigii de Riccarton, equitis...Jus Feudale tribus libris comprehensum*, Edinburgh, 1732: 3rd edition, ed. James Baillie), p. 24.

[2] 'he took the strongest for his companions and provided them with a source of upkeep.'

had formerly been maintained, the lord caring little whether his men occupied the land or merely consumed its yield ('utrum res ipsas, an fructus omnes ac utilitates assignar[et]'[1]), so long as he retained the actual *potestas*. (So that, despite the choice of words in the phrases just quoted, in assigning the *res ipsas* he would grant no more than a usufruct.) He therefore at first insisted on making all grants, whether of lands or pensions, precarious and at will; but in time came about that gradual development, known to us from the *Libri Feudorum*, towards the full heritability of fees, ending in the paradoxical climax that a mere usufruct has become perpetual, hereditary and forfeit only under strict codified rules.[2]

What we have here—whether it issues from Craig's mind or another's—can only be highly intelligent and indeed brilliant conjecture, designed to fill the gap which Hotman had noted and left between *comites* and vassals. Acknowledging that the feudal and barbarian laws do not provide a sufficient answer, some thinker has turned from the strictly legal analysis made by Cujas and Hotman, and has succeeded in linking three well-known facts rather of an economic order—that the *comites* fed at the board of their lord, that colonial tenures paying rents largely in kind increased under Germanic domination, and that the vassal or feudatory enjoyed the usufruct of the land granted him. This learned and plausible account of a social development can scarcely have been based on more evidence than that, and the modern reader is left with an acute sense of the adventurous vigour of the historical thought bred in the French law schools. At the same time, it emerges with clarity that study of the feudal law was peculiarly calculated to cause men's minds to pass from reflexions on the forms of the law to inquiry into the social and economic realities which underlay them.

Craig distinguishes three phases in the progress of the *feudum*: its infancy, in which it was entirely precarious or granted for one life, its adolescence, in which it became heritable by the son only, and its maturity, in which it became fully heritable, as did duchies, counties and baronies.[3] In a digression at the outset of this part of his argument, he makes the remarkable suggestion that the first

---

[1] 'whether he assigned them the land itself or the fruits and the use thereof.'
[2] Craig, pp. 26–7.   [3] Craig, pp. 27–30.

age may justly be compared to the *timar* system of contemporary Turkey. The Sultan ('Imperator Turcicus') grants out the frontier provinces of his empire in estates to be held 'sub ea lege ut ad omnes expeditiones certum numerum equitum paratum habeant pro quantitate et bonitate *Timarriae*'.[1] Since the historiography of our own age still holds debate with itself how far the term 'feudalism' may be applied to similar institutions which cannot be derived from western Europe in the tenth century, it is interesting to notice how early in the history of feudal studies the Ottoman empire began to furnish European scholars with illuminating comparisons. Thirty years before Craig's book was published, Hotman had suggested that 'quos Turcae Bassas appellant' might not unjustly be compared with the *vassi* and considered 'eodem ex fonte nomen sumpsisse'. Craig's comparison is notably better informed and he is aware of dissimilarities. On the death of the timariot, he observes, the holding reverts to the Sultan who regrants it to whom he will and for life only, and it is for this reason that the *timar* system can be compared only to the *feudorum infantiae*.[2]

It is out of this comparison, however, that the greatest difference between Craig's view of feudalism and ours emerges. He seems to think of the Germanic invaders, as of the Turks, as settling their conquered provinces with a strong centralized military class, instantly obedient to the prince's call; Hotman's emphasis on the origin of vassalage in the private blood-feud finds little place in his account of the matter, and the almost 'manorial' account of the rise of the *feudum*, given by Craig a page or two earlier, does not recur. The explanation of this must be seen in the fact that his notion of feudal society was drawn from the relatively ordered world revealed in the *Libri Feudorum*. The lords and vassals of Lombardy lived in a society which had been brought under a single rule at least to the point where a single code of feudal law could be drawn up and prove of some use, and, as we shall see, Craig looked upon feudal law as the law of a well-ordered and strongly monarchical society. He would be criticized by a modern student, also, for

[1] 'with the legal obligation to have ready for every military operation a certain number of cavalry, related to the size and value of the *timar*.'
[2] Craig, p. 30; Hotman, p. 13.

thinking of feudalism, at least in the first place, not as a disintegration of the heart of Carolingian society, but as a law which one people possessed and another could copy—an attitude more typical of what is usually attributed to Renaissance historiography than is much else in his writings. Because the feudal law he has is Lombard law, he assumes that it had been the law of the Lombards, at least in its essentials, for centuries before it was written down. Therefore Charlemagne must have discovered it in operation when he conquered the Lombard kingdom, and it must have been from this source that it spread to the rest of the Frankish empire. However, any tendency Craig may have had to give a naïve account of mere imitation and communication was checked by his awareness that the *feudum* had developed from a precarious to a hereditary tenure, and that the story of this growth was to be read in the constitutions of various emperors of whom Charlemagne was only the first. Conrad II, Hugh Capet and Barbarossa had brought the process to its culmination, and Craig's summary account of the matter is anything but unhistorical.

Sed nihil certius quam ex Caroli Magni, et Imperatorum qui eum sequuti sunt, constitutionibus primum in Gallia Cisalpina, quae nobis Transalpina est, quam hodie Longobardiam dicimus, coepisse; mox ad Transalpinam penetrasse: non ut unum universale jus de feudis a principio constitueretur, sed tantum ut peccata, quae ex diversa feudorum observatione eo tempore admittebantur, corrigerentur....Nec dubito quin toto illo tempore, quod inter Carolum Magnum et Fridericum primum intercesserat, multae aliae constitutiones Imperatorum promulgatae sint de feudis, saepe inter se diversae, aliquando contrariae, prioribus posteriores, tamen quae jus illud vagum et varium certis limitibus coercerent.[1]

[1] 'But there is nothing more certain than that the custom originated with the constitutions of Charlemagne and the Emperors who followed him, first in Cisalpine Gaul (Transalpine to us), today called Lombardy, and then made its way across the Alps; not that a single universal feudal law was set up from the beginning, but rather that the faults which were committed through the variations of feudal custom in that age were corrected....Nor can it be doubted that, in the long period between Charlemagne and Frederick I, many other Imperial constitutions were promulgated on the subject of *feuda*, and that these often differed among themselves, the later sometimes contradicting the earlier, but were calculated to bring this uncertain and varying custom within definite limits.' Craig, p. 34.

And the *Libri Feudorum*, he stresses—that is, the works of Gerardus Niger and Obertus de Orto—consist of a conflation of diverse Lombard customs made at the very end of this complex process. In an age when Machiavelli's praise of the legislator who had instituted the law and kingship of France was still widely read and admired, Craig can certainly not be accused of lacking a sense of the gradual development of institutions or of being blind to the partial and often contradictory actions of particular men through which that development pursues its course.

Having defined the *feudum* by a picture of its rise and progress in history, Craig turned to demonstrate the feudal character of Scots law. So convinced was he that his country's existing land law was essentially feudal and European that he taught that, where written and customary law failed them, Scots judges and jurisconsults might safely have recourse to the books of the continental feudists.[1] In the *Libri Feudorum*, as taught at Paris and edited by Cujas and Hotman, he saw a systematic exposition of the principles of tenure, forfeiture and inheritance which sufficed to render intelligible the laws of Scotland. This he was prepared to explain—first historically, by an account of how feudal law had arisen and come into Scotland; and next juridically, by a detailed analysis of Scots law based on the principles of the *Libri Feudorum*. But Craig was, in addition, aware that the history of his own country could only with the utmost care be separated from that of the neighbour kingdom—he was after all addressing himself to the king of both; and the peculiar importance of his book to the present study is that, publishing in the first year of the union of the crowns, he set out to show that the land law of England, no less than of Scotland, was feudal in character, and that the history of each country formed part of the history of law in Europe.

There is not much detailed analysis of English common law and reduction of it to feudal principles. Craig was not an authority on English law and he was but writing an introductory chapter to a book for Scotsmen. We may take it for granted that he was aware that, on Littleton's own showing, the basis of the common law of real property was the *feudum* and that, in the light of continental

[1] Craig, p. 52.

84

scholarship, it could hardly be denied what the *feudum* was; but he does not trouble to make this point. His arguments are really two. In the first place he remarks that nearly all the essential terms of French feudal law are in use in the English courts. From Rastell's book in exposition of the terms of English law and from the language employed in both common and statute law, it is safe to deduce the Norman and therefore French origin of all the land law in use among the English, 'et praecipue de wardis et maritatione heredum'.[1] Secondly, in a different place Craig gives a long list of the common law's better-known maxims and says that their Norman and feudal character is plain.[2] This seems to have sufficed, in his view, to demonstrate that feudal principles were an essential part of English law; he now devoted himself to the historical question of their introduction.

This he uncompromisingly ascribed to the Normans. For his authorities, Craig—true to his continental training—preferred to rely on recent European historians, rather than wrestle with the interpretation of medieval chroniclers; and he made considerable use of Polydore Vergil. Like another intelligent Italian, the author of a *Relation of England* penned about 1500, Vergil had been able, without (as far as is known) any special training in feudal law, to discern that the Norman settlement of England must have been based on some sort of feudal relationship, and to provide an account of it in those terms.[3] But Craig knew far more than Vergil of pre-Conquest society; in particular he had before him the Saxon and pseudo-Saxon laws collected by Lambarde; and his argument required him to show that the *feudum* had not existed among the Saxons. The proof he somewhat sketchily employs is drawn from his broad view of the history of feudalism. In Norman England we find a fully matured form of the *feudum*, in which the process of development from precarious to perpetual has reached its culmination. This corresponds exactly with the feudal law of Normandy in the earliest form in which we have it; whereas, if we test the social

---

[1] Craig, p. 39.   [2] Craig, pp. 43–4.

[3] Cf. the passage from Vergil's *Historia Anglica*, book 9, quoted by Craig, p. 39; and *An Italian Relation of England about the year 1500*, Camden Society, No. 37 (1847), pp. 38–9.

relationships of Anglo-Saxon England by the characteristics of the fully developed *feudum*, we find that they fall so far short of requirements as not to deserve the name. Craig's arguments are not very full or uniformly happy—he quotes a charter of Athelstan against one of William I to Hugh Earl of Chester and then has to confess that neither corresponds to the typical form of a feudal grant—but he regarded them with sufficient confidence to ignore the numerous assertions, ancient and modern, of the Conqueror's confirming the laws of King Edward, and to insist that the law had become wholly Norman and feudal at William's entry and had remained substantially so ever since.[1]

He allowed one important exception, which alone does no small credit to his historical insight. Although nearly all Anglo-Saxon law perished at the Conquest,

illud tamen *de pace domini Regis fracta*, licet ex Anglosaxonum Regum statutis descenderet, tenacissime Conquaestor retinuit, omnesque ab eo descendentes, quod maxime rationibus fisci conveniret.[2]

It is very doubtful if any other historian of 1603 had detected that the concept of the king's peace was the most noteworthy element of old English law to survive conquest, or that the reasons for this were largely fiscal. Though Craig allows for certain elements of pre-Conquest custom having survived or crept back into the Norman law, he will admit nothing of the story that later kings restored the Confessor's law to placate the English. The people, he says, did indeed beseech Henry I to do so, but the king cunningly eluded their requests by giving them a parliament instead, in which the ancient law may be amended and new law introduced, but nothing can be done but by petitioning the prince, who gives or withholds his assent as he pleases. This account of parliamentary origins—which owes something to Polydore Vergil—may be worthless, but it too gives some measure of Craig's energy and resource as a historian.[3]

[1] Craig, pp. 39–40.
[2] 'only the "breach of the King's peace", although derived from the laws of the Anglo-Saxon Kings, was resolutely retained by the Conqueror and all his successors, which was very convenient for fiscal purposes.' Craig, p. 42.
[3] *Ibid.*

Feudal learning did much for Craig, but it did not wholly free him from bondage to national myths. When he turned to consider the introduction of feudal law into Scotland, he made use of the apocryphal early laws, prefixed to certain editions of the *Regiam Majestatem*, to show that Scottish feudal custom, so far from finding its origin in conquest (like that of England) or in the activities of Norman barons from England, was already established in the reigns of Malcolm II, of Macbeth and even of Kenneth III (*c.* 970), and was 'ex contracta cum Gallis amicitia', the product of a tenth-century Auld Alliance.[1] Craig was perhaps influenced by the thought which almost obsessed his English brethren, that it was disgraceful for a country to derive its laws from conquest; more probably still, uppermost in his mind—as it was throughout his scholarly life— was the need to prove that the kingdom of Scotland was not held by homage to the English crown. If he could prove that for half a century or more the Scots had known of homage when the English had not, the original independence of Scotland would be unassailable. In the same way, he emphasizes that the feudal law of Scotland is purer and closer to its Frankish origins than that of England; nevertheless, English law can be regarded only as feudal and Norman, 'licet illi dissimulent, nullumque jus nisi suum agnoscere profiteantur'.[2] In both lands the law is feudal and he exhorts James VI and I to make full use of feudal principles in his government of each. It is a defect, as we have seen, of Craig's historical thought that he regards feudalism not as a dissolution of the state, but as a connected and unified body of law. It is another and consequent defect that he treats it as a system of royal and hierarchical authority binding all men to personal dependence on the king. Nothing, he says, could conduce more to the tranquillity of the king and his realms,

quam ut hujus Feudalis juris praecepta et consuetudines quam arctissime observentur: nam si tota Britannia in partes vel minutissimas secetur, nulla

---

[1] Craig, pp. 46–9. The words quoted are from the summary prefixed to ch. VIII.

[2] 'although they deny it and profess to acknowledge no law save their own.' Craig, p. 44.

erit quae non in feudo de M[ajestate] T[ua] teneatur, (ut in foro loqui solemus,) nulla quae non fidem debeat.[1]

Possessed of little more than a reasonable acquaintance with the *Libri Feudorum* and the French commentaries upon them, Craig had been able to construct an impressively broad historical synthesis, explaining the general history of European law since the barbarian invasions and fitting both Scotland and England into their place in this pattern. If we are to think of him as a product of what is called the Reception in Scotland, it is plain that in him at least reception of civil-law principles produced no contempt for or desire to displace native customs; rather, a new understanding and respect, produced by his new-found ability to see them in their historical context as part of the universal law of the western world. Only if the Scottish crown had been able to enforce feudal tenure as a universal dependence on the sovereign's will might Craig's admittedly over-centralized view of feudalism have become a source of danger to the traditional law of his country; as it is, we are told, 'to this day the land law of Scotland is the most feudal of all the systems of land law which exist',[2] and Craig would certainly not have lamented the fact.

The evident paradox is that Scotland's poverty in law had much to do with the breadth and clarity of Craig's historical thought, while England's unique possession of an organically evolved system of native law was a positive bar to the progress of historical self-knowledge. It would be merely cruel to compare Craig's history with Coke's; what is much more striking is that *Jus Feudale* anticipates by twenty-three years most of the main conclusions in Sir Henry Spelman's *Archaeologus* (1626), the first book in which an Englishman recognized and analysed in something like fullness the feudal element in his country's history. Englishmen, it is plain, felt little need to study the *Libri Feudorum* and apply their lessons to

---

[1] 'than that the rules and customs of feudal law should be observed with the utmost rigour; for were all Britain divided into the minutest fragments of land, there would still be none which was not held in fee of your Majesty (as we say in the Courts) or did not owe you fealty.' Craig, p. vii (dedication).

[2] Lord Cooper, *The Dark Age of Scottish Legal History* (David Murray Foundation Lecture), Glasgow University Press, 1952.

their own law; and they had not in fact the Scots lawyers' motives for doing so. Scotland in Craig's day stood in a position somewhat analogous to that of England in the twelfth century: that is, she was still borrowing from the civil law the principles around which to organize the diversity of customs pleadable in her courts. The Scot, therefore, went abroad as he had always done, to see his own law the better. From the mid-sixteenth century on, he came in the French universities under the influence of the new historical approach to jurisprudence. In the civil law he studied not merely the law of the late Roman empire, but the books of feudal law which had been added during the Middle Ages and were now receiving new and instructive emphasis. He returned armed with general ideas which enabled him not only to systematize his native customs but to understand their historical origins; with a legal and historical definition of the *feudum* which made him see that his own law was feudal and write its history, however sketchily, into the history of Europe. The failure of his country to achieve a common law of her own compelled him to be a European and view his law in a wider context and therefore historically.

But there was no need for the English common lawyer to look abroad, for there was no feature of English law which the presumption of immemorial custom did not explain to his satisfaction. It was several hundred years since he had been compelled to borrow ideas abroad if he was to have a law at all, and as learned a man as Selden could not imagine that there had ever been such a time. The recurrent theme of his *Dissertatio ad Fletam* is that civil-law influences have never been more than incidental to the unbroken development of English custom. The common lawyer was confident that the history of English law could be explained entirely by reference to the English past; and the more he developed the myths to which this inevitably gave birth, the greater his repugnance grew to any suggestion that his law might have sprung from an alien stock. To the end of his days Spelman was to complain of the common lawyer's refusal to look abroad and view his law from a European standpoint; but where the Scot was compelled by the needs of his practice to do so, the Englishman's professional outlook actively discouraged him. If an ultimate origin was sought, it must be in the custom of England, as interpreted by the judges; and there were enough records here to keep a man happily drowning all his lifetime in the search for precedent before precedent. There was no reason why a common lawyer should compare his law with that of Europe, except an intellectual curiosity arising and operating outside the everyday needs of his profession. The discovery of England's place in the legal history of Europe was therefore made by antiquarians, not by lawyers; it was made—if we date it from Spelman's *Archaeologus*—almost a quarter of a century after Craig's publication of his conclusions; and it faced a long and hard struggle for acceptance. It must therefore be admitted that the whole effect of the common law upon the Englishman as historian was to keep him isolated, a provincial, on the edge of European learning.

CHAPTER V

The Discovery of Feudalism: Sir Henry Spelman

I

THE English were to discover feudalism in the way fore-shadowed by Craig: in the form, that is, of a single code of law which, it was believed, had been observed, or borrowed from in, every nation of the west; they were to borrow definitions from the Lombard books and their French commentators and apply these to their common law. But they were to do this very late. The common lawyers resisted the discovery, and it was not made by English civilians. It may be that the influence of Gentili and the *mos Italicus* distracted the latter's attention from the work that had been done at Bourges. Civilians were certainly not encouraged to undertake independent investigations of the common law, but in neither Fulbecke nor Cowell, the two doctors of James I's reign who did attempt comparison of the two laws, do we find historical work comparable to Craig's.[1] There are the beginnings of it in Cowell's *Interpreter*: he took definitions of feudal terms (including *feudum* itself) from the *Libri Feudorum*, Hotman and other Continental feudists and pointed out that they were applicable and useful in the study of English law, and suggested that the close similarity of the Norman *Grand Custumier* to feudal law on one hand and common law on the other provided an obvious clue to the manner in which such law had come into England.[2] But Cowell continued to

---

[1] Cowell, *Institutiones juris anglicani ad methodum et seriem institutionum imperialium compositae et digestae* (1605 and 1630); *Interpreter or Booke containing the Signification of Words* (1607, 1637 and many subsequent editions). Fulbecke, *Parallele or Conference of the Civil Law, the Canon Law and the Common Law of this Realme of England* (1601 and 1618).

[2] *Interpreter*, ed. 1637 (not paginated), articles on 'Ayde', 'Baron', 'Bayliffe', 'Fealtie', 'Fee', 'Maner', 'Parlament' and elsewhere. Note also 'Custom' for Cowell's purely technical and conventional treatment of 'time out of mind'.

believe in the *Mirror of Justices*;[1] and more generally, he did not attempt the reinterpretation outlined by Craig, which would suggest that there had been a period in the past when English law was explicable only on the assumption that the principles of feudal law belonged to it also. The first English civilian to say dogmatically that the common law presupposed the *feudum* in the continental sense of the word, and that this had been imported with the military tenures of the Normans, seems to have been Richard Zouche, and he wrote after Spelman and acknowledged his debt to him.[2] Cowell made useful suggestions and supplied useful material to Spelman, but he did not anticipate his conclusions to the extent that Craig had done.

Nevertheless the English set to work in a fashion very different from Craig's or any lawyer's. If neither civilians nor inns-of-court men made the discovery of feudalism in the English past, it was the work of a different if closely connected group of men: the anti-quarians, and particularly some of the members of the Society of Antiquaries that flourished about 1614. It seems fairly clear that a diffused and piecemeal knowledge of the *Libri Feudorum*, of Cujas and Hotman and of their importance to English learning was making steady progress about this time, but we do not yet know by just what stages this happened or to what extent the giants of Jacobean scholarship—Camden, Cotton, Ussher, Selden, Spelman—assisted one another in this branch of their all but universal erudition. This chapter is devoted to Spelman, not because it is desired to suggest that he and he alone made the rediscovery of feudalism, or even because he was probably the greatest of those who made it; but because he reveals in great detail the way in which the antiquarians set to work, and because, more than any other scholar of his age, he showed to what uses it might be put. In his writings we see, more fully than elsewhere, the revolution which it wrought in traditional English historiography.

[1] *Interpreter, sub* 'Approvour', 'Maner'.
[2] In *Elementa iurisprudentiae...quibus accessit Descriptio iuris et iudicii temporalis secundum consuetudines feudales et normannicas...* (Oxford, 1636); see prefatory letter *Iuventuti iurisprudentiae studiosae.* Cf. Holdsworth, vol. IV, pp. 17–20, 24–5 (for the slightly later work of Arthur Duck).

The Discovery of Feudalism: Sir Henry Spelman

These writings, however, are scattered. Spelman's work divides itself into four parts. First, there is *Archaeologus*, the glossary of obsolete and barbaric words in the ecclesiastical and legal vocabularies, of which one volume was published in 1626 and another lay in manuscript until, long after its author's death in 1641, William Dugdale sent the whole work to the printers in 1664. Spelman's enormous labours in writing and editing the *Concilia* occupy a second place. Next, there is a series of works of a high-church character, vindicating the sanctity of tithes and deploring lay ownership of sacred property.[1] The *History of Sacrilege*, most interesting and most startling of these, was not published until 1698. Last, there is a group of tracts and treatises, mainly legal and antiquarian in character, which Spelman left in manuscript at his death; almost all were published, also in 1698, by Edmund Gibson in his *Reliquiae Spelmannianae*, but one—the *Codex Legum Veterum*—had to wait until David Wilkins brought out his edition of the Anglo-Saxon laws in 1721. The matter relevant to our present purposes is to be found in both parts of the *Archaeologus*, the *Reliquiae*, the *Codex* and the *History of Sacrilege*. Spelman's writings on feudal and legal history are consequently scattered and unsystematized, and many of them could have no effect on the public mind until long after his death.

Like Cotton, Twysden, Dugdale and many others of the great antiquaries—perhaps most of them, if we except the churchmen—Spelman was a man deeply imbued with the spirit of the common law, yet not fully committed to the outlook of the practising lawyer.[2] After a brief stay at Cambridge he entered Lincoln's Inn, from which he was withdrawn at the age of twenty, and for thirty years led the life of a prominent Norfolk gentleman, much employed both in county office and on commissions for the crown, one of which took him into Ireland. At the age of fifty—this would be about 1614—he removed to London and was so fortunate as to spend twenty-seven years more in intensive and productive scholarship.

[1] They include *De non temerandis ecclesiis* (1613); and the *Larger work of tithes*, published posthumously in 1646.

[2] The main authorities for Spelman's life are: his preface to the 1626 *Archaeologus*; Gibson's life, prefixed to *Reliquiae Spelmannianae*; Sir Maurice Powicke, 'Sir Henry Spelman and the *Concilia*', Raleigh Lecture on History, *Proc. Brit. Acad.* (1930); *D.N.B.*

In his writings he laments his early withdrawal from common-law studies;[1] but had he remained in the atmosphere of readings and year-books, it is easy to imagine him developing an intellect as powerful and (historically speaking) as misdirected as Coke's, for he was not by nature free from the common beliefs and prejudices of his age. As it was, however, his county activities ensured that he was well acquainted with the common law, while his decision to devote himself to general erudition left him free to regard it from a more detached point of view than that of the professional lawyer. The law never filled his intellectual horizon. When he returned to London at fifty, he was fully as much interested in ecclesiastical studies as in legal, and he continued all his life to conduct them side by side. Indeed, there have been those who have thought that the latter were too much sacrificed to the former.[2] Be that as it may, a turning-point in Spelman's life as a scholar was reached when he realized that the problem of obsolete and barbaric words was common to both branches of his studies, and determined that he must himself provide some sort of glossary to these before his work, and that of his friends and correspondents, could make further progress. *Archaeologus* was the fruit of this resolution, and it is a book devoted as much to ecclesiastical as to legal terminology. Nevertheless, it was in this glossary[3] that Spelman began systematically to study the common law from the point of view of the scholar, not the lawyer, and to treat it as material from which to extract answers to his own questions. The difference between Coke's approach and Spelman's is profound: for one the history of the law consists of precedents and justifications for present-day rights and actions, for the other it is a question of words no longer used and of meanings that words have now lost. Spelman was an antiquarian and his attitude to the common law was, to this extent at least, scholarly and critical from the start.

Archaeologus, then, is a study of words; but Spelman's interest in

[1] In the preface to the 1626 *Archaeologus*.

[2] Powicke, *loc. cit.* p. 34, quotes a letter of Ussher, dated 6 November 1638, to this effect.

[3] In a note to the 1626 edition, headed 'Clavis', Spelman described the book as less a glossary, although having that form, than a collection of general commentaries.

philology remained that of an ecclesiastical and legal scholar, and the words he chose to study were all the names of usages, offices, ranks, ceremonies and rules in the medieval church and law. In studying the name he studied the thing, and this historical dictionary of several thousand words is designedly a historical inquiry into the past of an organized society. Furthermore, it was of the very greatest importance that Spelman did not confine himself to elucidating words from English historical sources, but sought to understand them better by comparing them with

peregrini labii vocabula; Gothici, Vandalici, Saxonici, Germannici, Langobardici, Normannici, etc.—ignotae functionis ministeria, Officia, dignitates, Magistratus, et infinita huiusmodi.[1]

His correspondence with French, German and Netherlandish scholars—who outnumber the English and Scots in the list of his acknowledgments by twelve to seven[2]—helped him acquire an enormously varied knowledge of European laws, customs, cartularies, decrees, chronicles and documents of all kinds, and consequently of the legal and ecclesiastical aspects of medieval society in the west. Yet the range of his erudition is not so important as the comparative use he made of it. All this material he studied minutely for the words it employed and the usages it revealed, and he took note of a multitude of resemblances to the laws and terminology of his own country. Studying language for the sake of law, he approached the English past as part of the history of Europe; he did more than any English scholar before him to initiate the comparative investigation of the English and continental Middle Ages, and the gratitude of Peiresc, Bignon and other Frenchmen was energetically expressed.[3]

[1] 'words of foreign origin—Gothic, Vandal, Saxon, German, Lombard, Norman etc.—services, offices, dignities, magistracies of unknown function; and an infinity of things of this kind.' *Archaeologus*, 1626, 'Praefatio'.

[2] Peiresc, Bignon, Maussac, Gaulmin, Rigault, Salmasius, Meursius, Lindenbrog, the Pithou brothers, Goldast, Lydius; Camden, Ussher, Lord Keeper Williams, Cotton, Selden, Cowell and Skene.

[3] Some of Spelman's correspondence with foreign scholars may be found in British Museum Additional MSS. 34599, ff. 51, 60, 74, 81, 84; 34601, f. 14; 25384, f. 13. See also L. Van Norden, 'Peiresc and the English Scholars', *Huntington Library Quarterly*, vol. XII, no. 4 (1948–9), pp. 369–89.

Spelman went to work as he did because he fully accepted the fact—established by Nowell, Camden and Verstegan—that Anglo-Saxon and Old English formed part of a family of early Germanic tongues; nor was it news in his time that Anglo-Saxon law showed marked similarities with the *leges barbaricae*. He noticed also that when medieval English institutions resembled those of Carolingian France or Norman Sicily, the relationship could often be traced back to something recorded of the barbarian invaders. Spelman therefore decided that English law was largely Germanic in its origins, but this conclusion did not lead him to adopt any romantic or primitivist cult of the rude Gothic forbears. On the contrary, its value to him was that it placed a definite check on the exaggerations of those who sought to trace the law back into times more remote still—to assert with Fortescue that it was older than the Romans, or to engage in the not yet extinct fantasies of Geoffrey of Monmouth. In a paper originally composed for the Society of Antiquaries in 1614, but later enlarged and rewritten, he attacked those who derived the law from 'Brutus, Mulmutius, or the Druids'; the context points to Fortescue, but could equally well be aimed at Coke's *Third Reports*.[1] In Spelman's mind as he viewed the thought of his age, to prove that English law could be traced to a Germanic origin and to the time of the Anglo-Saxon settlements was to limit its antiquity, to prove it neither mythical nor immemorial, and to compel the reader to think of it in relation to the

---

[1] 'The Original of the Four Terms of the Year', especially foreword 'The Occasion of this Discourse'. Dr L. Van Norden, 'Sir Henry Spelman on the Chronology of the Elizabethan College of Antiquaries', *Huntington Library Quarterly*, vol. XIII, no. 2 (1949–50), pp. 131–60, uses this foreword in an attempt to revise the hitherto accepted dating both of its composition, and of the period at which the Society was most active; her arguments appear most convincing. The passage referred to runs (*Reliquiae*, p. 103): 'They therefore that fetch our Laws from *Brutus, Mulmutius,* the *Druides,* or any other *Brutish* or *British* Inhabitants here of old, affirming that in all the times of these several Nations, (viz. *Britains, Romans, Saxons, Danes* and *Normans*) and of their Kings, this Realm was still ruled with the self same customes that it is now (*viz.* in the time of King *Henry* VI.) govern'd withal; do like them that make the *Arcadians* to be elder than the Moon, and the God *Terminus* to be so fixed on the *Capitoline-hill,* as neither Mattocks nor Spades, nor all the power of men nor of the other Gods, could remove him from the place he stood in.' The reference to the time of Henry VI points plainly to Fortescue.

history of other peoples instead of indulging in the manufacture of purely insular legends.[1]

Spelman did not think that German custom had retained its pristine purity, because he too owed his debt to Gerardus Niger and knew that the laws of the barbarians had undergone important developments after their entry into the empire. He had read the *Libri Feudorum*—we do not know when or on whose suggestion—in the editions of Cujas and Hotman; he was acquainted with the work of Loyseau and Pasquier; and, though he does not seem to have read Craig, he was familiar with Scottish feudal law through the writings of Sir John Skene, who held views very like Craig's on the date of its introduction into Scotland. Spelman amicably dissents.[2] He therefore held, as all these writers did, that an important process had taken place in the structure of barbarian law, namely the rise and diffusion of the *feudum* and its evolution from a precarious grant to a perpetual and hereditary tenure. Like Craig, but in far greater detail, he saw that this general concept could be employed in the effort to understand the history of his own country. The stages by which he reached this understanding have to be collected and pieced together from many scattered paragraphs and references, but in all they amount to what is probably his most important single contribution to historiography.

Under the heading 'Feudum', Spelman gives us his account of general feudal history. He shares with Craig the apparently universal delusion that 'feudal law' was an hierarchical system imposed from above as a matter of state policy; thus land was granted to the great nobles not for their own enjoyment, but so that they might provide soldiers for the defence of the realm and particularly of its frontier provinces.[3] (There is, however, no Turkish analogy in his writings.) He is most like Hotman in his cautious acceptance of a Germanic origin for the *feudum*: its terminology is predominantly German, it has arisen only among Germanic peoples, and under careful inspection (*oculatius*) the *comites* described by Tacitus

[1] See the article 'Lex' in the 1626 *Archaeologus*, p. 435: 'Iactent igitur, etc.'
[2] *Reliquiae*, pp. 27–8.
[3] 1626 *Archaeologus*, p. 256 (misnumbered p. 254), cols. 1–2. ('Feudum' begins on p. 255, continues to p. 262.)

certainly appear the most likely ancestors of the vassals. It is noteworthy, however, that the characteristic of the *comites* on which
Spelman bases this opinion is not their military union with the
chieftain, but their obligation 'principibus pagorum *consilium ad-
fuisse et authoritatem*';[1] in the light of his later writings it is probable
that he was already preparing the way for a treatment of the lord
and his vassals as constituting not only a war-band, but a feudal
court. On these grounds, then, Spelman holds that the origin of
the *feudum* is German, but not that it existed fully grown among
the primitive Germans. In the first written Lombard laws we find
mention of the *feudum* never and of the *beneficium* hardly at all;
yet it was among the Lombards, much later, that the feudal law
was first reduced to writing. What we do find in the earliest Lombard, Frankish, Anglo-Saxon and barbaric laws generally is 'plurima
quae apprime huc conducunt'.[2] The *feudum* evolved slowly, taking
rise from a multitude of Germanic customs, and the decisive
point at which it assumed its full classical form in medieval
Europe was the visit of Conrad the Salian to Italy and his decree
extending the right to inherit from the son to the grandson or
nephew. Later emperors added further legislation, Spelman says,
but the essential history is that set down by Gerardus Niger—whom
he proceeds to quote *in extenso*, if not with perfect accuracy—
tracing the successive stages through which the *feudum* passed on its
way from precarious to perpetual.[3] He adds that Hugh Capet,
acquiring the French throne a generation before Conrad went to
Italy, made not only *feuda*, but duchies, counties and baronies
hereditary and perpetual, from which time the nobles began to call
themselves by the territorial names of their several fees.[4]

---

[1] '. . . to provide the district chieftains with advice and authority for their
doings.' P. 257 (misnumbered 158), col. 1. This seems to be Spelman's
adaptation of the last words of Tacitus, *Germania*, 12.

[2] 'many things which come very close to it.' Same page, col. 2.

[3] Same page, cols. 1–2. Gerardus had not identified his Conrad, but
Spelman rightly calls him Conradus Salicus. In the *Treatise of Feuds and
Tenures*, however, he confuses him with Conrad I, and dates his journey to
Rome in 915—an error by a great scholar which, though it does not affect
his essential argument, should serve as a warning to all (*Reliquiae*, p. 4).

[4] Same page, col. 2.

The Discovery of Feudalism: Sir Henry Spelman

Spelman now proceeds to use the stages through which Gerardus describes the *feudum* as passing to account for a wide variety of customs, found among different peoples, which he evidently regards as survivals of the barbarians' evolution towards the true feudal law. Thus the phase in which the *beneficium* was divided equally among the sons is the explanation of Kentish gavelkind[1] and of the similar custom among the Irish (a people 'veterum Germaniae morum tenacissimos').[2] The period in which the feudal aids were not fixed, but imposed by the lord according to his needs, accounts for such Irish exactions as the 'cutting'.[3] The earliest stage of all, that in which tenure was merely precarious, survives in English copyhold, where the tenure is *ad voluntatem domini*.[4] Little as may be the permanent value of such a classification, it is important in Spelman's thought; it shows that he was systematically employing the categories of the *Libri Feudorum* to arrange and account for the phenomena that were occupying his mind, and it enabled him to distinguish sharply between usages such as the above, which to him were approximations to true feudalism, and the *feudum* proper, which must possess all the characteristics which Gerardus attributes to the last stage of its growth—above all that of being fully and perpetually heritable. He next applies this test to distinguish the tenures of the Anglo-Saxons from those which prevailed under the Normans.

The Saxons possessed many customs dating from earlier stages in Gerardus' scheme, and in this sense Spelman would allow that the origin of feuds was to be found among them. But if they had the origins, they had not the thing itself.

Feodorum servitutes in Britanniam nostram primus invexit Gulielmus senior, Conquestor nuncupatus: qui lege ea e Normannia traducta, Angliam totam suis divisit commilitibus. Innuit hoc ipsum (ut Authores taceam) codex eius agrarius qui Domesdei appellatur....Deinceps vero resonarunt omnia *Feodorum* gravaminibus; Saxonum aevo ne auditis quidem.[5]

[1] Same page, col. 1.
[2] 1626 *Archaeologus*, p. 312, *sub* 'Gavelkind'.
[3] 1626 *Archaeologus*, p. 63, col. 1, *sub* 'Auxilium'.
[4] 1626 *Archaeologus*, p. 257 (misnumbered 158), col. 2; see also p. 253.
[5] 'Feudal burdens were first introduced into Britain by William I, known as the Conqueror; who, bringing this law with him from Normandy, divided

The Discovery of Feudalism: Sir Henry Spelman

Spelman became involved in controversy over these words and once at least modified his doctrine by saying that it was not *feuda* that were new with the Conquest, but only their burdens such as wardship, marriage and relief;[1] but at the same time he argued that these services revealed the existence of a fully developed *feudum*, because they could only be charged on a hereditary tenure. For this passage from *Archaeologus* was challenged, years later, in a court of law, and Spelman wrote a classic treatise in order to defend it. In the important *Case of Defective Titles*, the Irish judges were asked to consider whether a grant of land by letters patent, admittedly void in what it said about tenure, was therefore invalid altogether. For the grantees it was argued that while the tenure concerned was feudal and therefore—on Spelman's authority— no older than the Conquest, grants were part of the common law and therefore immemorial, so that they could not be invalidated merely because they were void in respect of the tenure. In condemning the grant, the judges denied Spelman's historical opinion and invoked the rival authority of Selden to support the view that feudal knight-service, with all its incidents, existed among the Anglo-Saxons. Spelman replied in 1639 with the *Treatise of Feuds and Tenures by Knight-service in England* (not printed until 1698) in which his version of feudal history was set forth in detail.[2]

He expanded his earlier argument:[3] the test of knight-service is not merely military service done in respect of tenure, but the subjection of the tenant to wardship, marriage and relief; the tenure must therefore be hereditary. Now feudal tenure is the product of an

up all England among his companions. This is indicated (to say nothing of the chroniclers) by his agrarian survey which is called Domesday Book....From that time we hear constantly of all the obligations of feudal tenure, which are unknown in the Saxon epoch.' 1626 *Archaeologus*, p. 258, col. 2.

[1] *Reliquiae*, p. 46.

[2] The whole controversy, with the relevant passages from the Irish judgment, is set forth in Gibson's preface to *Reliquiae*. The official report of the case was printed at Wentworth's command and appears as an appendix to the 1725 edition of Molyneux's *The Case of Ireland Truly Stated* (1st ed. 1698), whose arguments it is intended to support.

[3] What follows is a summary of an argument so rich that it is almost an impertinence to compress it, and there seems no necessity to assign every statement to the page which authorizes it.

evolution common to all the Germanic nations, and the roots from which it grew can no doubt be found among the Anglo-Saxons as elsewhere; but on the Continent it followed a well-marked evolution towards heritability, whose stages are known and which culminated in the actions of Hugh Capet in 988 and Conrad II in 1026. The Normans can be shown to have reached the final stage shortly before the Conquest, by comparing their usages in England with those they followed in Sicily, where they were established by 1031. It is in the first place improbable that English law, which we know to have undergone no French or imperial influence before the Conquest, should have anticipated this continental evolution on its own account. But we need not rely on this argument. We possess, in the *Libri Feudorum* and from French and other sources, many details of the hereditary *feudum* and the burdens it imposed, and it is perfectly possible to ascertain whether this relationship existed among the Anglo-Saxons.

Spelman proceeded to demonstrate that the military service performed by English thanes neither arose from homage nor was imposed together with a grant of land by a lord; and that since no such relationship existed there was nothing that could properly be called a *feudum*, still less a hereditary *feudum*, and consequently no rights of wardship, marriage or relief. Moreover, none of the words in which these things were described in the language of all other nations could be found in English documents before 1066; whereas all the relevant words and all the customs characteristic of the *feudum* could be found in plenty once the Normans were established. He had achieved his end in two ways: he had learnt the set of characteristics by which the *feudum* could be identified anywhere and distinguished from those social relationships which more or less resembled it, and he possessed a theory of its growth which satisfactorily explained why it should have appeared in England at a particular time and no earlier. In this way he had proved that the mature *feudum* had been imported into England by the Normans and had played an important part there. For, he added—both in *Archaeologus* and in the *Treatise*—it was now possible to see why Littleton had defined the *feodum* as 'idem quod haereditas'. That was no more than the culminating step in the age-old evolution of the *feudum* towards heritability. Sir Thomas Smith had been wrong in suggesting that Littleton's definition was unsound; the common-law *feodum* was a true *feudum*, even when treated 'pro haereditate et perpetuo rei immobilis dominio, licet ex more feudali, dominum agnosceret superiorem'.[1] For every piece of land in England did in fact (said Spelman) recognize a superior lord, namely the king, and it was therefore clear, both that common-law tenure naturally formed part of the feudal evolution, and that all the land of England had once been held feudally, in the *Libri Feudorum* sense of the word. The Conqueror must therefore—as the best chroniclers declared— have divided the whole country among his followers to hold in *feuda* of the Lombard and Norman pattern.

Spelman had thus established that the basic tenure of English law had at a time past involved the whole complex of lord-vassal relationships described by Gerardus, Obertus and a great company of continental writers on feudal and customary law. It could now be seen that a large number of these relationships were in fact mentioned or implied in the books of the common law and could be explained by reference to a common origin. It was this which constituted the seventeenth-century revolution in English historiography. By comparative study it had been discovered that English law had a great deal in common with the laws of other western nations, and that most of these common characteristics could be explained by using the academic definitions of feudalism to be found in the *Libri Feudorum* and their French editors. The feudal relationship as thus defined—a thing existing only in the past as far as England was concerned—could now be employed to bring about a radical reinterpretation of the whole body of English law as it had existed in the Middle Ages, simply by explaining every feature susceptible of that treatment as one of its consequences. This was the beginning of the genuinely historical study of English institutions and the only possible alternative to the pseudo-historical thought of Coke and the common lawyers. Because the latter lived in a closed

---

[1] 'as the inheritance and perpetual lordship of a piece of real property, although by feudal custom it should acknowledge a superior lord.' 1626 *Archaeologus*, p. 262, col. 2: 'Cum autem eo perventum esset, etc.'; cf. *Reliquiae*, p. 6.

intellectual world, the new technique possessed a highly abstract and even *a priori* character. 'Let us then see', Spelman once wrote, 'how the practice of those ancient ages agreed with this Theoreme',[1] and the words fairly describe his historical method. It was necessary to adopt a new definition of the basic English tenure from foreign sources, quite outside those of the common law, and to use this academic account of the *feudum* to redefine the whole body of the law as it had existed in times past. There is something reminiscent of contemporary advances in the natural sciences about this procedure; Bacon would surely have approved of this rearrangement of the evidence in the light of a single fundamental hypothesis independently arrived at. If, as Maitland intimated, Spelman's 'introduction of the feudal system' is too systematic and too abstract,[2] the fault lies mainly in the insularity of English thought.

II

It remains to see how far Spelman carried the remodelling of English history which he had made possible. The history of historiography contains far fewer examples of systematic revisions of entire fields of study, carried out in the clear light of day, than of the gradual emergence of a new standpoint from a mass of traditional preconceptions, and Spelman's thought is no exception to this rule. He recognized, however, that it was now theoretically possible to construct a completely new historical analysis of the law by distinguishing the elements of various origin which it contained. In the paper, already cited, which he first wrote in 1614, he pointed out that English law could be shown to consist, first, of primeval custom Germanic in its origins, heavily influenced by subsequent borrowings from the civil and canon law; and second,

in matters touching Inheritance, Fees, Tenure by Knights-service, Rents, Services, Wards, Marriage of Wards, Reliefs, Treason, Pleas of the Crown, Escheats, dower of the third part, aids, fines, Felony, Forfeiture, Tryal by battel, Essoine, Warrantie, etc. from the Feudal Law chiefly; as those that read the books of those Laws collected by *Obertus* and *Gerardus* may see apparently. Tho' we and divers other Nations (according as befitteth every

---

[1] *Reliquiae*, p. 61.   [2] *Constitutional History*, pp. 142–3.

one in their particular respects) do in many things vary from them, which
Obertus confesseth to be requisite, and to happen often among the *Longo-bards* themselves. I do marvel many times that my Lord *Cooke*, adorning our
Law with so many flowers of Antiquity and foreign Learning; hath not
(as I suppose) turned aside into this field, from whence so many roots of
our Law, have of old been taken and transplanted. I wish some worthy
Lawyer would read them diligently, and shew the several heads from
whence these of ours are taken. They beyond the seas are not only diligent
but very curious in this kind; but we are all for profit and *Lucrando pane*,
taking what we find at Market, without enquiring whence it came.[1]

This is impressive; and Spelman more than once shows himself
capable of distinguishing between the Germanic, civil, canon and
feudal elements in common law and studying particular aspects of
legal and juridical history in terms of their successive influences.
An instance is the discourse, dated 1633, *Of the Original of Wills and
Testaments and of their Probate*, in which he shows the Anglo-Saxons
first as primitive Germans knowing nothing of the testament, then
as moved to adopt it by Roman influence felt through ecclesiastical
channels, and increasingly transferring the probate to priestly hands.
Next he depicts the joint sitting of earl and bishop in the shire
courts, which brought pre-Gratian canonical ideas to bear on testamentary and many other types of case. The Normans put an end to
this phase by excluding ecclesiastics from the shire courts and by
introducing feudal tenures which virtually withdrew the land from
testamentary disposition. With a few remarks on the probate in
Norman times, Spelman concludes: 'I am now come to the lists of
the modern Common Law, and I dare venture no further';[2] an
interesting remark, if it means that he still looked on the law, as
revealed in its records, as being the professional mystery of the
lawyers, and did not presume to apply himself to its historical
development once the records had begun.

There was nothing in the common law which Spelman need
regard as immemorial, and he had dissolved the notion of custom
into a series of influences of diverse origins. Thus there seems no
reason in theory why he should not have analysed it into its com-
ponent elements and written its history at least to the time of the

[1] *Reliquiae*, pp. 98–9. [2] *Reliquiae*, pp. 127–32.

first records. Even if every statement it contained had required subsequent correction, this work by an English Cujas would have been one of the most important books in the national historiography. But it remained unwritten. Spelman neither completed the writing of *Archaeologus* nor printed all that he had written. About 1630 he seems definitely to have turned away from legal and towards ecclesiastical studies,[1] and though he wrote some short papers on legal history during the 1630's, he was hardly likely to embark on a general history of the law before he had finished his study of the legal vocabulary. The truth is that no one man could finish all that Spelman had begun, and it would have been in keeping with his age if he had felt that the history of the common law were better left to 'some worthy Lawyer', despite the improbability that any member of the profession would undertake a task so destructive of cherished convictions.

But the *Codex Legum Veterum*, which he completed in 1627, the year after printing the first volume of *Archaeologus*, and designed to publish in 1640, but which was not printed until 1721,[2] shows that traditional ideas of the law's antiquity had not yet lost their hold on him. The *Codex* combines an account of how the Normans introduced feudal tenure into England with the older doctrine—to which Spelman had already given some countenance in *Archaeologus*—that they confirmed the law of Edward the Confessor. The Conqueror, in the first place, was no conqueror:

conquestus enim in antiquis chartis illud notat quod jure haereditario non habemus a parentibus, sed quod labore comparatum est vel parsimonia.[3]

None the less, he brought in feudal tenures. Spelman explains how the *feudum* had become established in Europe and had grown to be hereditary among the Normans, while remaining unknown in its true sense among the Saxons, and considers the evidence for holding that William brought all English land under French feudal tenures

[1] See Sir Maurice Powicke's lecture, cited above.

[2] In Wilkins, *Leges Anglo-Saxonicae*, pp. 284 ff. All references to the *Codex* are to this edition.

[3] 'for "conquestus" in the old records means that which we do not inherit from our parents, but acquire by our labour or thrift.' Wilkins, p. 285, cols. 1–2.

and converted earldoms into hereditary titles involving tenure in chief of the crown. But 'distributis praediis, de *Legibus* cogitat innovandis';[1] he meditated introducing the Danish law, under which he had been brought up, but was deterred by the prayers of the *proceres* and instead restored, with much solemnity and after verification by twelve men of each shire, the laws of Edward the Confessor. This, however, he did not do, as contemporaries tell us, without amending them heavily by the introduction of Norman customs. Spelman repeats the assertion, already made in *Archaeologus,* that the *leges Confessoris,* whether we take them from Hoveden or from 'Ingulf of Croyland'—in whose authenticity he believed—cannot be the law exactly as it was in the Confessor's time; they contain far too many French words and feudal customs which can only be Norman in origin.[2] While it is known that William inserted Norman customs in the Confessor's law, these have never been collected and are not easy to distinguish from those of the preceding age; Spelman identifies them, however, by discussing the difference between Saxon usages and Lombard feudal tenures and noting the presence of the latter in William's so-called *leges Confessoris.*[3] Nevertheless, he does not deny that a text of the Confessor's law existed and was confirmed, though amended, by the Conqueror. William Rufus and Henry I built up their credit with the English by promising them their ancient law, and Henry issued his charter confirming the *leges Confessoris*; this example was followed by Stephen and Henry II; and so the story runs until Magna Carta, of which Spelman's interpretation—even though he singles out and emphasizes every feudal element in the document—is as 'Confessorial' as the most ardent common lawyer could desire. He does not carry his narrative beyond the early years of Henry III.

In the *Codex,* evidently, Spelman was trying to pour his new wine into old bottles. He described at length the feudal tenures introduced by the Normans and lost no opportunity of showing how much they had influenced English law and government thereafter; yet he attempted to reconcile this newly discovered

[1] 'having distributed estates among his men, he thought of making new laws.' Wilkins, pp. 287–8.

[2] Wilkins, p. 291, col. 2.

[3] Wilkins, pp. 288 ff.

pattern in our early history with the common-law 'myth of the confirmations'. We must not forget the weight of evidence and authority, both medieval and modern, which had made this legend an ingrained part of the English tradition. But we shall see in a later chapter that Robert Brady, the first true disciple of Spelman's feudal interpretation, while accepting the chronicle stories of William's confirming the ancient law, so far emphasized the feudal content of Anglo-Norman law as to rob the idea of confirmation of virtually all its meaning. Brady would never have written 'distributis praediis, de *Legibus* cogitat innovandis', because he saw that the distribution of the land in feudal tenures was the fundamental fact which determined the character of the law: once this was accomplished, the law could not be other than feudal and attempts, then or now, to pretend that it was the old English law could be dismissed as hollow.[1] Brady, in short, followed the consequences of Spelman's discovery further and more ruthlessly than Spelman himself. The latter's conservatism may be accounted for by sheer caution, or—like his insistence that William was no conqueror—by the obstinate survival of inherited ideas; and it may not be irrelevant that the *Codex* was written in the year before the Petition of Right, and that Spelman is thought to have supported the view that the demands of that document amounted to a claim for the ancient liberties. But the author of the *Codex* was not likely to rewrite the whole history of the law in the way that the author of *Archaeologus* had made possible. Spelman instead turned his attention to the history of parliament, and in this no less important field achieved his most revolutionary conclusions.

What he did was to find means of reinterpreting the history of parliament in the light of the *feudum*. He had always been interested by what may be termed the curial aspect of the feudal relationship; we have seen how he selected words of Tacitus which implied that the *comites* were obliged to furnish their lord with counsel. In the article 'Felo, felonia', which forms part of *Archaeologus*, he carried this idea further. Felony, he pointed out, was a word used by both Hostiensis and the *Libri Feudorum* in the purely feudal sense of that dereliction of duty for which the vassal forfeits his fee. In England

[1] See ch. VIII, below, section II.

it had been applied especially to the relations between the king and his subjects and had come to mean the offence for which the king exacted the *pretium feodi*; and this term the common law had expanded to include the forfeit 'totius haereditatis, fortunarum omnium, ipsiusque vitae'. It was like Spelman to see that the central concept of English criminal justice was developed from the feudal relationship; and in working out the history of *felonia* he traced, parallel to the evolution of the *feudum* from precarious to perpetual, the evolution from a state of things in which the vassal could be dispossessed at the mere will of the lord to one in which dispossession was controlled by law and legal only in the case of certain specified felonies. The stages in this development he took from the imperial constitutions included in the *Libri Feudorum*, and he thought that it had culminated in a constitution of Conrad's which declared that tenants were to be dispossessed only 'convicta culpa, et approbata iudicio parium curiae'. Just as—he went on—the vassal's one-time liability to dispossession at will was reflected in the English copyholder's tenure *ad voluntatem domini*, so too the judgment of the *pares curiae* corresponded to that verdict of the tenants of the manor by which alone the copyholder could be forfeited in the English court baron. Obertus had remarked that definitions of felony differed as widely as the usages of the various types of *curia*.[1] Spelman was clearly impressed with the versatility and wide distribution of the *curia* and its *pares*, and in the article 'Baro' he took the decisive step of applying these concepts to the history of parliament.

He knew—as did every educated Englishman; it was a matter of everyday knowledge of the law—that one of the essential marks of baronage was the right to a personal summons to parliament, and that there were three grounds on which this right could be claimed: tenure *in capite* of the crown, the hereditary receipt of a writ of summons and the possession of letters patent creating one or one's ancestor a baron with right to sit in parliament. But because he had already shown that *baro* was a feudal term common to most western nations and that in England it had formerly borne the purely feudal connotations by which it was recognized elsewhere,[2]

[1] 1626 *Archaeologus*, pp. 252–3.   [2] 1626 *Archaeologus*, pp. 77–9.

The Discovery of Feudalism: Sir Henry Spelman

Spelman concluded that of these three claims that based on tenure of the crown was the original and fundamental one; and, more important still, that the right by which the baron attended his king in parliament was the same as that which determined the composition of his own court baron.

> Illud certissimum est; eos olim maiores Barones habitos esse, qui de Rege tenentes in Capite, iudiciis praefuere Aulae Regiae; nuperius qui in Parlamentariis Comitiis Regi assident et suffragia ferunt, *Parlamentarii* inde *Barones* nuncupati Anglice *Lords of Parlament*....Quemadmodum itaque neque *Barones* ipsi *maiores*, neque *minores*, quempiam in Curiis suis ad iudicia consiliave ferenda de rebus sui dominii admittunt, nisi vassallos suos, qui de ipsis immediate tenent, hoc est, Milites suos et Tenentes libere: ita in summa Curia totius regni, nulli olim ad iudicia et consilia administranda personaliter accersendi erant, nisi qui proximi essent a Rege, ipsique arctioris fidei, et homagii vinculo coniuncti, hoc est, immediati vassalli sui, *Barones* nempe cuiuscunque generis qui de ipso tenuere in Capite, ut partim videas in *Brevi summonitionis*, partim in Charta libertatum Regis Iohannis inferius citatis.[1]

There had been a time when all barons had attended the king merely by reason of their tenure, and when parliament, so far as their attendance determined its character, had been simply a feudal *curia* in which the barons met their king, as vassals their lord, to discuss the affairs of his lordship. It had next to be shown how this state of things had come to an end. Like his great contemporary John Selden, Spelman attached much importance to the clause of Magna Carta in which it is said 'summoneri faciemus' the greater

[1] 'This much is certain: that those were once considered greater barons who held of the king in chief and presided over the judgments of his court; and more recently, those who sit with the king and vote in his parliamentary assemblies, deriving thence the name of *barones parlamentarii*, or in English "lords of parliament"....In the same way as neither greater nor lesser barons admitted anyone to their *curiae* to give judgment or counsel on the affairs of their lordships, except their vassals who held of them direct, that is their knights and free tenants; so in the supreme *curia* of the whole kingdom, none was formerly summoned in person to give judgment and counsel except those who were nearest to the king and bound to him by the strictest ties of fealty and homage: that is his immediate vassals, the barons of whatever degree who held of him in chief, as you may see in the writ of summons and in King John's charter of liberties, both of which are cited below.' 1626 *Archaeologus*, pp. 79–80.

tenants in chief by individual letters, and 'omnes alios qui de nobis tenent in capite ... in generali per vicecomites et ballivos nostros'.[1] He assumed that the assembly which this described was a parliament, and he thought that these provisions had been included in the Charter because it was desired to safeguard every tenant in chief's right to that summons to parliament which was an essential mark of baronage. As early as 1215, he suggested, the king was using his prerogative of issuing writs of summons to omit from parliament some who were tenants *in capite* and to summon others who were not; these discriminations tended to become permanent and those summoned to be known as barons whatever their tenure. 'Aegre hoc ferentes Proceres', they compelled John to guarantee every tenant his summons, while perpetuating the distinction between *barones maiores* and *minores* by means of the personal summons as opposed to the general. But the attempt failed; the use of the writ continued, under Henry III and Edward I, to act as a solvent on the purely tenurial nature of baronage; and

sic antiqua illa Baronum dignitas secessit sensim in titularem et arbitrariam, regioque tandem diplomate idcirco dispensata est.[2]

The creation of barons by patent completed the process, and in Spelman's own day those who claimed their baronies *ratione tenurae* did so by prescription or descent from the ancient baronial families, rather than because they now held in chief of the crown.[3]

Selden's interpretation of *summoneri faciemus* is discussed else-where;[4] it is broadly similar, and both men were prepared to envisage that baronage had once been a purely tenurial status and the whole kingdom a single feudal estate. But Spelman went further than Selden and applied this concept to the history of parliament as a whole. Believing as he did that the *summoneri faciemus* clause described the regular form of holding a parliament in the thirteenth

[1] Clause 14 in the 1215 Charter. Spelman took his text from Matthew Paris and the Red Book of the Exchequer.

[2] 'so that ancient dignity of baronage became by degrees a mere arbitrary title, and at length came to be granted by royal patent.' 1626 *Archaeologus*, p. 80, col. 1.

[3] *Loc. cit.* cols. 1–2.

[4] In ch. vi, below, pp. 137–8.

century, he could not but notice that parliament at that time had consisted exclusively of tenants *in capite*, great and small, all of whom attended in right of their tenure and all of whom were performing the vassal's duty to counsel the lord in his *curia*. It must therefore follow that the knights and burgesses of his own day, men who appeared in answer to the writ of summons because they had been chosen to represent their fellows and not because they owed the king personal service as his immediate tenants, had come into existence at a time subsequent to 1215. The historian's task now became to trace and explain the emergence of the Commons from a feudal background.

The practice of interpreting medieval law as the consequence of relationships based on the *feudum* had now resulted in a denial that parliament was immemorial, and in a very strong argument that the kingdom had once been a feudal estate, in which all relationships had been determined by tenure of the crown, and in which consequently the only kind of parliament that could be imagined as existing was a feudal council on the exact analogy of the *curia*. This is very probably the most important single discovery that has ever been made in the historiography of the medieval constitution, and the fact that Spelman made it dwarfs into insignificance the outmoded postulates which it contains and on which it is partly based. He believed that *summoneri faciemus* described a parliament which had met regularly, and it seems almost certain—this point will be further discussed when we compare his thought with that of his successor Brady—that he regarded the *omnes alios qui tenent in capite* as a class of knights who held direct of the crown and out of whom the knights of the shire had in some way developed. These are ideas which no one now accepts, but they enabled Spelman to approach the next great task of his historiography, that of ascertaining how the purely tenurial council had given place to the parliament of freeholders' representatives—which, with all the modifications which have subsequently been found necessary, is still recognizably the form in which we conceive the problem of parliamentary history.

The article entitled 'Parlamentum' which Spelman wrote for inclusion in *Archaeologus* was not printed in the 1626 volume, which extends only to the letter L, and consequently it was not published until Dugdale's complete edition appeared in 1664; and though it was through this essay that his interpretation of parliamentary history made its impact on the thought of the century, there is almost no sign of this before 1675. Spelman presented a theory of the origins of parliament and the rise of the House of Commons founded throughout on the conception that vassalage was the organizing principle of medieval society. The first step was to establish that though William I 'acquisivit, non conquisivit Angliam', he nevertheless caused every foot of land to be held of him by some tenant in chief 'per servitium plerumque baroniae'. Spelman next reiterated the identity of the medieval king's *concilium* with the feudal *curia*, and stressed that as the king was feudal lord of all the land, there were none but his barons whom he would admit to give him counsel:

rex perinde, qui totius regni dominus est supremus, regnumque universum, tam in personis baronum suorum, quam e subditorum ligeantia, ex jure coronae suae subjectum habet, consilio et assensu baronum suorum leges olim imposuit universo regno.[1]

Since there was no land that was not feudalized, there could have been no proprietors in the realm who were not either tenants *in capite* or their sub-tenants—the *allodium* being unknown in English law[2]—and Spelman believed it to be a universal feudal principle that the sub-tenant's assent was taken to be included in that which his lord gave in the king's court in matters touching his fee.[3] So long as feudal tenure endured unmodified, therefore, none but the king's tenants *in capite* could possibly appear to give him counsel in his court, and the advent there of persons who were not tenants must be a sign of the ending of the feudal world. As late as 1215, the Charter provided what Spelman evidently regarded as a classic

[1] 'the king likewise, who is supreme lord of the whole land and holds all the kingdom subject by right of his crown, whether by his immediate authority over his barons or by the allegiance which their sub-tenants owe him, once gave the whole kingdom laws by the counsel and assent of his barons.' *Glossarium Archaiologium* (1664; this is Dugdale's title for his complete edition of *Archaeologus*), p. 451, col. 1.

[2] See article 'Allodium' in 1626 *Archaeologus*.

[3] Further discussed in ch. VIII, section II, below.

picture of the feudal council in its maturity: the greater tenants summoned personally, the lesser generally through the sheriffs, but all attending out of the ancient obligations of the vassals.

When and how had this state of things come to an end? Spelman considered the evidence for the first summoning to parliament of the *plebs*—by which he clearly meant the commons who did not attend *ratione tenurae*—and, after rejecting various more or less remote dates, decided that there was no sign of their presence 'ab ingressu Gulielmi I ad excessum Henrici III'. He offered no single date at which they had first appeared, because the theory he was about to put forward was such as to preclude anything of the kind.[1] Though he is not perfectly explicit on this point, Spelman clearly thinks that the elected knights of the shire are in some way descended from the lesser tenants in chief of Magna Carta: that the latter, on receiving their general summons through the sheriff, elected some of their number to represent them, and that in time electors and elected ceased to be confined to the immediate tenants of the crown. In an unfinished paper, 'Of Parliaments', composed near the end of his life, he suggested that the fact that there were only two knights for each shire might be explained by supposing that the number of lesser tenants in chief had never been very great.[2] But he is noticeably vague on the manner in which the transition was accomplished. Here his thought might be held to suffer from a failure to make full use of the shire court. He knew that from an early time this body had included

omnis *Baronum* feodalium species, in uno quovis Comitatu degentium: Proceres nempe et Maneriorum domini, nec non libere quique Tenentes, hoc est, fundorum proprietarii. Anglice, *freeholders*,[3]

and it would have been easy to depict the shire court acting upon the general summons as the royal writ had acted upon the personal, altering the basis of parliamentary attendance until it was no longer tenurial. He preferred, however, to depict the change to freeholders' representatives merely as part of the general decline of

[1] *Glossarium* (1664), p. 451, col. 2.
[2] *Reliquiae*, p. 64.
[3] 1626 *Archaeologus*, p. 84, col. 2, *sub* 'Barones comitatus'.

feudal relationships. In 'Of Parliaments' he wrote that the *libere tenentes* of mesne lords,

> because they could not always be certainly distinguish'd from them that held *in capite*, (which encreased daily) grew by little and little to have voices in election of the Knights of the Shire, and at last to be confirm'd therein by the Stat. 7. *Henr*. IV and 8. *Henr*. VI.[1]

Here the shire court is the theatre in which the vital development takes place, but it is scarcely an actor therein. The nature of the process by which the lesser tenants *in capite* became indistinguishable from the other *libere tenentes* is not made clear, but, in his earlier-quoted discussion of the shire court, Spelman remarked that the county freeholders were formerly not so inconsiderable as they had later become, 'nam villas et Dominia in minutas haereditates nondum distrahebant'; and he may have thought that subdivision of land held of the crown had played a part in that blurring of distinctions between the crown's and other men's military tenants on which his whole theory of the rise of the commons depended.[2] But when all is said and done, Spelman's account of the social processes which brought feudal society to an end is never specific; he knows only that such processes must have occurred and that they must have been very gradual—so much so that he will fix no date for the origin of the commons, since no date can be fixed for the moment at which the lesser tenants in chief became finally indistinguishable from the freeholders. This is both a strength and a weakness in his historical thought: on the one hand it prevented him from giving too much importance to individuals and isolated actions and directed seventeenth-century attention to the gradual processes it was inclined to ignore; on the other the fact that Spelman knew that feudalism must have declined, but was unable to particularize the process or go into its causes, contained dangers for lesser minds. We shall see that James Harrington, possessing no better knowledge, imagined that feudal society had remained more or less intact until the legislation of the first Tudors.

---

[1] *Reliquiae*, p. 64.

[2] See ch. VIII, section II, below, for a discussion of the way in which his view of the knight's fee may have influenced his beliefs at this point.

The Discovery of Feudalism: Sir Henry Spelman

The idea of a gradual decay of feudal ties completes the account of parliamentary history given in 'Parlamentum'.

Post susceptionem plebis in comitia parlamentaria sensim decerpitur fastigiosa illa magnatum potestas, coercito alias eorum in tenentes imperio, et laxata alias plebis in eo servitute. Fit hoc statutis plurimis, adeoque labefactata est superbia procerum, ut adversus Regem nemo suscitare ausus est novorum quidpiam, si de regno non ageretur. Sed ecce novus iam Leviathan grassari coepit. Liberata iam ab imperio dominorum, offensa ex quavis causa, plebs quae ad arma hactenus absque voluntate dominorum nunquam convolant; iam non habentes quibus audiant in gravissimas insurgunt rebelliones, quod ne semel unquam factum est anterius.[1]

Whose were the statutes that relaxed the feudal ties—whether Edward I's or, as Harrington thought, Henry VII's or VIII's—Spelman does not tell us; but it is of far more interest to ask who precisely made up the 'new Leviathan' which waxed fat on its liberation from feudal authority until it became a grave danger to ordered society. Whoever they were, they menaced the crown when they swelled the power of the magnates; the king in parliament took steps to emancipate them, but thus raised up a new power which he could not altogether control. This statement occurs in the course of an essay on parliamentary history and the context makes it very tempting to assume that the *plebs*, the new Leviathan, is the parliamentary freeholders. If this is Spelman's meaning, we have passed at one stride into the world of James Harrington, and the rebellious conduct of the House of Commons is being explained as

---

[1] 'After the admission of the commons to parliament, the exalted power of the magnates was by degrees pared away, both because their authority over their tenants was restricted and because the services which these owed them were relaxed. This was brought about by many acts of parliament, and so far was the pride of the magnates brought low, that none dared to raise any new movement against the king unless it were a question of the crown. But now a new Leviathan began to prowl. The people, freed from the dominion of their lords, took offence at the slightest cause; and though they had never before resorted to arms unless by the will of their lords, there were no longer any for them to obey, and they broke out in rebellions of the utmost gravity, a thing which had never happened in previous centuries.' *Glossarium* (1664), p. 452. In the corrected manuscript of this paragraph (Bodleian Library MS. e Mus. 48, f. 471) the first sentence runs, '... potestas coercita, alias ...'. The emendation seems clear. It will be seen that Spelman's Latin is shaky.

the consequence of the creation of a new class as feudalism decays. But Spelman died in October 1641, when civil war was not yet universally foreseen; and we have no means of knowing whether this paragraph was written in the last years of his life. If the *plebs* are the parliamentary Commons, in what *gravissimae rebelliones* had they engaged of which Spelman might have been thinking? It is possible to gain some rather uncertain light on this problem by referring to his *History of Sacrilege*.

This book forms one of a number which Spelman wrote against lay possession of sacred things, in this case church lands and im-propriated rectories, his ownership of some of the latter having involved him in a vexatious lawsuit. He became convinced that the whole process of dissolution had been sacrilegious, and wrote largely to exhibit the effects of the divine displeasure under which England lay as a consequence; and he gave so many often scandalous instances of the decay of families who had acquired abbey lands that, in an age when country-house opinion was peculiarly strong and the possessors of church land decidedly touchy about their titles, none could be found to publish it until 1698, when White Kennett brought out an edition to forestall its appearance under impious auspices.[1] No class in the kingdom, said Spelman, had benefited by the dissolution, and certainly not Henry VIII.

I speak not of his prodigal Hand in the Blood of his Subjects, which no doubt much alienated the Hearts of them from him. But God in these eleven Years space visited him with 5 or 6 Rebellions. In *Lincolnshire*, Anno 28, and 3 one after another in *Yorkshire*, Anno 33; one in *Somersetshire*, Anno 29, and again in *Yorkshire*, Anno 33. And though Rebellions and Insurrections are not to be defended, yet they discover unto us what the displeasure and dislike was of the common People for Spoiling the Revenues of the Church; whereby they were great losers, the Clergy being mercifull Landlords, and bountifull Benefactors to all Men by their great Hospitality and Works of Charity.[2]

In the formidable agrarian outbreaks of the sixteenth century, which Spelman might see reflected in the not inconsiderable fen-land disorders of his own Norfolk generation, we have a possible alternative explanation of the new Leviathan and its *gravissimae*

[1] See his preface to the 1698 edition.   [2] *History of Sacrilege*, pp. 190–1.

rebelliones. But it remains true that logically the passage from 'Parlamentum' should refer to the freeholders. What of the gentry since the dissolution? Having described the many personal disasters which befell Henry VIII's peers, Spelman proceeds:

> Now I labour in observing the Particulars, seeing the whole body of the Baronage is since that fallen so much from their ancient lustre, magnitude and estimation. I that about 50 Years ago did behold with what great respect, observance, and distance, principal Men of Countries apply'd themselves to some of the meanest Barons, and so with what familiarity inferiour Gentlemen often do accost many of these of our times, cannot but wonder either at the Declination of the one, or at the Arrogance of the other.... To say what I observe herein, as the Nobility spoiled God of his Honour by putting those things from him, and communicating them to lazy and vulgar persons; so God to requite them hath taken the ancient Honours of Nobility, and communicat[ed][1] them to the meanest of the People, to Shopkeepers, Taverners, Taylors, Tradesmen, Burghers, Brewers, Grasiers; and it may be supposed, that as *Constantine the Great* seeing the inconvenience of the multitude of *Comites* of his time distinguished them, as *Eusebius* reporteth, into three degrees making the latter far inferior to the former; so may it one day come to pass among these of our times; and it shall not want some precedent of our own to the like purpose.[2]

Here we seem very close to Harrington and to a 'rise of the gentry, 1540–1640'. But whatever Spelman's estimate of the numbers of social upstarts, he does not present the whole class of the gentry as a people waxing rich and unmanageable. Certainly the king had to sell the church lands as fast as they came in to him, and his ancient crown lands as well, and all these passed into the hands of private proprietors;[3] but all Spelman's emphasis falls upon the fact that the purchasers received the new land subject to the reservation of a tenure *in capite*, which rendered them liable to the intolerable burdens of wardship. Among the Goths and Lombards, where blood-feuds abounded, there was an obvious case for seeing that the tenant did not marry among the lord's enemies, but there can be no justification for its extension to so many English land-owners since the dissolution.[4] A sense of anachronism, of the revival

---

[1] The text has 'communicating'. [2] *Hist. Sacr.* pp. 224–5.
[3] *Hist. Sacr.* pp. 225–7. [4] *Hist. Sacr.* pp. 229–35.

and perversion of ancient laws, of what we should call 'bastard feudalism', pervades all that Spelman writes on this topic. The gentry have not been delivered from feudal controls and left to grow omnipotent; they have been thrust back under a feudal service that was extinct (says Spelman) except among a few peers and owners of great estates. There is no hint that their dominance as a class is imminent.

It appears, on the whole, unsafe to suppose that Spelman was a Harringtonian before Harrington, or that the rebellious *plebs* of 'Parlamentum' can with any certainty be identified with the parliamentary freeholders or with what moderns call 'the gentry'. Nevertheless, the paragraph whose meaning we have been disputing reveals that Spelman had realized an historical truth which underlies the thought of Harrington and many other writers of the age. In the past the mass of people had been sub-tenants of the great lords and this had constituted a menace to the power of the crown. Now they were free of feudal services, and there was a growing impression that action on the crown's part had been largely responsible for this; but it had left the crown exposed to the attacks of people who were neither great lords nor bound to it by any sort of tenure. The crown had thus, by a kind of dialectic, raised up forces which it could not control. This generalization, which has remained potent in our historical thought to this day, appeared in the seventeenth century as soon as the existence of a feudal state of society in the past was at all widely realized. It owes much of its power and some of its unsatisfactoriness to the fact that it has always been easier for the English historian to anatomize in detail the workings of the feudal world than to particularize the processes of its decline; it is probably true that the average graduate of today knows the eleventh to thirteenth centuries far better than the fourteenth and fifteenth. This in its turn, in the obscure processes of the history of thought, can almost certainly be traced to Spelman's possession of a quasi-theoretical formula of the nature of feudalism which he could apply to medieval law and parliament with the most brilliant and astonishing results, but which left him with little more to say about the decline of the state of things founded on the *feudum* than that it must have occurred. The great value of his contribution, in being among the first to draw attention to this enormously important subject, must be offset by his inability to make any very useful contribution to its study. The feudal interpretation raised, but did not solve, the problem of the place occupied in English history by a monarchy which had once rested on a foundation of feudal relationships, had later contributed in some way to their decline and now survived them.

III

The main achievement of the feudal revolution in English historiography—of which Spelman was not the sole, but the principal architect—was to impose upon English history the division into pre-feudal, feudal and post-feudal periods which has ever since characterized it. The Conquest transformed Anglo-Saxon society by the systematic importation of Continental feudal tenures; the relationship of the barons to the crown from the eleventh to thirteenth centuries is to be understood in terms of vassalage and its obligations; the appearance of the county freeholders in parliament, where they were not obliged to attend by their tenures, could come about only in a society where feudal relationships were beginning to lose their exclusive importance. We may find much to criticize in this statement of the case, but it may be doubted whether we have found any more satisfactory set of generalizations to put in its place, or whether we have added anything which is more than a modification—except indeed the idea that the growth of the common law, centralized in the royal courts, had a unique and radical effect upon English feudalism and differentiated it from that of any other country. This we shall not find in Spelman, or apparently any other writer of the seventeenth century, because they were not yet capable of thinking independently and historically about the common law once its records had begun. But he and his peers created the only conditions of thought in which it could have been recognized that the common law had been the crown's means of acting within and upon feudal society and ultimately transforming its nature together with its own.

To the seventeenth century the feudal interpretation made another contribution of no less importance. It provided the only means of escape from the thought of the common lawyers and a powerful battery of critical weapons which could be used against them. Nothing would prevent Englishmen believing that their law and constitution were immemorial, unless it could be shown that at a time in the past both law and parliament, though they contained much that still existed today, had in fact been radically different and intelligible only on the basis of principles that were not those of the present age. This proof the feudal interpretation provided, and it did so the more effectively because of the abstract and systematic element which we have noted it contained. The revolution occurred because scholars had reduced the feudal relationship to a small number of simple general ideas and were willing to apply these, almost in the manner of scientific formulae, to the reconstruction of medieval society. They could now lay down a single hypothesis—that Anglo-Norman law and society were feudal law and society—and proceed to outline the whole past condition of England by pitting that hypothesis against the masses of evidence. In Spelman's hands this became a demonstration that England had once been a feudal lordship and the king's council a feudal *curia*, and that neither the Lords nor the Commons of the contemporary parliament could consequently be immemorial. Nor would any of the arguments in the armoury of the school of Coke suffice to prove that the common-law *feodum* was not the *feudum* of the feudal law, and without such a proof the whole theory of the ancient constitution lay open to devastating attack.

Here the feudal interpretation entered the sphere of practical politics. As the tides were running in England, the antiquity of parliament was soon to be a cry of greater political and intellectual importance than the antiquity of the law in general, and Spelman seems to have recognized this. The unfinished treatise 'Of Parliaments', which has already been quoted, opens with these words:

When States are departed from their original Constitution, and that original by tract of time worn out of memory; the succeeding Ages viewing what is past by the present, conceive the former to have been like to that they live in, and framing thereupon erroneous propositions, do likewise make thereon erroneous inferences and Conclusions. I would not pry too boldly into this ark of secrets: but having seen more Parliaments miscarry,

yea suffer shipwrack, within these sixteen years past, than in many hundred
heretofore, I desire for my understanding's sake to take a view of the
beginning and nature of Parliaments; not meddling with them of our time,
(which may displease both Court and Country,) but with those of old;
which now are like the siege of *Troy*, matters only of story and discourse.

It has been suggested that this treatise belongs to the very last
phase of Spelman's life and that 'these sixteen years' began in 1624
or 1625.[1] The evidence may seem flimsy; the sixteen years from
1614 to 1630 contain almost as many troublesome parliaments, and
Spelman's ideas of parliamentary history were probably well
formed by the last date. However, it is noteworthy that in July
1640 he obtained Chief Justice Bramston's *imprimatur* to the publication (which did not then take place) of the *Codex Legum Veterum*,
much of whose contents would have supported the argument in
'Of Parliaments'.[2] It may even be relevant that an attempt to
secure Spelman's election (despite his age and poor eyesight) as one
of the burgesses for the University of Cambridge miscarried about
this time.[3] But whatever the date of this treatise, Spelman was by
then convinced that historical error—and the error characteristic
of Englishmen in his time—was politically dangerous, but seems to
have thought that correction of the error could be undertaken
disinterestedly and without giving offence. How wrong he was he
might have learned had he completed 'Of Parliaments' and seen it
published; for the immemorial nature of parliament had become an
article of militant faith with not a few. But he began to set out, in
English instead of Latin, his feudal interpretation of parliamentary
history, with the intention—it seems fairly certain—of persuading
the House of Commons to see itself in historical perspective and
abate its more extreme claims.

Parliaments, he proceeds, are younger than kings, as is shown by

[1] *Reliquiae*, p. 57. Cf. L. Van Norden, *Huntington Library Quarterly*, vol. XII
(1948–9), p. 371 n. 17: 'can be dated by internal evidence, pp. 57, 58, between
the Short and Long Parliaments.' The passage quoted seems to be the only
piece of evidence of the kind.

[2] Thus an autograph note on the MS. itself, reported by Gibson in his
preface to *Reliquiae*.

[3] Spelman to Abraham Wheelock, 9 Nov. 1640, in Ellis (ed.), *Letters of
Eminent Literary Men*, Camden Society (1842), pp. 163–4.

the fact that kings summon them. Moreover, it was the kings who originally granted every man his land, in return for which he owed them loyalty and services, 'not *ex pacto vel condicto* (for that was but *cautela superabundans*) but of common right and by the Law of Nations (for so I may term the Feodal-law then to be in our Western Orb)...tho' no word were spoken of them'.[1] There follows the portrait of a feudal society: in such a world only the king's own tenants could be admitted to give him counsel, all others having their consent included in that of their lord and owing him besides a variety of vexatious services. The Commons, we feel, are to realize not only that their appearance in the councils of the realm is of comparatively late date, but that the very class of freeholders which they represent could not exist in a strictly feudal society. About the time of Henry II

there hapn'd...a notable alteration in the Commonwealth. For the great Lords and owners of towns which before manur'd their lands by Tenants at Will, began now generally to grant them Estates in Fee, and thereby to make a great multitude of Freeholders more than had been. Who by reason of their several interests, and being not so absolutely ty'd unto their Lords as in former times, began now to be a more eminent part in the Commonwealth, and more to be respected therefore in making Laws, to bind them and their Inheritance.[2]

The exact grounds for this statement that the character of sub-tenancy changed in the late twelfth century are not clear, but Spelman's purpose in making it is plain. For these are the freeholders—*libere tenentes*—who were later to blend with the lesser tenants *in capite* to elect knights of the shire and form the modern freeholder class; but since 'Of Parliaments' breaks off in the early years of Henry III we learn no more of how they came to do so.

The feudal interpretation of parliamentary history was to be used many times in the future to check the claims of the lower house. There were two lines along which it could point to royalist and even to absolutist conclusions: one was the argument that since the Commons were manifestly not immemorial, they owed their being to the king whose will had instituted them as a house; the other, that in virtue of his position as feudal suzerain the king stood

[1] *Reliquiae*, p. 57.   [2] *Reliquiae*, p. 62.

in a seigneurial relation to the whole of society and was entitled to
homage and loyalty from the proprietor of every piece of land—
much as Craig had pointed out to James VI and I. Both these
arguments are hinted at by Spelman, but he develops neither of
them and his thought on the whole question was on a much grander
scale; he depicts the Commons as coming into being as the result of
a historical process, far too complex to be the mere product of the
king's will, at the end of which the king's position as head of a feudal
hierarchy was a thing of the past. Thought which reached so far
was fundamentally more akin to that of Harrington. But the feudal
interpretation was to be used in both the ways just described, and
was to meet the stubborn, angry and usually uncomprehending
opposition of common lawyers, political pamphleteers and parliamentary theorists until the end of the century. The remarkable fact,
however, as we shall see, is the extreme slowness with which the
royalists took it up; not until the time of the Exclusionist crisis, forty
years after Spelman's death, was it put into action. The reason must
be found primarily in the extraordinary persistence of the common-
law tradition, which—it seems desirable to repeat—was the natural
way for all Englishmen, of whatever party, to think of their history
until they had been brought to perform the complex and unfamiliar
intellectual operations which we have studied in Spelman; or until
something had happened to jolt them out of the medieval reverence
for ancient law which was natural even to royalists, and accustom
them to think of the law as the product of the king's will and therefore, in a sense, of history. A subsidiary reason is Spelman's failure to
collect his scattered writings on the feudal law into a single reasoned
argument, or to arrange for the publication at his death of all
that he had written. All the writers studied in the present volume
worked without benefit of the *Treatise of Feuds and Tenures* or 'Of
Parliaments', and even the article 'Parlamentum', which was to
have so marked an effect in stimulating the growth of new ideas,
was not published till 1664 or noticed till 1675. Spelman's impact
upon his countrymen's conceptions of parliamentary history was
to be very long delayed and it was to be felt by a generation living
in an England very unlike that which he had known.

CHAPTER VI

Interregnum: the 'Oceana' of James Harrington

THE next part of this book must be in the nature of an interlude. Viewed as a whole, the work of Spelman shows that it was in his lifetime theoretically possible to subject the common-law interpretation of English history to destructive criticism and build up a new version on radically different lines; but it has already been pointed out that his work could not be viewed as a whole until 1721, eighty years after his death, and the line of advance he had indicated was not taken up until 1675 or 1680.[1] The probability that Spelman was far ahead of the scholars of his generation is supported by the fact that not until some of his literary remains had been published, and not until—some years later still—their true meaning began to be understood, was the feudal reinterpretation of constitutional history resumed in detail. In addition, the years after his death were revolutionary in their effect on the English use of history, as in so much else, and his work was reread in a new setting. It will be best to treat the mid-century as a period during which the minds of scholars and polemicists were prepared to make full use of Spelman's ideas when the meaning of these was at last made plain to them.

By 1649, the fundamental problem of the Interregnum had emerged: a truncated single chamber was ruling, and claiming powers to which there seemed no clear limit, in the name of the ancient constitution. Since the concept of an ancient constitution was embodied in the historical myth of the common lawyers, their version of history was still incessantly repeated; but so unparalleled a situation could not be without its effect even upon the myth. In the name of ancient law, the parliament had arrogated to itself what was constantly discovered, and as constantly denied, to be sovereignty, and it was bound to happen that elements of parliamentary and popular sovereignty should make their way into the mythical

[1] See ch. VIII, below.

accounts of early history.[1] Rather less began to be heard of the antiquity of the law, rather more of the antiquity of parliament. What must have been fairly common form by the end of the Civil War is recorded for us with admirable simplicity by a Russian, Gerasimus Dokhturov, who, arriving as ambassador to Charles I in 1645, was dismayed to find that the Muscovy merchants who greeted him at Gravesend were at war with their king.

The king wished—said the merchants—to govern the kingdom according to his own will, as do the sovereigns of other states. But here, from time immemorial, the country has been free; the early kings could settle nothing; it was parliament, the men who were elected, that governed. The king began to rule after his own will, but the parliament would not allow that, and many archbishops and Jesuits were executed. The king, seeing that the parliament intended to act according to its own wishes, as it had done from all time, and not according to the royal will, left London with the queen, without being expelled by anyone, saying that they were going away into other towns.[2]

Except in the matter of archbishops, Dokhturov would seem to have given an accurate enough account of what was said to him. But if the later Long Parliament and the Rump modified history to suit their new situation, those who attacked single-chamber government did so in the name of English history also. Some of these attacks were conservative, some revolutionary, and their treatment of antiquity varied accordingly; it is with a selection of them that this chapter and the next are concerned.

Something must be said first of the Leveller reinterpretation of the Norman Conquest, if only because it is usually misunderstood. The Levellers denounced Norman usurpation and looked backwards to Anglo-Saxon liberty; and on the assumption that, when Coke discovered law and parliament among the pre-Conquest English, he was indulging in fantasies of a golden age and primitive Germanic freedom, it is often maintained that the Leveller doctrine

[1] E.g. in Nathaniel Bacon's *Historical Discourse of the Uniformity of the Government of England* (1647–51), sometimes falsely attributed to Selden.

[2] The writer is indebted to his friend Liliana Archibald for this translation and for the reference, which is С. Н. Кологривов, 'Материалы для истории сношений России с иностранными державами в XVII веке' (St Petersburg, 1911).

was at bottom one with that of the common lawyers and made the same appeal to antiquity.[1] But, in reality, no two attitudes of mind could have been more deeply opposed. Coke's essential belief was that the common law had been proved good because it had lasted from time immemorial: there had been no Conquest and the law rested on the foundation of its antiquity and not of William's arbitrary will. What Walwyn, Lilburne and Winstanley said was the very reverse of this. Being engaged in a revolt against the whole existing structure of the common law, they declared that there had indeed been a Conquest; the existing law derived from the tyranny of the Conqueror and partook of the illegitimacy that had characterized his entire rule. Their historicism was not conservative. It was a radical criticism of existing society; the common-law myth stood on its head, as Marx said he had stood Hegel. Both parties indeed looked to the past and laid emphasis on the rights of Englishmen in the past, but what the common lawyers described was the unbroken continuity between past and present, which alone gave justification to the present; while the radicals were talking of a golden age, a lost paradise in which Englishmen had enjoyed liberties that had been taken from them and must be restored. If asked by what right Englishmen could claim the liberties they had lost, they could not appeal to the law, but to natural right and reason; and it is at this point that we notice they were talking the language of political rationalism.

[1] E.g. in D. B. Robertson, *The Religious Foundations of Leveller Democracy* (Columbia, 1951), pp. 112–13. There is a much more accurate interpretation in A. S. P. Woodhouse, *Puritanism and Liberty* (London, 1950), pp. 95–7 of the introduction, and Kliger, *The Goths in England*, pp. 263–7. Much may also be learnt on the difference between true anti-Normanism and the appeal to a past constitution, both among the Levellers and among radicals after 1780 and down to the Chartist movement, from Christopher Hill's 'The Norman Yoke' (see p. 54 n. 2 above). Mr Hill's Marxist analysis is not specially illuminating on conservative thinkers, but his eye for different shades of radicalism is most informative. He is particularly interesting on the tendency of some Leveller and near-Leveller writers to find ancient precedents for the subordination of parliament to outside assemblies exercising a direct popular sovereignty; he finds this marked in Nathaniel Bacon. J. Frank, *The Levellers* (Cambridge, Mass., 1955), brings out the ambiguities of an anti-historical doctrine expressed in historical language.

Ye were chosen [wrote Richard Overton to parliament] to work our deliverance, and to estate us in natural and just liberty agreeable to reason and common equity, for whatever our forefathers were, or whatever they did or suffered, or were enforced to yield unto, we are the men of the present age, and ought to be absolutely free from all kinds of exorbitancies, molestations or arbitrary power.[1]

The Leveller attitude to history is a strange hybrid. Their anti-Normanism, as it is sometimes called, amounts in the end to a rejection of history and existing law; there has been a fatal breach in the continuity of law, six centuries of usurpation during which we have had only fragments of our natural liberties, and now we are free either to reconstruct our society according to reason and equity, or to await the next operation of the Spirit that works in us all. But so inescapable by this time was the clutch of history on English political thought, that this fundamentally anti-historical theory could only be expressed in historical language; the past could only be rejected through a reinterpretation of the past. Here, it may be conjectured, we have a possible explanation of the strange fact, which has puzzled historians of thought, that the anti-Norman ideas of the Levellers reappear in the democrats of 1780 and after, between whom and the men of 1648 there can hardly be any direct continuity.[2] If history was the natural language even of political rationalists, it is intelligible enough that the next time there arose a radical criticism of existing institutions, it too should have seized upon the same weak point in conservative historiography and reinterpreted 1066 as a means to the rejection of the historic constitution.

But the revolt of the lower ranks of the army was only the first of a long series of attempts to reduce the power of the Interregnum parliament within bounds, and anti-Normanism was only one of many attempts to do so by a reinterpretation of English history. The problem proved insoluble by either commonwealth or protectorate, and the rewriting of history to this end went on steadily, and not altogether vainly, until the Restoration. The most remark-

[1] *A Remonstrance of Many Thousand Citizens* (1646), in Haller (ed.), *Tracts on Liberty in the Puritan Revolution* (New York, 1933), vol. III, pp. 354–5.

[2] For a study of the historical ideas of the Yorkshire Association in 1780, see H. Butterfield, *George III, Lord North and the People* (London, 1949), pp. 344 ff.

able, the most systematic and the most ambitious of these attempts was *Oceana* (1656), in which James Harrington was moved to put forward a new account not merely of English, but of European history and a new theory of political power. He is included in the present study because it is evident that the feudal scholars had a profound effect on his work.

Harrington owes his prominence in nearly all text-books on the history of political thought to two interpretations which are normally made of his fundamental doctrine that property is the basis of political power. In the first place, it is usually taken for granted that, in saying this, Harrington imported into political theory some consideration of the economic foundation on which any political society must ultimately rest. The statement that he did so may well be true, but needs to be precisely interpreted. It is a commonplace that Harrington overrated the political importance of land and neglected that of trade; but it is usually pointed out that, according to modern economic historians, the economic society of the day was such that Harrington may be excused—in the light of such facts as the investment of commercial profits in land—for thinking that the distribution of real property provided a sufficient explanation of the distribution of political power.[1] But it needs to be further emphasized that Harrington is not looking, even in the most primitive manner, at the economic society of his day and arriving at the conclusion that land is the most important factor in the economic determination of power. He is not doing this, because he has no conception whatever that there exists a complex web of economic relationships between men which can be studied in itself and which determines the distribution of power among them. Compared to the best Tudor writers on social reform he is not so much ignorant of as uninterested in the realities of an agrarian political economy, and it has not occurred to him that the exchange of goods and services on an agrarian basis either can be studied in order to determine its own laws, or ought to be studied in its relation to political power. There were men in the sixteenth century far ahead of him in this regard; Harrington is thinking

[1] R. H. Tawney, 'Harrington's Interpretation of his Age', *Proc. Brit. Acad.* vol. XXVII (1941), pp. 221–2.

about something else. His sole comment on the economic relations between men—and the sole foundation of all that he has to say about property as the basis of power—is, 'an army is a beast that hath a great belly and must be fed'; he that has the land can feed the soldiers. Harrington, we must keep in mind, was a Machiavellian, and the starting-point of his thought was Machiavelli's perception that in a republic the soldiers must be citizens and the citizens soldiers; if the soldiers follow private men for reward, then the republic cannot survive. To this Harrington's historical studies had added the further reflexion that the soldier normally lives on the land; if the land is in the hands of one man, or of a few, then the soldier will be the tenant of a lord and pledged by his tenure to fight for him. Only when the land is distributed among a class of freeholders, therefore, can the soldiers be citizens (or freemen) and the citizens soldiers.

That is the sum total of reflexion on the relation between property and power which will be found from one end to the other of Harrington's collected works. Economic it certainly is, in the sense that it points out the connexion between that which keeps a man alive and the direction his political action will probably take; but it considers the man solely in his capacity of soldier, and never comes near to asking how the relations which he enters into as producer and consumer will determine his action as a citizen. It is important—in view of what eminent authorities have said—to realize that Harrington had no concept of economic society as an aspect of human life possessing laws of its own, and therefore none of economic history as the evolution of economic relationships according to a logic of their own. When Acton praised Harrington for having discovered that there existed a great department of human life outside the control of the state, when G. H. Sabine commented that it was strange that a man who saw so far into the economic causes of political power should have placed so much reliance on constitutional apparatus, both made the mistake of assuming that Harrington knew there existed a sphere of economics apart from the sphere of politics and influencing it.[1] Harrington made no such

---

[1] Acton, *Historical Essays and Studies*, p. 380; Sabine, *History of Political Theory* (New York, ed. 1945), p. 505.

assertion; he was studying the military and consequently the political results of a system of dependent tenures, and inquiring what happened when such a system was removed. That is the reason for his inclusion here; it is also his claim to originality as a political thinker.

The second reason for ascribing a peculiar importance to his thought has been the belief that in the century or so before his time there had occurred a major transference of land into the hands of the gentry and a consequent rise of the gentry to political power. Harrington said that this had in fact occurred, and so long as our belief coincided with his it was the fashion to praise him as a man of profound insight into the social developments of his own day, to speak of him as an interpreter of his age and, somewhat less explicitly, to speak as if his discernment of the principle that 'property determines power' were developed from his diagnosis of this process occurring in contemporary English life. But, granting for the moment that a 'rise of the gentry' was going on, we may still legitimately inquire how it was that Harrington—the sources of whose information and the working categories of whose thoughts differed most widely from ours—knew it. The belief that the thought of an age reflects its social developments does not deliver us from the obligation to show how this process of reflexion takes place. Granted that there was a rise of the gentry, and granted also that Harrington says there was, did he mean what we mean by the statement and did he arrive at his conclusion by means of thoughts which have anything in common with ours? If we do not face and answer these questions, we risk inferring that Harrington anticipated in some unexplained and therefore miraculous manner the conclusions of modern economic history and should be praised on this account. This will be no explanation of how he actually thought.

It has been left for a historian who doubts the whole concept of a rise of the gentry—Professor Trevor-Roper—to ask just what grounds Harrington had for stating that the gentry in his day had engrossed the major part of the land.[1] Now if we examine the manner and the context in which Harrington makes this statement, we shall notice that though it is of course fundamental to his

[1] H. R. Trevor-Roper, 'The Gentry, 1540–1640' (*Economic History Review Supplement*, no. 1, Cambridge, 1954), *passim*.

diagnosis of contemporary England, he nowhere puts it forward
as his own discovery or regards himself as having conducted investigations which lead to this conclusion. It is not a conclusion of
his thought at all, but rather a presupposition. He does not make
himself an authority for the statement, nor does he organize the
development of his ideas around it; he merely takes it for granted,
as a truth everybody knows, and proceeds to show how it came
about and what its consequences must be. In these circumstances, it
does not seem very likely that Harrington reached the conclusion
that most of the land had passed to the gentry as a result of some
train of thought peculiarly his own and was stirred and excited by
this discovery to the point of formulating his general theory that
landed property determined power. It is perhaps time to remind
ourselves of what he actually said, and in so doing to consider by
what means he arrived at both the particular and the general conclusion, and what their relation is to one another. We shall then be
in a position to decide whether profound insight into contemporary
social realities is really the foundation of Harrington's thought, or
its most interesting characteristic.[1]

Having enunciated the proposition that landed property determines power, Harrington does not merely select examples to
prove it: he goes further and gives a summary account of European
history since the second century B.C., designed to show how the
unequal distribution of land has determined, since that time, the
succession of different types of state. Starting with the presumption
that once there existed an 'ancient prudence', in which the form of
government was adapted to the existing distribution of land and
that distribution stabilized by an agrarian law, he goes on to fix
the collapse of this equilibrium in that age of Roman history which
preceded the advent of the Gracchi. Like Toynbee, he regards the
fatal breakdown of ancient civilization as occurring just after the
Punic Wars, and its consequences as felt even at his own day.
Latifundia perdidere Italiam: the lands which should have been
divided among citizen-colonists were engrossed by a few rich men,
and by the time of the Gracchi it was too late to restore, even by

[1] All that follows is taken from the 'Second Part of the Preliminaries' in
Liljegren (ed.), *James Harrington's Oceana* (Lund and Heidelberg, 1924).

force, the law which defined their proper distribution. For the great men were now able both to subvert the constitution and to defeat the armed efforts of the people; Sulla's dictatorship and Augustus's empire were maintained by settling on the land, which should have been the people's, colonies of veterans who became the clients and the private armies of their patrons. The empire was founded on the emperor's power to settle the armies on lands withdrawn from public control.

These *Military Colonies*...consisted of such as I conceive were they that are called *Milites beneficiarii*; in regard that the *Tenure* of their Lands was by way of *Benefices*, that is for life, and upon condition of duty or service in the War upon their own charge. These Benefices *Alexander Severus* granted unto the Heirs of the Incumbents, but upon the same conditions: And such was the *Dominion* by which the Roman Emperours gave their *Ballance*.[1]

Harrington proceeds to compare the Roman empire with the Turkish sultanate, which has timariots corresponding to the *beneficiarii*, and a bodyguard of janissaries whose counterpart was the praetorians. But whereas the Turkish is the perfect instance of absolute monarchy—all the land being in the sultan's hands and held of him by military tenants for life—the Roman was imperfect; the senate and people retained some part of their liberty and the emperor, caught between the opposing forces of constitution and army, was in perpetual danger of deposition and death. The empire was an essentially unstable government and continued so until Constantine dispersed the praetorians and until

the *Benefices* of the Souldiers that were hitherto held for *life*, and upon duty, were by this *Prince* made *Hereditary*, so that the whole Foundation whereupon this *Empire* was first built, being now removed, sheweth plainly, that the Emperours must long before this have found out some other way of support; and this was by *Stipendiating* the *Gothes*...for the *Emperours* making use of them in their Arms (as the *French* do at this day of the *Switz*) gave them that, under the notion of stipend, which they received as *Tribute*, coming (if there were any default in the payment) so often to distrein for it, that in the time of *Honorius* they sacked *Rome*, and possessed themselves of *Italy*.[2]

The historical logic is extremely clear. The advent of the barbarians was not a conquest by a horde of invaders, but an infiltra-

[1] Liljegren, pp. 40–1.   [2] Liljegren, p. 42.

tion of over-mighty mercenaries brought into the empire as the result of its own inner weaknesses, weaknesses which Harrington is prepared to trace in logical sequence from a single mistake committed by the later republic; after which power oscillated from one to another of a series of unstable forces, until the introduction and establishment of the Goths came as the natural culmination. With their arrival there ended the transitional period between 'ancient' and 'modern prudence', and 'modern prudence'—which has been defined earlier as an essentially arbitrary mode of government in which the law fails to prevent the establishment of power in the hands of one or a few—is synonymous with 'the Gothic balance'. And the Gothic balance is feudalism: for

> to open the ground-work or *ballance* of these new *Politicians*. *Feudum*, saith *Calvine* the *Lawyer*, is a *Gothick* word of divers significations; for it is taken either for War, or for a *possession of conquered Lands, distributed by the Victor unto such of his Captains and Souldiers as had merited in his wars, upon condition to acknowledge him to be their perpetuall Lord, and themselves to be his Subjects.*

The Goths established three ranks of *feuda*, subinfeudated one to another and held by nobles, barons and vavasors; '*and this is the Gothick Ballance, by which all the Kingdoms this day in Christendome were at first erected*'.[1]

As has already been pointed out, the basic tenet throughout *Oceana* is that a man's tenants must fight for him, while a freeholder will fight for himself; and in the historical section of the work the rise and progress of 'modern prudence'—government by one or a few in their own interest and not according to law—is depicted as the rise and progress of dependent military tenures, of which a simplified version of feudalism is the last and culminating phase. Not only this, but the earlier phases—the devices of military clientage by which the Roman emperors overthrew the republic and prepared the way for the Goths—had all, and more than once, been advanced by the feudal scholars of the sixteenth century as possible origins of feudalism.[2] The possibility that veterans' colonies

---

[1] Liljegren, pp. 42–3; cf. Calvinus, *Lexicon juridicum juris romani* (Frankfort, 1600), *sub* 'Feudum'. Italics Harrington's.
[2] See ch. IV, above.

or the later *limitanei* were the seed from which the *feudum* had developed was extensively canvassed by Torelli and others, and as extensively refuted by Hotman in the *De feudis commentatio tripertita*, and by Craig in *Jus Feudale*—both works which might very easily have come Harrington's way. Although, as may have been noticed, Harrington ignores Gerardus Niger's belief that the *feudum* had developed from precarious to perpetual after the barbarian settlements, still he locates a similar development of the 'benefice' among the military settlements of the empire. Lastly, the analogy between feudalism and the Turkish system and the emphasis that the timariot holds for life are already familiar to us from Craig. Although Johann Kahl's *Lexicon Juridicum* is the only authority quoted, it looks very much as if earlier discussions on the history of feudalism were behind Harrington's thought in some way. There is good reason to think, first, that Harrington's essential notion of the way in which landed property determines power is derived from consideration of the power which a feudal lord draws from his vassals; and secondly, that in the attempts of sixteenth-century scholars to derive feudalism from Roman military clientage he found instances of earlier institutions embodying the same fundamental principle. Although the Roman dependent tenures had been excluded on technical grounds from the history of the *feudum* itself, they helped him to understand how the power of the emperors had been established among the ruins of the republic, why it too had declined and why, in comparison, the similarly based power of the sultanate seemed to be lasting. Since Harrington was not only writing the history of feudalism, but applying a principle drawn from it to the history of European society, he could combine, where others must compare, the history of Roman clientage with the history of the *feudum* proper; and because he thought of both as instances of what happened when an original balance of property was disturbed, he could see one disequilibrium as leading to another in a dialectical process which continued until, as the result of a miscalculation two centuries before Christ, all Europe became a prey to military nobles in the fifth century of our era. We have here an unorthodox form of historical thought, very unlike that of Craig or Spelman, but indebted ultimately to the same stimulus:

the power of feudal institutions to direct the student's thought from the law to the soil beneath it.

When Harrington turns from the history of Europe in general to recount that of England (or Oceana), it is still feudalism that is his guiding and connecting theme. Throughout this part of his work his authority is a single book by John Selden, the enlarged version of the *Titles of Honour* published in 1631. Selden, we have seen, was quoted by the Irish judges in 1639 for the view, as against Spelman, that feudal tenures were older than the Conquest and part of the immemorial law; it was to this book that the judges referred. It is true that he repeatedly refers to Anglo-Saxon thanes as 'feudal'; he says that the king's thanes held of him in chief and by knight-service, and he identifies 'middle thane' with 'vavasor'.[1] Yet, strangely enough, he held a view of the nature of the knight's fee far more in accord with subsequent research than did Spelman, or any contemporary scholar except Robert Cotton;[2] but he does not tell us whether this too existed before the Conquest. Why he adhered to opinions of this sort is uncertain; he was a most careful scholar and it is unlikely that he was actuated by the common desire to represent all English institutions as immemorial. To Harrington, however, who did not of course know Spelman's *Treatise of Feuds and Tenures*, the identification of Norman with Saxon tenures had a definite value. It aided him to think of feudalism as a single and simple body of institutions established everywhere by the Gothic conquerors, and to carry out the simplification of history which his theme required and which probably accounts in part for his choice of a half-mythical form. He wished to write of the rise and fall of the Gothic balance as the key to post-classical history; to have been compelled to depict it as everywhere subject to modification and development would have been no more than a distraction.

He therefore describes the Saxon ('Teutonic') system of government as a simplified form of feudalism, with ealdormen, king's

[1] Selden, *Titles of Honour* (1631), pp. 612, 622, 624–7. None of this matter seems to appear in the 1614 text.

[2] *Titles of Honour*, pp. 691–7. See D. C. Douglas, *The Norman Conquest and British Historians* (David Murray Foundation Lecture, Glasgow, 1946) for a discussion of the views of Cotton.

thanes and middle thanes as the three ranks of feudatories. This society is of course typical of the Gothic balance, with the land dominated by the nobility and the people in dependence on them; and though Harrington finds it necessary to say that the present House of Commons is descended from a representation of the people in the witan—and to employ a positively ultra-Cokean argument to support his claim[1]—it is clear from the context that these Saxon commons must have been virtually powerless. This is a curious passage; an insistence on the antiquity of the commons is unnecessary on a strict interpretation of Harrington's own theory, and its inclusion seems to represent a survival of traditional prejudices in his mind. For, as we shall see, his theory of the rise of the people to power is not clearly connected with a rise of the House of Commons to predominance in the constitution.

To an England already so thoroughly feudalized Norman conquest could make little difference. The Normans ('Neustrians' in the language of *Oceana*) brought an interlude of quasi-absolutism, while the barons who had inherited the lands and tenures of the thanes felt their security in a newly won country to be dependent on the powers of their king; but these

> were no sooner rooted in their vast *Dominions*, than they came up according to the infallible consequence of the *Ballance Domesticke*, and contracting the *Nationall* interest of the *Baronage* grew as fierce in the Vindication of the *Ancient rights and liberties* of the same, as if they had beene alwaies *Natives*.[2]

It was still the ancient constitution for which the barons had fought, but to Harrington this was no more than an expression of class conflict. The Norman polity, like the Saxon before it and all other examples of the Gothic balance, was inherently unstable. The nobility had too much land to be properly controlled by the king, yet their own divisions made it necessary that they should have a

---

[1] Liljegren, p. 45 and note, pp. 270–1. The argument (to be found also in Lambarde's *Archeion*) is that the existence of parliamentary boroughs which have been decayed since time out of mind is proof of the existence of borough representation since time out of mind—and consequently before the Conquest. For its use by Hobbes (of all people), see ch. vii, below. See also Coke, Preface to *Ninth Reports* (T.F. vol. v), pp. xxii–xxiii.

[2] Liljegren, p. 47.

king over them. The king therefore was constantly trying to extend his authority, the nobility constantly frustrating him; but as often as they overthrew a king, the necessities of the Gothic balance constrained them to set up another in his place. The establishment of parliamentary government was an expression of this conflict of forces, and at the same time contained the seeds of the Gothic balance's future decay. On the one hand, the barons of Henry III's time exacted the restoration of the ancient parliament of the Saxons; on the other, the kings had by this time found means of introducing into it creatures of their own. So in all government by estates:

> By which meanes this *Government* being indeed the *Master-piece of Moderne Prudence* hath beene cry'd up to the *Skyes*, as the only invention, whereby at once to maintaine the soveraignty of a *Prince*, and the liberty of the *people*: whereas indeed it hath beene no other than a wrestling match, wherein the *Nobility*, as they have been stronger have thrown the *King*; or the *King* if he have been stronger, hath thrown the *Nobility*; or the *King* where he hath had a *Nobility*, and could bring them to his party, hath thrown the *people*, as in *France* and *Spain*: or the *people* where they have had no *Nobility*, or could get them to be of their party, have thrown the *King*, as in *Holland*, and of latter times in *Oceana*. But they came not to this strength but by such approaches and degrees, as remain to be further opened.[1]

Like the Levellers, Harrington condemns the historic constitution as the fruit of Norman misgovernment; but he blames not their tyranny so much as their inefficiency, and regards the Saxons as no better. But if it was in parliament that the people rose to power and overthrew the king—as the foregoing passage certainly suggests—then we should expect to hear that it was through the House of Commons that they did it. We should expect to be told that the new men whom the thirteenth-century kings introduced into the re-founded parliament—in doing which they 'set awry' the balance—were the representatives of the commons. But we are not; Harrington is utterly unable to give any account whatever of the medieval commons and their place in parliament. For an explanation of this remarkable fact we must turn back to Selden's *Titles of Honour*.

In the section of that mighty work that dealt with the English title of baron, Selden wrote an account of parliamentary attendance

[1] Liljegren, pp. 47–8.

as one of the distinguishing marks of baronage.[1] Like Spelman in *Archaeologus*, five years earlier, he was aware of the differentiation of the order into barons by tenure, by writ and by letters patent, and thought that Magna Carta's distinction between the modes of summoning greater and lesser tenants in chief marked the decisive moment at which the ancient principle of a baronage purely of tenure had been abandoned. But, as we have seen, Spelman thought that the *summoneri faciemus* clause of 1215 represented a collective reaction of the whole body of tenants in chief against the king's use of the writ of summons to exclude some of their number from his councils. Selden gave a different emphasis and treated *summoneri faciemus* as an attempt by the greater tenants to exclude the less from individual summons and monopolize the title of baron: a fatal breach of feudal principle which prepared the way for the writ to continue undermining the purely tenurial nature of baronage and for the king to exclude from his councils some who were tenants in chief and to summon some who were not, until in Richard II's time the creation of barons by letters patent sealed the divorce between baronage and tenure. Substantially, both men were in agreement, but whether because his brief was only to write about baronage, or because he did not share Spelman's determination to view the history of England as the introduction and decline of feudal principles, Selden did not press his thesis so far as to inquire what became of the parliamentary attendance of the smaller tenants in chief; and neither here nor elsewhere did he advance Spelman's theory that a lower house of small tenants in chief had evolved into a lower house of freeholders.

As we have seen, all Spelman's detailed statements of his theory were contained in writings not published when *Oceana* was written; and Harrington consequently lacked knowledge of a doctrine which his own argument badly needed. His account of parliamentary history follows Selden and makes no mention whatever of the Commons between the Conquest and the reign of Elizabeth I. The passage, earlier quoted, on parliament as a wrestling-ground between king, lords and people occurs as part of an account of the manner in which barons by writ—whom at this point he manages

[1] *Titles of Honour*, pp. 701–45, in particular pp. 708–15.

to confuse with the lords spiritual[1]—and barons by letters patent appeared in parliament. It was jealousy between the old barons and the new that led to the deposition of Richard II, and, having once tasted blood, the nobility formed itself into factions and continued to overthrow kings and put up new until the Tudors struck at the roots of their power.

This account of the strange weakness of Harrington's argument, just at the point where we expect it to be most complete, has been given to emphasize his virtual ignorance of later medieval history and inability to chart the decline of the classical feudalism of the Normans. If we now inquire by what stages the people got possession of the land and rose to political power, we shall be given no answer earlier than the reign of Henry VII. This prince, Harrington repeatedly declares, was the first who attacked the power of the nobility and set in train the destruction of the Gothic balance. He did this by means of his statutes of population, retainers and alienations: the first of these—Harrington is following Bacon here—by forbidding the lords to dispossess their tenants holding twenty and more acres, broke their feudal control over the yeomanry and guaranteed the latter in possession of their lands. The second deprived the lords of their cavalry as the former had of their infantry; and, forbidden to keep great households in the country, they resorted to court, became extravagant and began to sell their lands, a course which the statute of alienations thoughtfully encouraged. The next step was Henry VIII's, who

dissolving the *Abbeys*, brought with the declining estate of the *Nobility* so vast a prey unto the Industry of the people, that the *Ballance* of the *Commonwealth* was too apparently in the *Popular party*, to be unseen by the wise

---

[1] Liljegren, p. 48 and note. Liljegren's comment is interesting. Harrington placed at this point the marginal reference '49 H. 3', the date of the oldest extant summons of knights of the shire to a parliament; and his argument seems so imperatively to demand a discussion of the rise of the House of Commons that Liljegren considers at length the possibility that he is referring to this. But the text at this point contains no mention of knights or burgesses, but only of barons by writ, whom Harrington declares to have consisted of sixty-four abbots and thirty-six priors; and in *Titles of Honour*, pp. 723–4, will be found a list of this number of spiritual persons, whose summons is recorded on a close roll of 49 H. 3. This reference (which Liljegren also gives) is the only one to which Harrington's marginal note can be taken to point.

Councel of *Queen Parthenia* [Elizabeth I], who converting her reign through
the perpetuall Love-tricks that passed between her and her people into a
kind of *Romanze*; wholly neglected the *Nobility*. And by these degrees
came the House of *Commons* to raise that head, which since hath been so
high and formidable unto their *Princes*; that they have looked pale upon
those assemblies.[1]

This is literally the first mention of the House of Commons since
it was observed that a powerless and nominal representation of the
people may be presumed to have survived the Norman Conquest.
It is clear that, as Harrington was unable to incorporate the history
of parliament into his account of the later Middle Ages, so too he
believed feudal society to have survived more or less unchanged
until the advent of the Tudors. Such was certainly the opinion of
that sometime member of the Rota Club, John Aubrey. He wrote:[2]

> For the government till the time of Henry VIII, it was like a nest of boxes:
> for the copy-holders, (who till then were villaines) held of the Lords of the
> Manor, who held perhaps of another superior lord or duke, who held of the
> king.... The lords (then lords *in deed* as well as in title) lived in their countries
> like petty kings, had *jura regalia* belonging to their signories, had their
> castles and burroughes, and sent burghesses to the Lower House: had
> gallows within their liberties where they could try, condemne, hang, and
> drawe....Then were entails in fashion (a good prop for monarchie).
> Destroying of petty mannors began in Henry VII to be more common:
> whereby the meane people lived lawlesse, nobody to govern them, they
> cared for nobody, having on nobody any dependence; and thus, and by
> selling the Church landes, is the ballance of the government quite altered,
> and putt into the handes of the common people.

The thought in the last sentences is obviously Harrington's.
Interspersed with these accounts of a feudal world, and forming
part of them, are references to the retainer system, the last rem-
nants of which Aubrey's older contemporaries could remember
from the closing decades of Elizabeth I's reign: younger sons and
servants riding behind some magnate, armed and in his livery, and
engaging in riots and rufflings in his cause. It is easy to see how the

[1] Liljegren, p. 49.
[2] A. Powell (ed.), *Brief Lives and Other Selected Writings by John Aubrey*
(London, 1949), pp. 2–4.

still living tradition of such customs could blend in the antiquary's mind with the accounts of feudal vassalage given by the scholars, and help create the image of a feudalism surviving until the previous century; but such a confusion could take place only if the means of charting the decline of classical feudalism had not yet been discovered. We have seen how Spelman, unable to give any account of the positive forces which had worked to bring feudal tenures to an end, had written rather vaguely of a general decline; but at least he had insisted on the gradualness of this process, and some of its details of which he had knowledge—such as the replacement of the feudal justiciar by the professional chief justice—he had dated as far back as the reign of Edward I.[1] But Harrington and Aubrey, lacking both Spelman's awareness of the complexity of feudal tenure and (in Harrington's case at least) his concept of the rise of the House of Commons, telescoped history and substituted for the gradual decline of feudalism its sudden and more or less complete overthrow by Tudor legislation.

Now it is the argument of this chapter that Harrington was primarily a historian of feudalism and only in a most rudimentary sense an observer of contemporary social processes. This interpretation seems to be borne out by the account of his thought which has just been given. For when we come to his version of what we call 'the rise of the gentry', it amounts to little more than the statement that under the early Tudors the feudal system was abolished. Henry VII freed the yeomen from feudal dependence and encouraged the nobility to sell land; Henry VIII dissolved the monasteries and threw their estates into the hands of the commons. (To this point, the summary is exactly echoed by Aubrey.) Under Elizabeth I, the House of Commons began to wax in power. That is the most we can justly make of Harrington's account of this alleged development; and it may well seem likely that his 'rise of the gentry' is based simply on a comparison of his own with feudal society, and a very imperfect notion of how the latter in fact disappeared. Mr Trevor-Roper has remarked that Harrington and others who thought like him were singularly vague as to the dates and stages by which their 'rise of the gentry' had come about—as if, he says,

[1] See the article 'Justiciarius' in the 1626 *Archaeologus*.

they were trying to derive the present situation from some ideal state of things imagined in the past.[1] In Harrington's case, ignorance of late medieval history seems to explain the vagueness, and the ideal state of things is an extremely generalized description of the classical type of feudalism. Harrington, we may suppose, noted the obvious fact of the political power possessed by the land-holding commons in his own time, and cast back into the past as a means of accounting for it. There he encountered the description of a feudal system in which those who were now the freeholding gentry had been subordinate vassals. Unable to describe the decline of this state of things, he supposed that it had endured through the fourteenth and fifteenth centuries, and guided by Bacon[2] hit upon Tudor legislation—aimed in reality at emasculating the retainer system, checking enclosures and resuming the crown lands—as marking the destruction, almost at a blow, of classical feudalism. The picture thus created was completed by reference to the effects of the dissolution.

It is true that the belief that land had passed or was passing into the hands of the gentry was fairly widespread at this time, and that by no means all its expressions—the statistics of Thomas Wilson the younger, for example—can be explained as resulting from a comparison between a freeholding society and an imperfectly understood feudalism or half-remembered retainer system. It may well be that ideas like Wilson's helped to shape Harrington's thought. But he does not allude to or make use of them; as far as he is concerned, the preponderance of the freeholders is a *datum*, and he is seeking to explain it by contrast with feudalism. It is even not impossible that the study of feudal society—and exaggeration of its longevity—first convinced him of the importance of landed property to the victory of the commons in his own day. But perhaps it does not greatly matter how Harrington arrived at his conviction that a transfer of land into the gentry's hands had occurred during the sixteenth century, because that does not seem to be the most important or interesting part of his thought. It is not the product of an analysis of the contemporary distribution of land,

[1] Trevor-Roper, *op. cit.* pp. 45–6.
[2] For his citations from Bacon see Liljegren, pp. 9, 49, and notes.

because it does not claim to be. As a piece of history, it is fundamentally vitiated by Harrington's ignorance of anything between the establishment of classical feudalism and the legislation of the Tudors. Nor does it seem to have been the origin of the doctrine that the possession of land determines political power, for Harrington expounds that far more convincingly by showing what happens when land is engrossed by an aristocracy: by comparing the history of dependent tenures in general, and feudal tenures in particular, with the land laws of the ideal legislators. The rise of the English freeholders merely makes possible the return to 'ancient prudence'.

It seems reasonable to regard this part of Harrington's political theory as mainly the product of reflexion upon feudal tenures. They provided him with the clearest explanation of how the many, who should be citizen-soldiers, might be converted into the private armies of a few. Roman military clientage provided the link between the Gothic Middle Ages and the ideal republics in which things had been better ordered. The comparison between the tenure for life only of the Turkish timariot and the western benefice's tendency to become hereditary showed him how a despotic monarchy erected on a foundation of military tenures should be maintained, and how it should not. Lastly, the contrast between the vassalage of feudal England and the predominance of freehold about him provided him with a means of explaining his own day, and convinced him that he had lived to see conditions in which the classical republic was once more a practical possibility. These things together amount to the doctrine that the distribution of land determines political power—for no other reason than that it determines whether the soldier shall fight as a citizen for the public power or as a dependent for his patron or lord.

We have now been led to abandon the belief that Harrington was primarily a political economist or a serious authority for a recent or contemporary 'rise of the gentry'. There remain, happily, excellent reasons for holding this amiable man in high respect. If he did not study political power in terms of economics, he wrote its history in terms of land; and he was a very remarkable speculative historian. The 'Second Part of the Preliminaries' to *Oceana* is a connected, logical and consistent history of the transformations of political authority in Europe from the Roman republic to the English civil wars. It starts, admittedly, from an ideal antiquity and it ends with the prospect of an ideal future; but within those limits it is based on the rise and fall of a single phenomenon—dependent military tenures—and it succeeds by means of this generalization alone in accounting for a great many facts and weaving them together in a single narrative. The reader travels far, in Harrington's company, from the allegedly typical humanist historian who searches the past for general principles and the examples which illustrate them; for in Harrington's hands the examples become links in a chain of causation and the principle a key to unlock the whole course of western history. A regular series of causes and effects connects the Gracchi with Cromwell, and since the fundamental idea on which this history is constructed is that of the disturbance of an original balance—of a sometime equitable distribution of the land—the sequence of events that follows the original disturbance is, as has already been observed, dialectical. Excess in one direction produces excess in another, until the oscillations of the 'balance' gather sufficient force to sweep away an inherently unstable system of government. An emperor brings in the Goths, who overthrow both him and his land-hungry armies; a king, to check the nobles, raises up the people, who destroy him and them impartially.

In this dialectic of eighteen centuries the last step—the rise of the people—is, as we have seen, the least satisfactorily explained; and it might be observed also that Harrington shared with Marx the delusion that a historical dialectic might come or be brought to a stop, and a static unhistorical equilibrium succeed it. Just as, in the dialectic of production, the triumph of the proletariat leads to the classless society and the consummation of the historical process, so too, in the dialectic of land distribution, the triumph of the freeholders leads to the foundation of an impersonal machine of government so evenly balanced that there is no reason why it should not last for ever. But these extravagances need not blind one to the fact that the construction of a dialectical process on this scale was a notable achievement of the historical intellect. If it is true that each main point in Harrington's historical thought arose originally from the consideration of feudal tenure, then that branch of study had done as much to broaden his perception of history as it had done for that of Craig or even Spelman.

Another aspect of his historiography can best be appreciated by comparison of his thought with that of his master Machiavelli. The Italian, following Polybius, had spoken of forms of government giving preponderance to the one, the few and the many, each breaking down through the excess of its own peculiar qualities and giving rise to its successor, doomed to perish in its turn. From this sorrowful wheel the legislator might deliver his people by setting up a government so compounded of all three elements that the degenerative tendencies held one another in check. Such a system, like that of Lycurgus, might endure for many centuries; Machiavelli only doubted whether some force, innate human folly or the blind stroke of fortune, would not overthrow even this in the end. But if asked exactly what forces impelled the degeneration of each un-mixed form of government and kept the Polybian cycle turning, he could only reply: the inherent instability of terrestrial things. There was in human affairs, as in everything sublunary, an innate tendency for things to perish by the mere excess of their own being, for each virtue to produce its corresponding vice and for the latter in the end to prevail, for fortune to throw down what it had built up. This cosmology, typical of late medieval thought, lingered on long in humanism, and it has lately been shown how a dominant theme of German historiography in the seventeenth century is that the individual must either struggle with or escape from irresistible fortune.[1] In Harrington there is much of this to be found: riches (including land) are 'the goods of fortune', it is still the legislator's part to found a government immune from change. But for all that an immense alteration has taken place. Governments no longer degenerate because of the operation of a tendency inherent in all nature; they do so because man has ignored, for almost two thousand years, part of the logic of the situation in which he finds himself. The consequences of his blindness follow according to a law of their own, but once they have brought him another opportunity to

[1] Leonard Forster, *The Temper of Seventeenth-century German Literature* (London, 1951), pp. 7–12.

establish stable government, and the process of history is understood, then the original blunder can be remedied and the degenerative cycle brought to a halt. Thus, though history was earlier identified with fortune, the concept of fortune has practically disappeared; history has a law which may be comprehended. Harrington denies Machiavelli's conviction that a people once thoroughly corrupt cannot be saved even by the wisest legislator: the causes of corruption are in an unjust distribution of land, or in the existence of a constitution at variance with the distribution, and its causes being known can be remedied. The dialectic can be solved.

Harrington hints that his conclusions are to be compared to the discovery of the circulation of the blood,[1] and Machiavelli, we may reflect, lived in a closed Greco-medieval universe, Harrington in an expanding scientific one. But that is not all. If degeneration has ceased to be essential and become accidental, that is because Harrington has located its causes, not in man's nature, but in his situation; and he has done this by writing history in terms, not of man's character, but of the social structure. He does not look deeper into agrarian society than the military tenures, but this is far enough to give him a vision of a particular pattern of social relationships, which may be replaced by another and may change from causes lying within itself: a vision to which Machiavelli never attained. Machiavelli lived in a city state, which he could easily identify with Athens or Rome, and where politics could be reduced to the fierce, kaleidoscopic and essentially personal factions and reactions of the piazza; he therefore wrote history in terms of human nature, which he viewed in isolation and thought unchanging. But Harrington lived in a territorial and agrarian community, where law and justice, custom and tenure, mattered and had always mattered more than the logic of the individual's conduct in politics; where institutions, far more than actions, determined the nature of political life. He therefore wrote history in terms of the changing structure of society. Feudalism, as was happening everywhere in English historical thought, helped him to see how the pattern of custom, law and government had changed in modern history, and helped him to see also that law might be largely a matter of land, and

[1] Liljegren, p. 13.

social relationships a matter of tenure. It is the marriage between this and the essentially classical and Italian concepts of the one, the few and the many, of the degenerative cycle, of the legislator, of the citizenry as a voting militia and the militia as an armed citizenry, that produces the thought of the 'Preliminaries', which posterity has agreed to consider the important part of Harrington's legacy. Viewed in this light, *Oceana* is a Machiavellian meditation upon feudalism.

CHAPTER VII

Interregnum: the First Royalist Reaction and the Response of Sir Matthew Hale

I

DURING the Interregnum there also occurred the first signs of a royalist reaction in the field of historiography; but this reaction, though it produced some new and valuable criticisms of the traditional accounts of constitutional history, did not of itself lead to a radical reassessment of the whole subject. That could come only when feudal institutions were given their proper place in English history, and the royalist writers before and just after 1660 lacked many of Spelman's works and did not fully understand those which they had. They sought merely to provide a history of the constitution which would emphasize the original and essential nature of the king's authority; and while this was not without its value as a means to criticizing the concept of the immemorial, its power to bring about a deeper understanding of history was limited. It is noticeable, too, that the reinterpretation they did provide depended rather on changes taking place in royalist political theory than on developments in the field of scholarship; and this may help to explain the curious fact that a genuine royalist historiography seems to have been delayed until at earliest the years between the first and second civil wars. Royalists of the school of Hyde, for instance, remained common lawyers in their predilections and consequently believers in the ancient constitution; the limit of their political beliefs was the assertion that a freely functioning royal prerogative formed an essential part of the constitution, and the limit of their use of history was the attempt to find precedents proving its existence. Hyde himself, in his last years and second exile, criticized Hobbes's *Leviathan*[1] partly on the grounds that the

[1] *A Brief View and Survey of the Dangerous and Pernicious Errors to Church and State in Mr. Hobbes' Book Entitled Leviathan* (1676); especially pp. 109, 110.

laws of England were derived from immemorial custom and not from the will of a conquering sovereign, and after his death was himself criticized by Robert Brady, a royalist in a far more radical sense, as one of the school of common lawyers who had built up a myth so dangerous to the crown.[1] But the beliefs of Hyde continued to satisfy many royalists even as late as the Revolution, and they may be found turning the concept of an immemorial constitution to support the doctrine of an immemorial prerogative.[2] From thought as conservative as theirs no new interpretation of history was to be expected.

What Hyde especially disliked in Hobbes was the latter's willingness to believe that William I had ruled as a conqueror, that the laws had continued to exist only by his will, and that his right over them had consequently been absolute and had descended intact to his successors. The theory of conquest, fatal alike to the doctrine of constitutional monarchy and to the concept of the law's antiquity, had for many years been peculiarly odious to common lawyers and parliamentarians, and from Lambarde and Camden far into the eighteenth century they never tired of refuting the suggestion that William I had conquered England. We have seen how the great Spelman himself had thought the idea worth repeated denials. What is curious is that the suggestion seems to have been refuted times without number, but very seldom actually made. Neither James I nor Sir Robert Filmer, normally regarded as the twin dragons of theoretical absolutism, made any serious use of it— Filmer indeed made none—and though it is now and then adduced by figures of no greater stature than Henry Ferne, for a systematic exposition of its meaning we must turn to so untypical and unpopular a thinker as Thomas Hobbes. Conquest struck few roots in royalist thought, though from the writings of its opponents one would think it the most dreaded and ever-present of dialectical menaces.[3]

[1] See p. 217, below.

[2] A good instance would be *Antidotum Britannicum*, an attack on Nevile's *Plato Redivivus*, written by one W. W. and published in 1681. This man believes in sovereign monarchy and regrets the abolition of the feudal tenures, yet he transcribes without acknowledgment the passage from Davies's *Irish Reports* in which the immemorial law is extolled. See his pp. 8–9.

[3] Ranke himself seems to have been misled by this anomaly. In his *History of England in the Seventeenth Century* (English edition, 1879), vol. IV, pp. 123–4,

The reasons for its insignificance are probably various; one—brought to light by the mention of Hyde—is that a great many royalists were believers in law and held that in defending the king they were defending the ancient constitution. Others may lie in the nature of the conquest theory itself. Viewed superficially, it seemed to offer royalists the chance of proving that all the subject's liberties were the gift of the king's grace and could not constitute a fundamental law before which he might be brought to book; but under examination it revealed disadvantages. It was essentially an appeal to the sword; if this was no more than an appeal to force, to God's judgment as expressed in success, then it conferred as good a right on Cromwell as on Charles. The royalists sought to establish that kings ruled by a right intelligible to human reason but independent of human consent, and a right ultimately derived from the arbitrament of war could not but seem impermanent and subject to fortune. Furthermore, in the writers on *jus gentium*, by whom the theory of conquest had been most fully worked out, it proved to mean no more than that a conquered people were entitled to derive their laws from the conqueror's will in the absence of any more secure foundation;[1] and Ferne stipulated that the right of conquest could not be alleged where there was a legitimate heir to the defeated king. Royalist thought inevitably turned from the theory of conquest to establish monarchy on the basis of some more permanent principle. Some sought it in *ius divinum* and

he discusses Algernon Sidney's *Discourses on Government* and says that Filmer, against whom Sidney was writing, 'takes his stand upon the Norman Conquest and the right it gave, which he however extends so far as to destroy all national freedom'. In point of fact, Filmer did not use the argument from conquest and, as is shown in this chapter, rather disliked it when he found it in Hobbes. Sidney, however, refuted it at length, as if Filmer had indeed used it; and it is to be feared that in this particular the great German took his notion of Filmer from Sidney.

[1] It was used to justify obedience to a usurping power by several writers during the Interregnum (e.g. Ascham and Dury): Zagorin, *A History of Political Thought during the English Revolution* (1954), pp. 64–73. Hobbes might of course be considered as one of these. It was in this sense that a few 'de facto Tories' sought to justify their acceptance of William III on the grounds that he ruled by right of conquest. The case of the unfortunate licenser of books, Edmund Bohun, in 1692, illustrates the argument's appeal and its dangers.

express divine command, in which case the argument was conducted in scriptural terms and altogether outside the sphere of English history; others, as we have seen, sought it in the immemorial custom of England, and argued from assumptions and presuppositions which did not differ at all from those of the common lawyers.

But the theory that a legislative sovereign was logically necessary, while it did not automatically involve recourse to the notion of conquest, made a wide appeal to royalists and could be couched in constitutional and historical language. During 1648 Sir Robert Filmer began to publish tracts containing the political ideas he had worked out in the still unprinted *Patriarcha*: these were *The Freeholder's Grand Inquest*, *The Anarchy of a Limited or Mixed Monarchy*, and *The Necessity of the Absolute Power of all Kings*.[1] *The Freeholder's Grand Inquest* dealt entirely with constitutional law and history, and there is some interest in the fact that he should have laid it before the public earlier than the tracts which expound his doctrine in the language of political theory; there is a sense, besides, in which it inaugurated the political and historical debate of the next forty years. The work appeared in January 1647–8, a moment at which it was still just possible to hope for an agreed dissolution of the Long Parliament and the issue of writs for a new election by the king's command; and Filmer's purpose in publishing it was to remind the prospective elector of the legal significance of his choice and in particular to convince him that the knights and burgesses he would be electing did not constitute a chamber of unlimited powers. To this end Filmer chose the form of a close examination of the writ which enjoined the sheriff to hold elections, and he undertook to prove three things:

I. That the Commons, by their Writ, are only to perform and consent to the Ordinances of Parliament.

II. That the Lords or Common Council by their Writ are only to treat, and give counsel in Parliament.

III. That the King himself only ordains and makes laws, and is supreme judge in Parliament.[2]

[1] For the order and circumstances in which he published see Laslett, *Patriarcha and other Political Works of Sir Robert Filmer* (Oxford, 1949), pp. 7–9, and the bibliographical notes to the several tracts. From this edition all subsequent quotations from Filmer are taken.　　　　[2] Laslett, p. 129.

The argument of the whole tract runs somewhat as follows.
By study of the writ of summons, and of the form in which legislation is now and has in the past been promulgated, it can be shown
that the king is sole judge and sole legislator; his Lords and his Commons are those whom he summons by writ to aid and advise him
in work which is properly his alone. But they do not do this on an
equal footing: the writ issued to the Lords summons them 'to
treat with us and give us of your counsel' (*tractaturi vestrumque consilium impensuri*), that to the Commons only 'to execute and consent'
(*ad faciendum et consentiendum*) to those things which the king and the
common council may determine. Filmer concludes that the Commons do not, properly speaking, form any part of the common
council, nor, if the terms are interchangeable, of parliament. The
Lords alone form the common council and are called to give advice;
the Commons are called to stand at the bar ('no magistratical
posture'), to present petitions to the king, and to consent and give
effect to the decisions arrived at by the king with the counsel of the
lords. There may, Filmer says, be many other things which the
king permits the Commons to do; but the limit of what they can
claim is the function named in the writ of summons, and this too—
like the Lords' function of giving advice in the common council
proper—has no other origin but the king's command. Therefore,
once again, all legislation is the act of the king alone, and as both
houses derive from him their mere existence, so their privileges can
have no other origin but his grace.

Down to this point in the argument, Filmer is merely extracting
from authoritative constitutional documents evidence for his
fundamental thesis—that the king must be sovereign and that all
law and right must be the work of his will. But in the first few
pages of the *Freeholder's Inquest*, he turned aside to meet the inevitable
reply that the knights and burgesses had formed part of the common
council from time immemorial, so that there was no need for their
membership to be made explicit in the writ. He denied the antiquity
of the Commons and asserted that there had been a time when the
common council had met without them.

For clearing the meaning and sense of the writ, and satisfaction of such as
think it impossible, but that the Commons of England have always been a

part of the common council of the kingdom, I shall insist upon these points: 1. That anciently the Barons of England were the common council of the kingdom. 2. That until the time of Henry I, the Commons were not called to Parliament. 3. Though the Commons were called by Henry I, yet they were not constantly called, nor yet regularly elected by writ until Henry III's time.[1]

Attacks such as this on the antiquity of the Commons were to be the matter of debate until the Revolution and even after, and it is desirable to see what, in this early stage of the doctrine's history, Filmer meant by it. The reference to Henry I need not detain us: Polydore Vergil and Selden had been inclined to accept a story that 'all the people' had assembled at that king's coronation and made laws, but Spelman had rejected it and it does not figure prominently in subsequent controversy. But the statement that a regular summons by writ began under Henry III presumably alludes to the fact that the first extant summons of knights of the shire by writ to the sheriff was dated in the forty-ninth year of his reign. Filmer indeed mentions '49 H. 3' without suggesting that the commons were sent for,[2] but this was the year fixed on in the angry debates of the next generation between those who wished to date the origin of the Commons and those who wished them to remain immemorial. To all the disputants, the point at issue was less whether the Commons had originated in this year or that, than whether they could be shown to have originated in any identifiable year at all. If they could not, then they were immemorial and their privileges were secure; but if they could, then they owed their being to some pre-existent authority—always assumed to be the king—which must to the end of time retain the sovereignty over them. What the king's remotest ancestor had given, his remotest descendant could take away. There was now no need to prove a Norman conquest, unless that happened to be the best means of

[1] Laslett, p. 136.

[2] Laslett, pp. 139–40. It may be appropriate to mention here that the year 1265 figures prominently in this and the next chapter, but is always alluded to by its regnal dating of 49 H. 3. This was the mode invariably adopted by contemporary writers, and to translate it into *anno domini* would seem to depart from the character of their historical thought, rooted as it was in the English public records.

dating the origin of the Commons, and this may partly account for Filmer's neglect of the argument. As far back as 1581, when they had imprisoned Arthur Hall of Grantham for denying that they were immemorial, the Commons had shown their fear of some such attack as this; but the fact that it had hardly been levelled until now is evidence of the extraordinary sway which common-law historiography exerted over even the royalist mind. Spelman, from his own advanced standpoint, had framed a criticism in 'Of Parliaments' but had probably not meant to argue that the Commons, being late in origin, were in all things subject to the crown. But in Filmer's view this was a necessary consequence; and it was only when a clear doctrine of sovereignty had been framed that royalists, lacking the peculiar impulse afforded by Spelman's thought, began to see the full utility of impugning the antiquity of the Commons. From now on, however, to do so might be to provide arguments for Filmerian absolutism. If the Commons were not immemorial, had they any rights against the crown at all?

The immediate impact of the *Freeholder's Inquest*, however, was rather different from this; but before considering this aspect of the subject, we should observe that to derive the whole constitution from the will of the king did not necessarily bring about a general readjustment of historical ideas. As a statement, it was scarcely susceptible of historical proof, and it could never have the stimulating and deepening effect on historical thought which the discovery of feudalism had had on that of Craig, Spelman and Harrington. Of this branch of learning Filmer was apparently devoid. Though he had been one of the group of scholars who first met at Westminster late in James I's reign, though he had known and could quote Cotton, Selden and Spelman, he shows no sign of knowing that the giving of counsel was an obligation of tenure or that the tenurial relationship was of any special importance in the medieval kingdom. He tells us, for instance, that before the summoning of the Commons the council was composed of barons, but his account of the origin and nature of baronage is given in the words of a peculiarly old-fashioned passage in Coke,[1] and on this subject at least he had clearly read *Archaeologus* and the *Titles of*

[1] Laslett, pp. 140-1, with Filmer's reference to Coke.

Honour in vain. Here we may perhaps blame his political philosophy. For Filmer

the difference between a Peer and a Commoner, is not by nature, but by the grace of the Prince: who creates honours, and makes those honours to be hereditary (whereas he might have given them for life only, or during pleasure, or good behaviour) and also annexeth to those honours the power of having votes in Parliament, as hereditary councillors, furnished with ampler privileges than the commons.[1]

If the difference between one social rank and another comes simply from the sovereign's command, there is no need to investigate the social structure of which they form part; and if the sovereign is an absolutely free agent, we need not inquire whether the relations between him and one class of his subjects are of a special nature and differ essentially from those he has with all other classes. Filmer's absolutism caused him to ignore the complexities of the medieval structure and diminished the extent to which his thought was genuinely historical. He could not see the origin of the Commons as Spelman had seen it, as an aspect of the transition from a feudal to a freeholding society. Filmer's argument means no more than that since the Commons originated late, they are not sovereign but subject to a sovereign.

To us, with the whole of Filmer's political thought before us, the absolutist interpretation of the *Freeholder's Inquest* is evidently the correct one. We need to remember, however, that this tract was first read by a public quite unacquainted with Filmer's doctrine of patriarchalism and none too familiar with that of political sovereignty. To minds such as these, it would be perfectly possible to read it as an essay in constitutionalism rather than absolutism, an appeal to the documents of the ancient constitution rather than a demonstration that the constitution itself was the creation of the king's will. It was in this sense that William Prynne read it; for though this formidable Puritan and common lawyer was profoundly influenced by the *Freeholder's Inquest* and cited it and developed its arguments throughout the rest of his pamphleteering life, he criticized the antiquity of the Commons in order to bring them not

[1] Laslett, pp. 156–7.

so much under the authority of the sovereign as within the bounds of the ancient constitution.

The alliance of two such minds—there is no trace of its having been known to Filmer—seems fantastic to contemplate, but it lay in the nature of the political and constitutional developments of the Interregnum. From late 1647 onwards, the fundamental dilemma of that period became increasingly plain. A single chamber, styling itself parliament, soon claimed sovereign power in the name of the ancient constitution; the only force capable of checking its pretensions was the army, which meant that the power of parliament seemed about to be made subject not to law, but to the sword. To those who wished to end this state of affairs, and were detached from Cromwell's increasingly desperate attempts to do so by means of synthetic constitutions, it was evident that to restore the ancient constitution was the only solution and in time it emerged that the restoration of the ancient constitution meant the restoration of the crown. What was needed was a government not destructive of liberty, but equally not open to the reproach that any man who had not given his consent to its foundation might withhold his obedience, and it might be argued that the monarchy satisfied this need and was beyond the reach of consent as much because it was immemorial as because it was sacred. Every man knew who had made the Protector, but none knew who had made the king unless it were God himself; and if the divine origin of kingship were expressed in terms of ancient English custom rather than of scriptural warrant, it became plain that the immemorial monarchy was the best guarantee of the immemorial law. The Restoration of 1660 was the greatest triumph which the cult of the ancient constitution ever enjoyed, and perhaps the greatest service it ever rendered.

As the theoretical debate of the 1640's and 1650's worked itself out to this conclusion, it became plain that the case for the ancient constitution could be identified with the case for the crown. Possibly none was better placed to discern this conclusion than the conservative Presbyterians, always constitutionalist, monarchist and counter-revolutionary. From the time of the army's march on London and the first expulsions of Presbyterian members of parliament, William Prynne—who was himself to be expelled by Pride—

saw that he was faced with a subversion of the whole parliamentary structure, and he was intelligent enough to see that the root of the trouble was his own house's claim to virtual sovereignty. It was not that the army had dictated to parliament, but that the Commons were taking it on themselves to try the king, abolish the Lords and expel their own members by majority vote. If the right of the secluded members to sit was to be restored, it must be established that the writ under which they had been returned was not within the exclusive control of the lower house acting alone; it must therefore be shown that the summons was issued by the king and that the Commons were not the whole of parliament. At the beginning of 1648, the *Freeholder's Inquest* supplied Prynne with the arguments he needed. It appeared in January;[1] not later than March[2] he published *A Plea for the Lords*, in which he cited Filmer's tract four times and made use of its case against the antiquity of the Commons. (Ten years later he reissued the *Plea* in a greatly expanded form, and the *Inquest* appeared seventeen times amongst his authorities.) The right of the Lords in parliament, he urged, was independent of that of the Commons:

their sitting, voting and judging therefore in Parliament, being so ancient, cleare and unquestionable ever since their first beginning till now; and the sitting of Knights, Citizens, and Burgesses by the peoples election in our ancientest Parliaments and Councells not so cleare and evident by *History* or *Records* as theirs: we must needs acknowledge and subscribe to their Right and Title, or else deny the Knights, Citizens and Burgesses rights in Parliament rather than theirs, who have not so ancient or cleare a Title or right as they.[3]

Next year he pressed the attack further in *The First Part of a Historical Collection concerning the Ancient Parliaments of England, from...673 till...1216.* Throughout these centuries, he wrote,

(and many yeers after), our Parliaments were constituted and made up onely of our *Kings, Princes*, Dukes, Earles, Nobles, BARONS, *Spirituall and Temporall Lords*, and those who in later ages we stile the HOUSE OF PEERS, without any *Knights of Shires, Citizens, Burgesses*, elected by the people as their Representatives, or any House of Commons, not known, nor heard of

---

[1] Laslett, p. 128.   [2] Copies are dated 1647.
[3] *A Plea for the Lords* (1647–8), p. 4 (wrongly numbered for p. 12).

in these elder times, though those who now stile themselves the *Commons*, endeavour to cashier both *King* and *Lords* from being Members of our Parliaments, contrary to our *Laws, Statutes, Oathes* and *Solemn League and Covenant*, and the practice of all former ages; at whose Door and Barr themselves have waited, and stood bare upon all occasions, till within these few months, as their professed Superiours, and the onely Judges in Parliament, being but so many *Grand Jurie* men to present the Kingdomes grievances to their Superiour Tribunall and crave their redress and censure of them: A sufficient refutation of their present usurpation over them.[1]

The influence of the *Freeholder's Inquest* is plain, and Prynne now assumed for the rest of his life the role of an historical scholar, the aim of whose researches was to restore the usurped ancient constitution. From 1650 to 1653 he was imprisoned ('of purpose', in his own estimation, 'to debarr me from publishing any thing of this Nature, or against their New *Tyrannical Usurpations*'),[2] but on his return embarked on those labours among the Tower records which were to dominate the last phase of his career. 'In Caesar's Chapel, under the leads of the White Tower', he found great decaying masses of records: writs of summons, returns and other documents relevant to parliamentary elections. These he set himself first to rescue, then to digest and publish; and his toil bore fruit in the *Brief Register of Parliamentary Writs*, published in four volumes and more than two thousand pages between 1658–9 and 1664. In this vast survey of every writ of summons then extant and known we have the repetition on a gigantic scale of the *Freeholder's Inquest*; all the old arguments recur. The writ is issued by the king; it confers a status inferior to that of the Lords; the Commons are formally entitled to discuss only those matters which the king and the Lords lay before them. Above all, the subordinate position of the Commons is proved by the fact that they are not immemorial; Prynne assembled more documentary evidence than had ever been known before to support the view that no summons of knights and burgesses could be traced earlier than the first extant writ in 49 H. 3.

[1] *First Part of a Historical Collection...* (1649), pp. 5–6. No second part appeared and the work's function was carried on (after Prynne's imprisonment) by the *Brief Register of Parliamentary Writs*.

[2] From the preface 'To the Ingenuous Readers' of the *First Part of a Brief Register* (1658–9).

By the time the Long Parliament reassembled in 1660, Prynne could rise to argue that the writs for the new parliament should be issued in the name of Charles II—no decision to recall whom had yet been taken—as a mere matter of obedience to existing law.[1]

But Prynne used the arguments of the *Freeholder's Inquest* to support a view of the constitution ultimately very different from Filmer's. Where the latter maintained a theory of sovereignty which must at bottom mean that all law was the king's creation and consequently had originated at some point in time, Prynne believed in the immemorial constitution with all Coke's extravagance crossed with his own fanaticism. The law he was upholding had been constitutional law since the time of the Britons. The immemorial custom of England was visibly embodied less in the authorities of the common law than in the records of the Tower. The chaotic heaps of documents among which contemporaries saw him labouring assumed in his mind a peculiar sanctity; they were the repository of all constitutional truth, all political wisdom, and he was defending the constitution not merely intellectually by his pen, but physically by protecting these precious evidences and guarding them against neglect, decay and the malice of their enemies. He compared himself to Hilkiah the High Priest, who 'found the Book of the Law in the House of the Lord', and to Shaphan the scribe, who 'carried the Book to the King and read it before the King'. In dedicating the *Third Part of a Brief Register* to Charles II (1662), he told his sovereign that one and the same miraculous resurrection had restored him to the throne and raised up the records of the constitution from oblivion (at Prynne's hands).[2] He was, as usual, fabulously exaggerating his case; but he was only giving expression, in his own way, to a time-honoured belief. He was not therefore stating the view of constitutional history which Filmer had inaugurated and which was to become royalist orthodoxy some twenty years later. In his mind, all that he had proved was that the constitution was immemorial, that the king and the Lords were immemorial, but that the Commons were not. They must therefore

---

[1] *D.N.B.* 'William Prynne'.
[2] Prynne added that Hugh Peters's proposal to burn the records was the worst deed that sinner had advocated except the execution of Charles I.

accept subordination, not as in Filmer to the will of a sovereign legislator, but to the ancient law of England.

We look, therefore, to Prynne even less than to Filmer for a revival of Spelman's approach to the study of constitutional history. In one respect, it is true, he shows insight superior to Filmer's, but the promise comes to nothing. Filmer, as we have seen, failed to connect baronage with tenure because he thought of it merely as a rank conferred by royal favour; but Prynne wrote the first version (1648) of *A Plea for the Lords* to defend the upper house against Leveller assailants, some of whom had alleged that the Lords owed their title to the king's summons alone and were a nobility foisted upon the country by Norman usurpers. Prynne replied that the Lords had sat in parliament 'by right of peerage and tenure' for centuries before the Conquest, and in the *First Part of a Brief Register* (1658–9) he continued to defend them against the imputation of sitting by the king's will alone, declaring both that their right in parliament was immemorial and that the royal summons alone could not make a hereditary peer, unless the recipient either held *per baroniam* or had a special patent creating a hereditary title. In his anxiety to endow the peerage with a right more august than that of the representatives of the commons, Prynne remembered, where Filmer seems to have ignored, the ancient principle that tenure was a characteristic mark of baronage. He knew that the commons were a late adjunct to the king's council; he knew that before their advent the council had been composed principally of barons; he knew that tenure had been an essential of baronage. But he never quite succeeded in taking the next step and concluding that the barons had given counsel as an obligation incident to their tenures and that the growth of parliament had occurred as society developed away from a condition in which tenure and vassalage had determined the whole network of social relationships.

Prynne's study of the evidence again and again carried him to the point of remarking that before Henry III the council had consisted of barons, that these barons had held land and done homage, and that they had been summoned to give counsel on their homage and allegiance. But he never reached the stage of generalizing from the evidence, and for this we must blame his ignorance of the feudal history of countries other than his own—the basis on which Spelman had built up the concept of certain universal feudal characteristics which could be applied to the history of medieval England. Because Prynne could not do this, he could not explain that before the commons were added to it the council had been a body constituted on the basis of tenure in chief of the crown; and because he could not do this, his thought about parliamentary history continued to be a critical and sophisticated variant of that common-law thought which took the institutions of the present day and sought for their origins in the remote past. Spelman, having concluded that counsel had once been a function of tenure, decided that the parliamentary attendance of the commons had descended to them from the lesser tenants in chief; but when Prynne encountered the *omnes alios qui de nobis tenent in capite* of Magna Carta, or the knights of the shire summoned for specified purposes before 49 H. 3, he invariably argued that these persons could not be the commons, because they attended as tenants of the king and not as the elected representatives of their fellows. Before 49 H. 3 there were no commons; after that date there were the commons summoned in the writ. More than that Prynne could not say.

There was no alternative to an appreciation of the full meaning of Spelman's thought. When he published his last work, *Animadversions on Sir Edward Coke's Fourth Institutes* (1669), Prynne had in his possession Dugdale's 1664 edition of the complete *Archaeologus*, in which 'Parlamentum' had been published for the first time, and he actually quoted several of its most vital sentences; but clearly without understanding their true significance.[1] Spelman—thanks to the *Libri Feudorum* and his Continental learning—had framed a theory of feudalism and by its means established the existence of a feudal phase in the English past; Prynne had not done this, and it does not seem that it could have been done by study of the English evidence alone. He continued to believe that the constitution was immemorial, with the qualification that the House of Commons was not—and this perhaps he owed to Filmer. At the Restoration he was appointed, in recognition of his services to the constitution, to be Keeper of Records in the Tower, a post which he held to his

---

[1] *Animadversions on the Fourth Institutes* (1669), pp. 2, 6, 7, 8.

death in 1669, inaugurating a period in which the keepers were sometimes appointed for their work in propagandist historiography on medieval and constitutional themes; but significant figure though he is, he yet founded no school and remained in essentials a survivor from the age of Coke. Filmer had denied the antiquity of the Commons as a means to proving the sovereignty of the king, Prynne out of concern for the ancient constitution; their criticisms provided a useful weapon for checking the claims of parliament, but none for altering the way in which Englishmen instinctively thought about their history. For that there was no alternative to Spelman, to the application of feudal knowledge to constitutional history. The appeal to 49 H. 3, however, did much to create a more critical atmosphere: one in which the thought of Spelman, once it re-appeared and was understood, would be taken up and used, as much for its polemical as for its scholarly value. The true royalist counter-offensive, when at last it began, was a mingling of Spelman's ideas with Filmer's.

II

Thomas Hobbes, it is generally agreed, is far from typical of royalist thought—not least in his willingness to make use of the argument from Norman conquest—but, in the field which we are surveying, his writings assist us considerably to understand the case against the common-law mind which a penetrating intellect could build up out of the new historical ideas becoming current in the middle decades of the century. Students of his thought have perhaps neglected to note how much space he devoted to refutation of such ideas as that law is law because it is immemorial custom: several paragraphs of *Leviathan*, the greater part of the *Dialogue of the Common Laws* and much of *Behemoth* are directed to this end, and in all these writings we find English history interpreted in the light of Hobbes's characteristic ideas to form a radical criticism of the traditional beliefs of his countrymen. Coke, as we should expect, was his principal target, and Hobbes set himself to refute two of the chief justice's fundamental contentions: first, that most law was law because immemorial custom, second, that law of this kind constituted an 'artificial reason', the accumulated and refined wisdom of many generations, which none but a professional could comprehend and no individual intellect, however great, could have produced. On the contrary, Hobbes replied, law was two things: first, it was the dictate of a perfectly simple and universal 'natural reason', which enjoined those things which were good for our self-preservation; and second, it was made law by the command of the sovereign, not because he possessed greater or less 'natural reason', but because he had been instituted by men in the state of nature to enforce a certain mode of living which 'natural reason' enjoined.[1] The first part of this argument earned him a highly Burkean rebuke from Chief Justice Hale; it was in connexion with the second that he made most of his allusions to English history. Hobbes's position as regards custom is practically identical with that taken up by Filmer, which may be termed the historical limitation of right: law may be custom, but custom alone has no binding force; for custom to become law requires that there should already exist an authority capable of making law by his injunctions. Therefore no law can be immemorial; before there can be law there must be a sovereign; and every law must have been made at a particular point in time. To state such an argument as this was to give every royalist a vested interest in historical research. Logically, every law must have a beginning in time, the point at which the sovereign commanded it; practically, let that point only be found and the law's derivation from the command of a pre-existing sovereign was demonstrated.

Hobbes, however, did not spend much time in his *Dialogue* searching for the historical beginnings of specific English laws. He was concerned instead to demonstrate the presence in English history of such a legislative sovereign as he believed must exist on *a priori* grounds, and to this end employed such arguments as that the king made judges and gave them their authority to judge, that the king determined punishments where the existing law prescribed none, and that the king had in past ages made the law of England with the assent of the Lords and Commons in parliament, but without consulting the judges.[2] (It is pleasant to observe that for once in a way Coke was right on a point of history and Hobbes,

[1] Hobbes, E[nglish] W[orks], vol. VI, pp. 5–7, 14–15, 62–3 and generally.
[2] E.W. vol. VI, p. 15.

as many contemporary scholars might have told him, demonstrably wrong; his argument might also tend to exaggerate the antiquity of parliament.) But Hobbes also made use of the concept of a Norman Conquest, and the way in which he did so merits study. He had discussed, in *Leviathan*, conquest as one of the two modes of acquiring dominion over others (the second being the acquisition of paternal dominion by begetting children), and Filmer had deplored his having done so. For—Sir Robert pointed out—Hobbes made it plain that the conqueror's dominion was created, not by his sword but by the wills of the conquered constituting him their sovereign out of fear of his sword, so that all difference between a sovereign by conquest and a sovereign peacefully instituted by social compact disappeared: each was absolute, each was the creature of covenant. This Filmer was unable to understand. How could an absolute sovereign guarantee the well-being of his subjects, and how could a sovereign instituted by the will of his subjects to a specific end be absolute? Moreover, it was clearly at the back of Filmer's mind that an appeal to conquest could not but justify the successful usurper. Hobbes's clarity of mind had exhibited to the perspicacious Filmer the two fundamental reasons why conquest could never be a theory long acceptable to royalists. Under close analysis it proved to be a mingling of force and covenant; and the royalists, especially under the Interregnum, could stomach neither.[1] But to Hobbes nothing could be more acceptable; in his view the will had little to do, at the best of times, but to consent to inescapable force and seek to turn it to its advantage, and the notion that the English kings acquired their sovereignty from William the Norman's conquest of the land was perfectly sensible and not particularly alarming. The mode of acquisition merely illustrated the essential nature of sovereignty. Granted that it must be above the law, it was indifferent how it came there.

> But say withal, that the King is subject to the laws of God, both written and unwritten, and to no other; and so was William the Conqueror, whose right is all descended to our present King....[2]

[1] See Oakeshott (ed.), *Leviathan* (Oxford, Blackwell's Political Texts; undated), pp. 130–3; and Laslett, pp. 239–40.

[2] *E.W.* vol. VI, p. 21.

Statutes are not philosophy, as is the common law, and other disputable arts, but are commands or prohibitions which ought to be obeyed, because assented to by submission made to the Conqueror here in England and to whosoever had the sovereign power in other places.[1]

The quotations fairly illustrate the subsidiary and illustrative character of the Norman Conquest in Hobbes's theory of English sovereignty. Neither in the *Dialogue of the Common Laws* nor in *Behemoth* did he place the fact of conquest at the centre of his argument or attempt, save by way of illustration, to derive the laws and liberties of England from it; but the considerations that made him regard it as not of the first importance made him also unafraid of it. Nor did it necessarily provide him with reasons for criticizing all the allegations of antiquity made about the various institutions of England. In the *Dialogue*'s closing passages the Lawyer and the Philosopher agree that it is in the sovereign's interest to surround himself with the chief men of the realm and make laws with their consent. But what of the composition of this council; what of the antiquity of the Commons? The Lawyer puts forward the old argument, found in Lambarde and Harrington, that the existence of totally deserted and decayed boroughs, still returning representatives to parliament, proves the extreme—and, it is taken for granted, pre-Conquest—antiquity of this right. Consider Old Sarum; its burgesses should be rabbits. The Philosopher agrees: in the time of the heptarchy there were many kings, each with his parliament and burgesses in each parliament; when one parliament met for all the kingdom, each borough sent its representatives. This may account for the preponderance of boroughs in the west, 'being more populous, and also more obnoxious to invaders, and for that cause having greater store of towns fortified'. The *Dialogue* ends on this cordial note.[2] But when the antiquity of the Commons is mentioned in *Behemoth*, an account is given which blends Filmer and Selden with a hint of Harrington:

The knights of shires and burgesses were never called to Parliament, for aught that I know, till the beginning of the reign of Edward I, or the latter end of the reign of Henry III, immediately after the misbehaviour of the

[1] *E.W.* vol. VI, p. 24.   [2] *E.W.* vol. VI, pp. 157–60.

barons; and, for aught any man knows, were called on purpose to weaken that power of the lords, which they had so freshly abused. Before the time of Henry III the lords were descended, most of them, from such as in the invasions and conquests of the Germans were peers and fellow-kings, till one was made king of them all; and their tenants were their subjects, as it is at this day with the lords of France. But after the time of Henry III, the kings began to make lords in the place of them whose issue failed, titulary only, without the lands belonging to their title; and by that means, their tenants being no longer bound to serve them in the wars, they grew every day less and less able to make a party against the King, though they continued still to be his great council. And as their power decreased, so the power of the House of Commons increased; but I do not find they were part of the King's council at all, nor judges over other men; though it cannot be denied, but a King may ask their advice, as well as the advice of any other. But I do not find that the end of their summoning was to give advice, but only, in case they had any petitions for redress of grievances, to be ready there with them whilst the King had his great council about him.[1]

Hobbes, we may take it, was by this time aware of the advantages of proving that the Commons originated late and consequently by the king's will. But it cannot escape notice that the passage just quoted unmistakably associates the decline of the barons' feudal power with the rise to importance of the House of Commons; and this raises the interesting question of Hobbes's knowledge of feudalism and the use he made of it. The opinion of the learned seems to be that these two dialogues were written within a short space of time, the *Common Laws* after 1666, *Behemoth* about 1668.[2] Hobbes could therefore have been acquainted with the complete edition of Spelman's *Archaeologus* that appeared in 1664. However that may be, both dialogues contain a definite and consistent appeal to feudal principles, which occurs first in the context of universal rather than English history.

Then let us consider next the commentaries of Sir Edward Coke upon Magna Charta and other statutes. For the understanding of Magna Charta it will be very necessary to run up into ancient times, as far as history will give us leave, and consider not only the customs of our ancestors the Saxons,

[1] *E.W.* vol. VI, p. 261.
[2] J. Laird, *Hobbes* (London, 1934), pp. 35-6, and his references to the work of G. C. Robertson.

but also the law of nature, the most ancient of all laws, concerning the
original of government and acquisition of property, and concerning courts
of judicature. And first, it is evident that dominion, government and laws
are far more ancient than history or any other writing, and that the beginning
of all dominion amongst men was in families.[1]

The father of the family—Hobbes does not call him the patriarch,
but we may legitimately do so—possesses absolute power over his
wife and children. This is in accordance with the principles of
Leviathan, where it was pointed out that paternity was one of the
origins of dominion, but that the father's authority was derived not
from the mere fact of his paternity, but from his children's submission to his power (another doctrine which Filmer could by no
means accept). Landless individuals may attach themselves to the
family for security and submit themselves to the patriarch's authority
in exactly the same way as his children. If a family so constituted
conquers another and seizes its lands—which the law of God permits
if it is the only way of procuring subsistence or removing a just
cause of fear—the lands so won become the property of the patriarch. The Lawyer points out that this denies all right of property to
the subject members of the tribe. The Philosopher assents: when the
subjects placed themselves under the patriarch's authority, they did so
for the sake of security; they are entitled to nothing else, and this
does not of itself confer a title to land.

Did not Joshua and the High Priest divide the land of Canaan in such sort
among the tribes of Israel as they pleased? Did not the Roman and Grecian
princes and states, according to their own discretion, send out the colonies
to inhabit such provinces as they had conquered? Is there at this day among
the Turks, any inheritor of land besides the Sultan? And was not all the
land of England once in the hands of William the Conqueror? Sir Edward
Coke himself confesses it.[2]

The Saxons and other German peoples—with whose history and
institutions Hobbes appears to be identifying those of the Normans
—dwelt in families and under patriarchs in this way. When they
conquered land in England, it became the absolute property of the
sovereign, first of the heads of independent tribes, later of the king.
But the subjects were not without definite rights in the land, for—

[1] *E.W.* vol. VI, p. 147.　　　　[2] *E.W.* vol. VI, p. 149.

says the Philosopher—it is necessary to distinguish two sorts of property: the *allodium* and the fee. In a monarchy, none could possess allodial property but the king; all subjects must (as the common law declares) hold in fee, that is by the tenure and service of the king. The king lived, partly by his own demesnes—which Hobbes identifies with the forests—partly by the services which all men owed him. For in addition to the great men of the land, endowed with

much more land than they had need of for their own maintenance; but so charged with one or many soldiers, according to the quantity of land given, as there could be no want of soldiers at all times ready to resist an invading enemy: which soldiers these lords were bound to furnish, for a time certain, at their own charges,[1]

all men took an oath of allegiance to the king in the tithings and hundreds; and those who held 'by the service of husbandry', together with villeins and even women and children, were obliged to help to defend the kingdom in such manner as they were able, by the law of nature. But a special obligation rested on those who held by military service. Hobbes notes with approval the form of words employed in doing both homage and fealty, and looking at them through his eyes we can see how exactly an unlimited and unconditional yielding of one's self and one's services fitted the notion of compact set forth in *Leviathan*. In vassalage royalist thought was beginning to find the irrevocable contract of unqualified and absolute subjection which it had sought for so long. The patriarch was becoming identified with the seigneur, the seigneur with the king, and all three with Leviathan. Thanks to the centralized nature of the English monarchy, it was possible to perform the remarkable intellectual feat of making feudalism an argument for sovereignty.

Hobbes rehearses the feudal services and other rights due to the king; but, he says, speaking of homage and fealty,

both these services, and the services of husbandry, were quickly after turned into rents, payable either in money, as in England, or in corn and other victuals, as in Scotland and France.

[1] *E.W.* vol. VI, pp. 154–5.

However, this could not of itself do away with the military tenant's obligation to serve in person if summoned,

which, methinks, should ever hold for law, unless by some other law it come to be altered....The ancient kings had means enough, by their various feudal rights, to defend their kingdom and keep the peace. And so had the succeeding Kings, if they had never given their rights away, and their subjects always kept their oaths and promises.[1]

These remarks are the nearest Hobbes came to admitting that he was writing after the feudal tenures had been formally abolished, by *rex in parliamento*, in 1660. There were some royalist thinkers, as we shall see, who openly regretted this step, and it may not be unreasonable to attribute a trace of this nostalgia to Hobbes. He had forecast, in considerable detail, the case which royalists of greater erudition were to construct out of English history between 1675 and 1688: the denial of the immemorial, the appeal to a logically necessary sovereign, the attack on the antiquity of the Commons and the attempt to use the king's feudal suzerainty as an argument for his political sovereignty. All these were to be repeated, consciously or otherwise, by later royalists, though his appeal to the Norman Conquest won little favour.

Feudalism might, in addition, be used to demonstrate that parliament and the common law in their present form could have come into being only as feudal society declined. There is something of this in Hobbes: he observes that there seems to have been no Court of Common Pleas before Magna Carta, and

perhaps there was not so much need of it as you think. For in those times the laws, for the most part, were in settling, rather than settled; and the old Saxon laws concerning inheritance were then practised, by which laws speedy justice was executed by the King's writs, in the courts of Barons, which were landlords to the rest of the freeholders; and suits of barons in County courts; and but few suits in the King's courts, but when justice could not be had in those inferior courts. But at this day there be more suits in the King's courts, than any one court can dispatch.[2]

This is not particularly complete, but it shows a willingness to trace the growth of the modern common law from a feudal background. To the history of parliament, however, Hobbes could make

[1] *E.W.* vol. VI, pp. 156–7.   [2] *E.W.* vol. VI, pp. 43–4.

no further application of feudal principles than appears in the passage quoted earlier; he was aware that the barons attended the council as obliged by the homage which they did for their fiefs, but he never quite reached the point of saying that the council was a court of tenants. As the above passage shows, he did not distinguish Saxon from Norman law, and he held that lordship and tenure were institutions common to all the ancient Germans and indeed to all mankind in its primitive age. If, like Spelman, he had realized that a special form of tenure and a body of laws consequent upon it had been brought in and imposed upon England by the Norman conqueror, he might have gone on to reconstitute the early council on a tenurial basis. As it was, this was not done before the rediscovery of Spelman.

III

A reply to the *Dialogue of the Common Laws* was written (but not published or even perhaps completed) by Sir Matthew Hale, Chief Justice of the King's Bench, who also wrote, at an undetermined date before his death in 1675, a *History of the Common Law* which was published in 1715 and is still rightly regarded as one of the early classics of its kind. A train of thought which runs from Hale's reply to Hobbes to its maturity in the *History* deserves study as part of the present work, because in it Hale, one of the finest minds to work within the old legal tradition, revived and developed in a new direction the fundamental premiss of common-law historiography, that law was custom.

This was the point at which Hobbes had attacked Coke's doctrine of 'artificial reason'. Coke, it will be remembered, had presented law as customary and judge-made, the fruit of centuries of constant adaptation, and had argued that each maxim or rule of law embodied reason and experience so great and ripe that no individual mind with its limited horizon could attain to the height of its wisdom. Behind this doctrine there clearly lies the notion that law is custom and custom perpetual adaptation. Hobbes, wishing to deny both that law was immemorial custom and that the judges possessed any esoteric knowledge to which subject and sovereign should defer, had sharply replied that on the contrary law was first,

the simple commands of reason, and secondly, the simple commands
of the sovereign; no law rested on anything more mysterious than
a rule of reason, apparent to any individual who reflected, and the
immediate command of the sovereign who had last enjoined it.
Hale, therefore, when he came to Coke's defence, was in a position
analogous to that of Burke attacking the political rationalists and
believers in a simple sovereignty of 1789; and that this is something
more than an analogy will be suggested presently.

Hale's reply is printed as an appendix to the fifth volume of
Holdsworth's *History of English Law*. The gist of his highly compressed argument is that the wisdom of the law should not be too
readily subjected to the criticism and amendment of individual
reason. We cannot, he argues, lay down the simple rules of law, if
for no other reason than that morals is not an exact science. The
reason which we exert in our juridical activity is then a purely
empirical one, and we aim at no more than establishing rules of
conduct to which all can agree and which will give satisfaction in the
greatest possible number of the cases which come before the courts.
Yet even in this relatively humble activity we have to bear constantly in mind that the field we are dealing with—human society—
exhibits the most unimaginably complex interrelations between all
its parts, so that we cannot in fact tell what the outcome of our
decisions may be:

it is a thing of greatest difficulty, So to Contrive and Order any Lawe that
while it remedyes or provides against one Inconvenience, it introduceth not
worse or an equall. A Man that hath a prospect at one, or a few thinges may
with ease enough fitt a Lawe to that, or those thinges. Qui ad pauca respicit
facile pronuntiat. But the texture of Humane affaires is not unlike the Texture of a diseased bodey labouring under Maladies, it may be of so various
natures that such Phisique as may be proper for the Cure of one of the
maladies may be destructive in relation to the other, and the Cure of one
disease may be the death of the patient.[1]

Life, in fact, overflows the intellect—the image of an organic
body is regularly used by Hale when he wishes to suggest the in-
comprehensibility of the totality of human affairs—and we are
compelled to admit that the most we can do in framing a particular

[1] Holdsworth, *History of English Law*, vol. v, p. 503.

law is to base it upon experience of as many as possible of the kind of cases it concerns, in order to diminish the probability of an unforeseeable complication appearing and upsetting its workings. This being so, it is immediately evident that the experience of many men outweighs the experience of one; and since the reason of the law is founded on men's experience instead of on abstract reasoning, it follows that the reason of many outweighs the reason of one. I ought to prefer the wisdom of an ancient law even though my reason protests against it.

There are many things especially in Laws and Governments that mediately, Remotely and Consequentially are reasonable to be approved, though the reason of the party doth not presently or imediately and distinctly See its reasonableness. For instance, itt is reasonable for me to preferre a Law made by a hundred or two hundred persons of age wisdom Experience and Interest before a Law excogitated by my Selfe that [am] it may be a Simple unexperienced younge man, though I discerne better the reason of that Law that I have thought of then the reason of the Law of those wise men.

Againe it is a reason for me to preferre a Law by which a Kingdome hath been happily governed four or five hundred yeares then to adventure the happiness and Peace of a Kingdome upon Some new Theory of my owne tho' I am better acquainted with the reasonableness of my owne theory then with that Law. Again I have reason to assure myselfe that Long Experience makes more discoveries touching conveniences or Inconveniences of Laws then is possible for the wisest Councill of Men att first to foresee. And that those amendments and supplements that through the various Experiences of wise and knowing men have been applyed to any Law must needs be better suited to the Convenience of Laws then the best Invention of the most pregnant witts not ayded by such a series and tract of Experience.[1]

It is a corollary that no body of existing law can be reconstructed by abstract reasoning:

Now if any the most refined Braine under heaven would goe about to Enquire by Speculation, or by reading of Plato or Aristotle, or by Considering the Laws of the Jewes, or other Nations, to find out how Landes descend in England, or how Estates are there transferred, or transmitted among us, he wou'd lose his Labour, and Spend his Notions in vaine, till he acquainted himselfe with the Lawes of England, and the reason is because they are Institutions introduced by the will and Consent of others implicitly by Custome and usage, or Explicitly by written Laws or Acts of Parlement.[2]

[1] Holdsworth, vol. v, p. 504.   [2] Holdsworth, vol. v, p. 505.

To know the English law, then, there is no other way but to learn what the English have at various times decided shall be law. Since it is essentially an accumulation of judgments, decisions, amendments and refinements of age-old customs, to understand it is to understand the process by which this accumulation has been built up. Hale follows Selden in implying that the lawyer's knowledge is historical knowledge: in knowing the judgments and statutes of the past, he knows what ills they were designed to remedy and what the state of the law was which they remedied. In this way his understanding of the law's content is deepened, and he comes to see a greater part—never, perhaps, the whole—of the accumulated wisdom with which the refining generations have loaded it.

This is what Hale means by 'artificial reason', and it is obvious that he has anticipated and made his own several of the essential points of Burke's philosophy. The distrust of abstract reasoning, the belief that ancient institutions contain a latent wisdom greater than that of the individual, above all the concept of the law as the fruit of a great social process whereby society adapts itself to the consecutive emergencies brought to it by its experience in history—all these are Burke's; but they are foreshadowed, as we have already seen, not by Hale alone, but also by Coke and even by the French sixteenth-century partisans of *droit coutumier*. It is evident that they all arise from the idea of law as custom, or rather from that aspect of the idea of custom which emphasizes its universality and anonymity, the myriad minds who, not knowing the importance of what they do, have, each by responding to the circumstances in which he finds himself, contributed to build up a law which is the sum total of society's response to the vicissitudes of its history and will be insensibly modified tomorrow by fresh responses to fresh circumstances. The philosophy of Burke is descended from the concept of custom worked out in the late Renaissance during the first reaction against Roman law, and Hale marks a definite stage in its development.

But we saw in an earlier chapter that the idea of custom was twofold—men might treat it primarily as that which was continually adapted, or as that which was constantly preserved. The former emphasis would lead, as it does here, to the idea that law was the ever-changing product of a historical process; the latter to the idea that law was fixed, unchanging, immemorial. In Coke and Davies we studied how the cult of the immemorial was built up, through an incautious use of the idea of custom, in the minds of men who had shown themselves equally ready to employ it in its former sense. The interest of Hale is that, following the line established in his reply to Hobbes, he went back in his *History of the Common Law* to the fundamental notion that law was custom and developed it in a reverse direction from that taken by Coke, denying at all points that the law had remained unchanged since time immemorial and asserting instead that it was in continual change in response to circumstances, until he depicted it as altogether a response to history. He lays down a complex and impressive historical theory of law, which has won him, from very competent judges, high praise as a legal historian.[1] But to possess a developed historical sense and apply it to law may not be the same as to solve the actual problems of legal history. It is the argument of the present work that English legal historians in the seventeenth century faced problems which could only be solved by means that Hale did not in fact adopt; and at the end of this chapter it will be asked whether Hale's triumph in the field of legal history was not more apparent than real.

In the first chapter of his *History* Hale treated of the familiar distinction between written and unwritten law, and it is plain that he was warning his readers against making this distinction too rigid. There were, he said, statute laws which were treated as *lex non scripta* simply because they were dated before the coronation of Richard I, which 'according to a juridical Account and legal Signification' marked the limit of 'time of memory'. These were not pleadable as acts of parliament but 'obtain their Strength by meer immemorial Usage or Custom'. The term immemorial, however, is obviously at least in part conventional; and the real status of these laws was that they had been so much expounded by judges as to be 'as it were incorporated into the very Common Law, and become a part of it', absorbed by the body of immemorial unwritten law which it was the judges' business to deliver. If we had the records of the most ancient parliaments, which must be accounted

[1] Holdsworth, vol. VI, pp. 584–95.

lost, we should no doubt find that much of the *lex non scripta* now regarded as ancient custom was originally statute. Here, it will be noticed, Hale was following his brethren in their common assumption that if we had no records of a certain kind before a given date, that was proof that they had been lost rather than that the courts which preserved them had only then begun to function; but the immediate importance of the argument is that Hale was trying to establish that written and unwritten law were essentially one.[1]

In his second, third and fourth chapters he dealt with the *lex non scripta*, which he showed to have the fundamental meaning of the ancient custom of England; and it was here that his historical thought began to rise to its full stature. He devoted his fourth chapter to arguing that the origins of English law could not be known. In other hands this would assuredly have meant that it was immemorial in the Cokean sense, that there had been no time when substantially the same law had not been in force in England. But Hale's argument is rather that its origins cannot be known because its nature is to be in constant, fluid and largely imperceptible change, a flux in which nothing remains the same for long and the moment and reasons of its alteration are often unmarked and unrecorded. Hale enlarges the old notion of custom into a theory of the nature of law. He draws his principal argument

from the Nature of Laws themselves in general, which being to be accommodated to the Conditions, Exigencies and Conveniencies of the People, for or by whom they are appointed, as those Exigencies and Conveniencies do insensibly grow upon the People, so many times there grows insensibly a Variation of Laws, especially in a long tract of Time; and hence it is, that tho' for the Purpose in some particular Part of the Common Law of *England*, we may easily say, That the Common Law, as it is now taken, is otherwise than it was in that particular Part or Point in the Time of *Hen*. II when *Glanville* wrote, or than it was in the Time of *Hen*. III when *Bracton* wrote, yet it is not possible to assign the certain Time when the Change began; nor have we all the Monuments or Memorials, either of Acts of Parliament, or of Judicial Resolutions, which might induce or occasion such Alterations; for we have no authentick Records of any Acts of Parliament before 9 H. 3, and those we have of that King's Time, are but few. Nor have we any Reports of Judicial Decisions in any constant series of Time

[1] Hale, *The History of the Common Law of England*, 2nd ed., 1716, pp. 2–4.

before the Reign of *Edw.* I, tho' we have the Plea Rolls of the Times of *Hen.* III and King *John*, in some remarkable Order. So that Use and Custom and Judicial Decisions and Resolutions, and Acts of Parliament, tho' not now extant, might introduce some *New* Laws, and alter some *Old*, which we now take to be the very Common Law itself, tho' the Times and precise Periods of such Alterations are not explicitly or clearly known: But tho' those particular Variations and Accessions have happened in the Laws, yet they being only partial and successive, we may with just Reason say, They are the same *English* Laws now, that they were 600 Years since in the general. As the *Argonauts* Ship was the same when it returned home, as it was when it went out, tho' in that long Voyage it had successive Amendments, and scarce came back with any of its former Materials; and as *Titius* is the same Man he was 40 Years since, tho' Physitians tell us, that in a Tract of 7 Years, the Body has scarce any of the same Material Substance it had before.[1]

If the law can remain the same when the whole of its content has altered, it must be the continuity of the process of law-making which counts. Law is made as society adjusts itself to new situations, and under a system of unwritten law little record is kept of the actual moments at which such changes occur. Laws tend to grow more complex and their original meaning to be lost to sight.

It is very evident to every Day's Experience, that Laws, the further they go from their original Institution, grow the larger, and the more numerous: In the first Coalition of a People, their Prospect is not great, they provide Laws for their present Exigence and Convenience: But in Process of Time, possibly their first Laws are changed, altered or antiquated, as some of the Laws of the Twelve Tables among the *Romans* were: But whatsoever be done touching their *Old* Laws, there must of Necessity be a Provision of *New*, and other Laws successively, answering to the Multitude of successive Exigencies and Emergencies, that in a long Tract of Time will offer themselves; so that if a Man could at this Day have the Prospect of all the Laws of the *Britains* before any Invasion upon them, it would yet be impossible to say, which of them were *New*, and which were *Old*, and the several Seasons and Periods of Time wherein every Law took its Rise and Original, especially since it appears, that in those elder Times, the *Britains* were not reduc'd to that civiliz'd Estate, as to keep the Annals and Memorials of their Laws and Government, as the *Romans* and other civiliz'd Parts of the World have done.[2]

[1] Hale, pp. 57-9.   [2] Hale, pp. 60-1.

But the absence of historical records is not the main reason for our ignorance of the origins of our laws. Their history has been such that laws may be altered unconsciously and those who deliberately introduce changes may not realize the full import of what they are doing. A further complication is the fact that England has been several times overrun by peoples of different stocks, and

those Occurrences might easily have a great Influence upon the Laws of this Kingdom, and secretly and insensibly introduce *New* Laws, Customs and Usages; so that altho' the Body and Gross of the Law might continue the same, and so continue the ancient Denomination that it first had, yet it must needs receive diverse Accessions from the Laws of those People that were thus intermingled with the ancient *Britains* or *Saxons*, as the Rivers of *Severn*, *Thames*, *Trent*, etc., tho' they continue the same Denomination which their first Stream had, yet have the Accession of divers other Streams added to them in the Tracts of their Passage which enlarge and augment them. And hence grew those several Denominations of the *Saxon*, *Mercian* and *Danish* Laws, out of which (as before is shewn) the Confessor extracted his Body of the Common Law, and therefore among all those various Ingredients and Mixtures of Laws, it is almost an impossible Piece of Chymistry to reduce every *Caput Legis* to its true Original, as to say, This is a piece of the *Danish*, this of the *Norman*, or this of the *Saxon* or *British* Law: Neither was it, or indeed is it much Material, which of these is their Original; for 'tis very plain, the Strength and Obligation, and the formal Nature of a Law, is not upon Account that the *Danes*, or the *Saxons*, or the *Normans*, brought it in with them, but they became Laws, and binding in this Kingdom, by Virtue only of their being received and approved here.[1]

Hale has now used three distinct images, suggesting continuity in the midst of change, to convey the historical character of law. This continuity rests ultimately on the continuity of the society itself which constantly makes and unmakes the law, but Hale distinguishes three organs by which it does so—custom, judicial decision and act of parliament. It is never really clear whether these three are all thought essential to the law-making process; if they are, and the process cannot go on without each one of them, then there is clearly some danger that parliament and the courts will be thought immemorial on the grounds that they must have existed from the moment at which society began to make law. We have

[1] Hale, pp. 62–3.

seen that Hale was inclined to assume that parliament and the courts must be older than their earliest records. But as regards the content of the law, which is all that concerns him in the book he is writing, Hale's outlook seems entirely historical. Each law is the product of a moment's exigency; as time goes on, new exigencies will arise and the old law will survive or be modified or fall into desuetude, as it gives satisfaction or not in dealing with them. If it survives it will be accounted immemorial, but mainly in a conventional sense. This process may be insensible, for the making of law is partly an unconscious activity, particularly in that part of it which is custom, but the imperceptible formation of custom is one with the conscious activities of interpreting it in the courts and modifying it by act of parliament. Each law is the product of many past moments and is being tested at the present moment by a wisdom which in its turn relies on the past. Each law will change, but society and its wisdom will go on.

This vision of a historical flux seems as far from the thought of Coke as could very well be. Hale seems to have escaped the pitfalls which trapped his great predecessor into treating custom as immemorial and immutable; all his emphasis is placed not on antiquity but on process and continuity. But it is not clear that he has escaped falling into a different error. He can paint the picture of a historical process; but can he study a particular process, date its stages or explain its transitions from one phase to another? There are sentences in the passages just quoted which seem to suggest that the history of law cannot be known. If it is really impossible to trace any particular point of the law back to its origin, it would seem that no means exist of analysing the history of the law in general; we are back at the ancient problem of the unknowability of the flux. If, furthermore, it is unnecessary to do so—as Hale seems to be suggesting—because the courts will maintain the tradition handed down to them, then there is no place for a historian of English law, since nothing will matter except the interpretation which the courts adjudge correct. If Hale has been describing the historical process only to leave its course at the last mysterious and irrelevant, he is after all only half a historian. At this point we must investigate his dealings with the concrete problems of English legal history.

The greatest of these problems to a man of Hale's generation was the Norman Conquest: were we to see in that event the violent imposition of one man's will, or a continuation of the ancient process of custom, judgment and consent? Hale devoted a great deal of space to arguing that it was the latter, and both Maitland and Holdsworth deplored that he should have done so.[1] They regretted it for two reasons: in the first place, it appeared to interrupt the development of his historical narrative; in the second, they felt that a man of so much learning and historical sense should have been able to see the irrelevance and unimportance of the problem. Of the almost obsessive power which the question of the Conquest exercised over contemporary minds we have already had sufficient evidence; but on Hale's own principles there existed a road leading away from the problem, and the strangest feature of his thought is that he set foot on this road only to abandon it. The unhistorical element in most seventeenth-century thought about the Conquest was the assumption that if the laws had at one time existed at the mere will of a conqueror they must continue in some sort to depend on his will even at the present day. The desire to rid the laws of this stigma was Hale's express motive for dealing with the question in his long fifth chapter, but in its course he considered whether it was not possible that a government originally founded on conquest might in time be transformed into a rule of law, and concluded that this might indeed be in certain cases, one of which would arise

when by long Succession of Time, the Conquered had either been incorporated with the conquering People, whereby they had worn out the very Marks and Discriminations between the Conquerors and Conquered; and if they continued distinct, yet by a long Prescription, Usage and Custom, the Laws and Rights of the conquered People were in a manner settled, and the long Permission of the Conquerors amounted to a tacite Concession or Capitulation, for the Enjoyment of their Laws and Liberties.

Hale seems to imply that this tacit concession would in time become as binding on the conquerors as a formal covenant with their subjects. Time and use, custom and history, then, may be

[1] Maitland, *Collected Papers*, vol. II, p. 5; Holdsworth, vol. VI, pp. 584–7.

sufficient of themselves to turn the dictatorship of a conqueror into a rule of law:

> But of this more than enough is said, because it will appear in what follows, that *William* I never made any such Conquest of *England*.[1]

Hale made no attempt to bring his concept of gradual transformation out of the realms of hypothesis; abandoning it with obvious relief, he went on to plead the familiar case. William's victory was won over Harold, not over the kingdom; he merely proved by battle his right to succeed to the throne according to English law; he confiscated the lands of none except his active opponents; he confirmed the ancient law of the Confessor. It is evident that Hale's sense of history was not sufficient to convince him that even if there had been a conquest, it had occurred in a remote and alien world and could not possibly confer any rights on Charles II. His concept of law as constantly changing, however subtly conceived and eloquently expressed, remained a theory, not a vision of history in the concrete; he was not able to persuade himself that a right won by the sword did not descend untouched through the centuries; conquest remained an absolute which the history of England as he saw it could not absorb.

If men were to believe in a historic process which could absorb conquest, they must think in a manner more subtle even than Hale. They must see that conquest as occurring in a concrete historical situation, unlike that of their own day, and as capable of being understood only in relation to that situation. Then it would appear that the true problem was the transformation of that past situation into the situation of their own day: a process in which the nature of the conqueror's power could scarcely have escaped being changed. To think with Spelman that the chief effect of the Norman invasion had been to introduce feudal tenure, and that the main features of Anglo-Norman society must be understood as organized upon that basis, must in time bring about such a change in views—even though Spelman himself had found it necessary to go on denying that there had been a conquest. For then William would cease to be that abstract, juridical thing, a conqueror, and become some-

---

[1] Hale, pp. 81–2.

thing far more concrete and historical, a king whose power consisted largely in his lordship over feudal tenants; and in the effort to explain how the king of England, having been that, had become what he now was, the suggestion that his power might still be that of a conqueror would necessarily be lost to sight. Hale was unquestionably perceptive enough to have followed such a line of thought, but there is nowhere in his work any sign that he considered feudal tenure of any special importance in the history of the law. He can have had no concept that feudal tenure had been introduced at one time, had declined at another, and between those dates had been that in the light of which, above all else, relations of property, personal status, and political rights and obligations must be understood. Therefore there existed a great gap in his perception of history; he studied the Norman period in terms of the problem of conquest because he could not conceive that it could be studied in any other way; and though he was learned enough to see that the reigns of Henry II and Edward I were of particular importance in legal history,[1] his treatment suffered because he was unable to describe these kings as acting upon and modifying a system of tenures, or a system of legal relationships largely determined by the presence of a particular form of tenure. This deficiency prevented his history of the common law from achieving any narrative unity, and it prevented him from transforming his vision of a historical process into terms of concrete history. At the time of Hale's death in 1675, the whole development of constitutional historiography was held up, unable to make progress without the discoveries and the ideas so far peculiar to Spelman.

[1] It was for his treatment of Edward I's legislation that Holdsworth particularly praised him (*Sources and Literature of English Law*, p. 62); and it could be said that his account of Henry II's work is a remarkable piece of insight considering that he could not describe the substratum of feudal customs on which Henry's judges worked.

CHAPTER VIII

The Brady Controversy

I

BUT the royalist version of history was rapidly developing to a point where the ideas of Spelman could be of use to it. Feudalism could be used to prove Filmer's and Prynne's point that the House of Commons was no older than Henry III's reign; it could also be employed, as Hobbes had shown, to vest the monarchy with an authority which was sovereign and paternal rather than contractual. It should perhaps be emphasized once again that to the seventeenth-century English feudalism did not mean a dissolution of the state or even a private agreement between lord and vassal; it implied primarily that all land was held of the king on condition of homage and obedience. The time was not long, therefore, before the ideas of Spelman were revived and employed in party controversy; but the way in which this came about may repay study. In 1675, the year of Hale's death, Sir William Dugdale, the most eminent medievalist of his day, published the first volume of a work entitled *The Baronage of England*, and in the preface gave an account of parliamentary history in which the ideas are plainly Spelman's. Eleven years previously, he had brought out a complete edition of the *Archaeologus*, including for the first time the article 'Parlamentum',[1] and we have seen how William Prynne quoted this without apparently realizing its full significance. The remarkable fact is that Dugdale himself seems to have been distinctly slow to grasp what it really implied. For example, in a work of 1666, called *Origines Juridiciales*, he had opened by declaring the antiquity of the common law in language of which Coke himself need not have been ashamed: it was unwritten, immemorial, rooted in pure reason and had been sworn to by William the Conqueror.[2] Spelman

---

[1] *Glossarium Archaiologium* (1664). There is an account of how he undertook the task in the life of Spelman prefixed to Gibson's *Reliquiae*.

[2] *Origines Juridiciales*, pp. 3–5.

himself, it will be remembered, had proved unwilling to abandon
this myth altogether, and had Dugdale gone on to apply feudal
principles to constitutional history, this opening need have been no
more than a pious exordium. But in his fifth chapter, 'Of Parliaments',[1] he was guilty of a significant if unconscious distortion of
Spelman's meaning. There was sufficient evidence, he thought, of
the commons having been represented in the councils of William I
and his successors; he cited Anglo-Norman documents which
used such terms as *a clero et populo, communitas* and *baronagium*—the
last of which, following a suggestion of Lambarde's, he thought
should be interpreted to include all freemen. But it was clear, he
continued, from the words of Magna Carta that the council of
that period had included none but tenants in chief. Yet the charter,
as was well known, was no more than a confirmation of the ancient
liberties, so that there was a problem of reconciling this restriction of
the membership of councils with the right of every freeman to be
represented which, Dugdale took it for granted, had formed part of
the immemorial law. 'It must necessarily follow', he therefore
declared,

that the persons, who held of the King *in Capite*, were the representatives
of the rest of the Commons, called by some *Barones Minores*...and that the
dependent tenants consent was included in the assent of his immediate
superior Lord, whose presence was ever so required in those great Councills,
need not I think be doubted.[2]

There was some apparent justification in 'Parlamentum' for this
curious attempt to combine the tenurial council with the representative principle. Spelman had undeniably written:

et consentire inferior quisque visus est, in persona domini sui capitalis,
prout hodie per procuratores comitatus vel burgi, quos in parlamentis
KNIGHTS AND BURGESSES appellamus.[3]

[1] *Origines Juridiciales*, pp. 14–19.
[2] *Origines Juridiciales*, pp. 17–18.
[3] 'and every inferior was considered as giving his consent in the person of
his principal lord, just as today he gives it through the representatives of
shire and borough, whom in parliament we call knights and burgesses.'
Glossarium (1664), p. 451, col. 1.

But a passage in the treatise 'Of Parliaments' (still unpublished and presumably unknown to Dugdale) shows what manner of representation Spelman had in mind, and how far the not very happy analogy with knights and burgesses conveys his real thought.

...in those times, it belonged only to the tenants *in capite* to consult with the King on State matters and matters of the Kingdom; insomuch as no other in the Kingdom possessed any thing but under them. And therefore, as in Despotical Government, the agreement or disagreement of the Master of the Family concluded the menial and the whole Family; so the agreement and disagreement of the chief Lord or him that held *in Capite*, concluded all that depended on him or claimed under him, in any matter touching his Fee or Tenure. To this purpose, seemeth that in the Laws of *Edward* the Confessor, ratified by the Conqueror: *Debet etiam Rex omnia rite facere in regno, et per judicium procerum regni.*[1]

Spelman, in fact, had argued from the character of the *feudum* to give a new and quite unfamiliar meaning to the term representation; but Dugdale was employing his master's ideas to suggest that some immemorial right of representation had survived even into the feudal period. Since he was a convinced and lifelong royalist, there can have been no political motive behind these proceedings, and they merely offer one more instance of the astonishing strength and persistence of the common-law habit of mind. Dugdale was a master of feudal learning, and Professor Douglas has commented on his readiness to relate 'the principles of tenure...to the charters in which they were severally expressed',[2] but when he came to the history of the constitution, he could not perform a like feat; the habit of thinking in terms of immemorial liberties was too strong for him, and he attempted to interpret feudalism so as to harmonize it with the imposing structure of ancient law.

The account of parliamentary history which he gave in the preface to the *Baronage* is therefore not quite perfect when considered as a report of Spelman's findings; none the less it conveyed Spelman's essential thesis and was the occasion of the controversy in which this was driven home. From the Conquest to the reign of Henry III,

[1] 'The king ought to do all things in his kingdom in the proper way and by judgment of the chief men.' *Reliquiae Spelmannianae*, p. 58.
[2] D. C. Douglas, *English Scholars* (London, 1943), p. 58.

Dugdale explained, the king's councils had contained none but tenants *in capite*, and these were present not because the House of Lords was older than the House of Commons, but because they were the king's tenants, who owed their lord this service. But though it is right to gloss Dugdale's words in such a way as to emphasize that he was in effect making this latter point, he nevertheless still believed that the tenants in chief had in some way represented the commons, who held as sub-tenants under them. But in 49 H. 3—this date was not Spelman's and, if Dugdale took it from anyone, it could have been from Prynne—there appeared the first direct representatives of the commons in the form of the knights summoned by Simon de Montfort. Here Dugdale departed once more from the full complexity of his predecessor's thought. Spelman had seen the origin of the Commons as occurring in a process of transition whereby a class of lesser tenants *in capite*, promised a general summons in the charter of 1215, had evolved into a class of freeholders no longer confined to tenants *in capite*, who returned their representatives through the machinery of the shire. He had therefore refrained from mentioning any specific date for the first appearance of the Commons in parliament, and had treated the problem as part of the general decline of feudal relationships. But Dugdale assigned the origin of the Commons, almost without qualification, to the year 49 H. 3, and he attributed it to specific acts of deliberate statesmanship occurring in and soon after that year. To his way of thinking, the rebellious barons went in fear of the trains of knights by whose aid they had just defeated the king at Lewes, and therefore brought knights of the shire and burgesses into parliament; and "the Kings of this Realm ever since" saw in this device an admirable means of counter-balancing the power of the barons assembled in parliament. This would present Edward I, as was done as late as the time of Stubbs, as the conscious architect of state who appealed to one class against another.[1] Dugdale's theory of representation implies that the commons already existed and were in some sort represented in parliament; what they

---

[1] For the historiography of Edward I, there is an article by Mr Geoffrey Templeman, 'Edward I and the Historians', in the *Cambridge Historical Journal*, vol. X, no. 1 (1950), pp. 16–35.

received in 49 H. 3 was a change from indirect to direct representation. Dugdale did not understand, as Spelman did, that the growth of the knights of the shire was one aspect of a general change in social relations, and his historical thought must therefore be placed on a rather lower level.

But whatever its deficiencies as a piece of historical writing, the preface to the *Baronage* had confronted the antiquity doctrine with its most serious challenge to date. Prynne's attack had turned chiefly on the interpretation of documents, and the point that there was no record of a summons older than 49 H. 3 could be met with the usual *argumentum ex silentio*; but Dugdale's preface, and Spelman's 'Parlamentum' to which it soon drew attention, not only alleged that there had been no parliamentary commons before the late thirteenth century, but gave some formidable reasons for thinking that there could not have been. Historical controversy seems to have been relatively dormant for some time, but 1675 was the year of *Shirley* v. *Fagg*, when Shaftesbury and Holles were defending the jurisdiction of the Lords against the attacks of the Commons with arguments drawn from both William Prynne and James Harrington;[1] and perhaps it was in this connexion that William Petyt, a rising Whig barrister, began early in 1676 to collect materials for a reply to Dugdale. Petyt was a Yorkshireman whose career had been built largely on his acquaintance with the public records: it had earned him a new surname, a patent of gentility, membership of the Inner Temple, the friendship of Burnet and Essex and an increasing reputation for learning in circles opposed to the crown—though it is ironical that his first experience had been gained in the office of that more than royalist lawyer and antiquary, Fabian Philipps. In January 1676 three of his clerks were questioned about the writing of libels.[2] By April he was writing to various

[1] See various pamphlets in *State Tracts during the Reign of Charles II* (London, 1693); Holles, *The Case Stated Concerning the Judicature of the House of Peers in the Point of Appeals* (1675), and *The Case Stated Concerning the Judicature of the House of Peers in the Point of Impostures* (1676).

[2] The *D.N.B.* article on Petyt may be supplemented from the following sources. For the pedigree which he made out for himself and his brother, enabling them to take out a patent of gentility and change the spelling of their name, see *Calendar of State Papers (Domestic)*, 5 April, 31 August

correspondents about his reply to Dugdale and inquiring for evidence
which might justify the unhandsome accusation that 'Parlamentum'
was not Spelman's work but had been foisted into the *Glossarium* by
Dugdale or some other enemy of the laws and liberties.[1] However,
he did not now publish anything—perhaps for fear of offending
John Cotton, Dugdale's friend, in whose care was his grandfather's
great library[2]—and the new defence of the immemorial nature of
the Commons had to wait until the very different circumstances of
the year 1680; so that it appeared both as a contribution to Exclusionist propaganda and after the republished works of Sir Robert
Filmer had come upon the scene and transformed the whole
polemical situation.[3]

It has long been known that the posthumous republication of
Filmer played a major role in establishing that Tory ideology—
based almost for the first time on an unhesitating assertion of the
crown's sovereignty—to which the theorists of the opposition had
to find an answer. But because of the long neglect of that aspect of
English political thought with which this book is concerned, it is
less often pointed out that, after 1679–80, Filmer was used to attack
the Exclusionists on two fronts, with the *Freeholder's Inquest* as well
as *Patriarcha*, and that those who replied to him—with the interesting
exception of Locke—were at least as much concerned with the
origins of the English constitution as with the creation of Adam
and the events at the disembarkation of Noah. Yet the facts can
easily be established. James Tyrrell, Locke's friend, wrote to Petyt
in January 1680, addressing him as his superior in historical learning,
and urged him to reply to certain aspects of *Patriarcha* and to the

---

and 1 September 1676, and (for rumours of forgery) *Historical Manuscripts
Commission, VIth Report*, p. 232. The last reference mentions his association
with Philipps; see also Philipps to Brady, Caius College MSS. 607, fol. 5.
Inderwick, *Calendar of the Inner Temple Records*, vol. III, pp. xvi, xviii, 74.
Burnet, *History of the Reformation* (ed. 1865), vol. I, p. 7, gives details of Petyt's
help to Burnet. Petyt's *Antient Right of the Commons* is dedicated to Essex.
For the incident involving his clerks, see *Cal. S.P.D.*, 16 January 1676.

[1] Inner Temple MSS. (Petyt MSS.) 583 (17), fols. 483 and 483 b.

[2] Petyt to Cotton, Inner Temple MSS. *ibid.* fol. 482.

[3] For what is known of the circumstances of this republication, and a
consideration of its effects, see Laslett, *op. cit.* pp. 33–41.

Freeholder's Inquest;[1] and in his own work, *Patriarcha non Monarcha*, he included some discussion of historical and constitutional questions and for the rest referred the reader to Petyt's newly published book.[2] This work, *The Antient Right of the Commons of England Asserted*, seems to have been in circulation as early as October 1679,[3] though it was not published until 1680. Like *Jani Anglorum Facies Nova*, the work which William Atwood, Petyt's pupil and friend, soon produced in its support, it is directed as much against Dugdale and (through him) Spelman as against Filmer, and is irritatingly vague in naming or identifying its adversaries; but the above facts link it unmistakably with the Filmerian controversy. Algernon Sidney also, in his *Discourses on Government*, thought it necessary to answer Filmer at some length on historical grounds. The two branches of the debate were again united in Tyrrell's post-Revolutionary folio, *Bibliotheca Politica* (1694). The many chapters of this work mingle the ideas of Petyt with those of Locke, and this conjoint influence is traceable as late as William Molyneux's *The Case of Ireland Truly Stated* (1698). These facts seem both to establish the dual nature of the Filmerian controversy, and to emphasize how exceptional was Locke in omitting any discussion of English legal or constitutional history from the *Treatises of Civil Government* which he ultimately published.

It was not only the arguments of the *Freeholder's Inquest* which confronted the believers in an ancient constitution; the whole Filmerian thesis was aimed at dissolving and destroying the concept of immemorial law. Such a thing was impossible, wrote Filmer in *Patriarcha*:

for every custom there was a time when it was no custom, and the first precedent we now have had no precedent when it began. When every custom began, there was something else than custom that made it lawful,

[1] Inner Temple MSS. 583 (17), fol. 302; dated 'January 12'. Petyt's work was already complete.

[2] *Patriarcha non Monarcha* (1681), p. 124; cf. pp. 147–52.

[3] See letters in Inner Temple MSS. *ibid.* fols. 291 and 298, dated October 16 and 26, in which Ralph Cudworth and Bishop Thomas Barlow thank Petyt for copies of his book. Cudworth did not cut the pages of his copy, if it was the one shown the present writer in the library of Christ's College in 1949; it was in beautiful condition.

or else the beginning of all custom were unlawful. Customs at first became lawful only by some superior power which did either command or consent unto their beginning.[1]

This superior power, Filmer thought, must ultimately reside in the will of some one man, so that in the last resort the original sovereign was Adam. It was the essence of patriarchal doctrine that the absolute sovereignty enjoyed by the first man must—being by definition inalienable—have descended intact to his successor, the lawfully constituted king of today. Apart from the obvious difficulty of proving that Charles II was descended direct from Adam by primogeniture, it is important that we should recognize that this doctrine did not sound absurd to its opponents; they did not argue, on grounds of historical relativity, that sovereignty in Charles must mean something quite unlike the sovereignty possessed by Melchizedek. This is shown by the fact that, one and all, they angrily denied the occurrence of a Norman Conquest (which Filmer had not asserted). They did so because they unreservedly agreed that if William I in the eleventh century had ruled with absolute power, there was nothing to prevent Charles II in the seventeenth from revoking every law and liberty ever granted by the kings of England. We have been exploring the causes of this lack of historical sense throughout the present volume, and we may agree that if a writer as subtly aware of the processes of history as Sir Matthew Hale could not, when it came to the pinch, bear to admit that there had been a conquest, those causes lay deep and were hard to remove. Filmer is not to be ridiculed for a lack of historical sense all but universal among the Englishmen of his century; and it may be observed that, a few years before Charles's *quo warranto* proceedings and the French king's revocation of the edict of Nantes, there was nothing absurd, from a practical point of view, about the idea that grants made by a sovereign king might be revoked by any of his successors to the end of time. What Filmer did, in the passage just quoted, was to show that, on premises which his opponents accepted as fully as he did, the fact that any law or right must have had a beginning at some point of time within human history was in itself an argument for absolute power. If a man made law, he must

[1] Laslett, pp. 106–7.

have sovereign power; that power must descend to his heirs intact; and all laws, it was contended, must have been made by somebody—if necessary by Adam. Armed with this formula, the Filmerians could tax the battered champions of the common-law tradition with not knowing what they meant by immemorial and ask—as Robert Brady repeatedly did—whether the law of England had existed before the island was inhabited, or before the Flood or the Creation.[1] If the Whig writers could not prove this, must they not admit that the laws had in the first instance been made by some man, empowered by God to do so and consequently sovereign, whose heirs were sovereign to this day? We can now perhaps see why Filmer never thought it worth while proving that there had been a Norman Conquest. He could make his case equally clear without any questionable appeal to the sword, simply by insisting that every law had originated at some point in time and in the will of some man. His influence must therefore have tended to encourage the Tories in historical criticism of the doctrine of antiquity.

But it should still have been possible to meet his arguments by an appeal to custom, along lines similar to those followed by Hale. Laws are the product of custom, it might have been said; they come into being slowly, as the result of many men's agreement tacitly given over many years, and it is insensitive to demand that some established sovereign must have legitimized this process. If you seek a sovereign, some ultimate sanction, it is the people themselves, not indeed met in any legislative assembly, but living their daily lives over the generations; and it is the slow accumulation of their often wordless decisions that makes laws, so gradually that you cannot

---

[1] Brady, *Complete History of England*, vol. I (1685), p. xlvii (wrongly numbered lxvii); and *Introduction to the Old English History* (1684), p. 86: Petyt 'lays the great stress of his Argument upon the words, HATH EVER BE. What, were the COMMONS of *England* as now Represented by *Knights, Citizens*, and *Burgesses* ever an essential constituent part of the Parliament, from eternity, before man was created? Or have they been so ever since *Adam*? Or ever since England was peopled? Or ever since the *Britains, Romans*, and *Saxons* inhabited this Island? Certainly there was a time when they began to be so represented. And that is the question between us, which whether this Gentleman, or my self, be in the right, I leave to any impartial Judge.' 'Hath ever be' is correct; Petyt has been quoting a document of the fifteenth century.

say with certainty when any law that we now have first came into being, still less what authority sanctioned it. Hale could assuredly have answered Filmer in some such way as this, as he had answered Hobbes, but he had been dead five years, and no such mode of reply occurred to Petyt and Atwood. Their answer is purely obscurantist; they merely insist that parliament and the law are immemorial —that is, that at whatever time it is suggested that parliament may have originated, it was already ancient: an argument which of course runs straight into the logical absurdities pointed out by Brady. By insisting that the rights of Englishmen must be older than any potential sovereign, they left themselves the more exposed to the Filmerian reply that nevertheless some sovereign must have instituted them in the first place. They made no appeal to custom and do not seem to have understood that the doctrine that a law was immemorial rested ultimately on the presumption that such a law was custom. We have seen that the idea of an ancient constitution was founded, in England, on the customary character of the common law, and that ever since the time of Coke and Davies it had been possible to emphasize either that custom was immemorial or that custom was in perpetual adaptation. The latter idea, brilliantly and elaborately developed by Hale, could have been built into a powerful argument against patriarchalism; but in the Whig controversialists of the 1680's we have only the notion that law is immemorial blindly insisted on by men who seem to have forgotten that it is immemorial because it is custom. If Petyt and Atwood, rather than Hale, are typical of the common-law mind in the last decade of Stuart monarchy, that mind was far gone in ossification and the Filmerian attackers had an easier task than might have been the case if they had had a Hale before them.

Petyt, then, in *The Antient Right of the Commons*, set out to prove once more the traditional thesis that parliament and the laws were immemorial. This is a confused book, hurriedly put together in three sections. The central essay, which we are told was written first,[1] is a group of arguments designed to prove that the Commons were already immemorial, and known to be so, in 49 H. 3; we may perhaps detect in this the reply to Dugdale which Petyt had

[1] *Antient Right*, Preface (separately paginated), p. 74.

been preparing since 1676. But a Preface of more than half its length advances the familiar case for the immemorial nature of the law in general, and this as usual develops into a defence of the constitutional character of the Norman Conquest. Neither Filmer, Dugdale nor Spelman had in fact asserted that William had ruled as a conqueror, but a common lawyer defending the immemorial law would soon find himself denying the Conquest, whether an adversary had upheld it or not; and the doctrines of Filmer made a rehabilitation of the immemorial constitution seem a peculiarly urgent need. There is a deeper note, however, in Petyt's treatment of the Conquest, and this is particularly associated with the third section of his book, the Appendix. Earlier, in the Preface, Petyt makes use of the familiar argument that William did not confiscate the land of the whole kingdom, but confirmed much of it in the hands of those who had held it before the Conquest. This assertion had often been made—Petyt quoted Justice Shardelowe in Edward III's reign[1]—in order to demonstrate William's reverence for existing law and rights; but Petyt also used it to suggest that those whose rights were thus confirmed were freemen, who both before and after the Conquest must have enjoyed all the rights which the law accorded to freeholders, including that of representation in parliament[2]—a typical common-law argument, which we have seen was not without its appeal to Dugdale. Its full meaning, however, becomes apparent only when we read Petyt's Appendix,[3] in which an attempt is made to blunt the edge of Spelman's main argument. Petyt admits that the king regularly met his barons in the *curia regis*, which was a feudal court of a lord and his vassals discussing their joint affairs; but in addition to the *barones regis*, he declares, who were tenants *in capite* meeting in the *curia*, there were the *barones regni*, non-feudal freeholders, who met in the *commune concilium regni*, a true parliament of Lords and Commons, to discuss affairs of a far wider range than came before the purely feudal *curia*.

---

[1] *Antient Right*, Preface, p. 27. 'Le Conqueror ne vient pas pur ouster eux, qui avoient droiturell possession, mes de ouster eux que de lour tort avoient occupie ascun terre en desheritance del Roy & son Corone.'

[2] *Antient Right*, Preface, pp. 39–41.

[3] The Appendix (exclusive of documents) occupies pp. 129–48.

This argument was suggested to him by 'friends'—perhaps by William Atwood, who carried it on with a great deal of misplaced ingenuity in his works of this and subsequent years—and while its intrinsic value is emphatically negative, its importance lies in the very extensive concessions which it makes to Spelman's most revolutionary assertions. Petyt had in fact admitted that there was such a thing as feudal tenure, which had been imported into England by the Normans and had exerted a unique form of influence on the way in which the king took counsel and did the kingdom's business. He was merely determined to limit as far as possible the scope both of the phenomenon and of its influence, in order to leave parliament and the freeholders it represented securely immemorial; and this compelled him to adopt a new attitude to the Conquest. Up till now it had been treated, e.g. by Hale, as a purely juridical question, involving the relation of the Conqueror's will to the laws of the land; but when Petyt insisted that the Conqueror had not seized the whole land and that non-feudal freeholders had survived the establishment of Norman rule, he was implicitly admitting that feudal tenants held their land in a special way and would require special institutions for their governance. This was to take a long step in the direction of the new Spelmanist historiography, but Petyt took it unwillingly and was resolved to maintain as far as possible the view that contemporary institutions were immemorial.

II

Petyt wrote this part of his argument because the ideas of Spelman were now being circulated in the context of Filmerian controversy; a man who argued for a feudal phase in the history of law and parliament might be thought to argue against the antiquity of these things, and so for their continuing dependence on the will of the sovereign who had instituted them; and indeed some writers for the crown would soon be willing to argue in this way. It was a question, however, whether the royalists could bring themselves to abandon the traditional historiography to which they had clung for so long; we have seen that Dugdale was far from being detached from the notion of immemorial law. But a new combatant was at hand, who fully understood the thought of Spelman and was Filmerian enough to feel no compunction at throwing over the immemorial. In April 1675, Dr Robert Brady, Master of Caius, had written to Sir Joseph Williamson, then Secretary of State, offering to compose a history of England which would teach the people loyalty and obedience and frustrate the designs of the seditious.[1] Brady was at this time about forty-eight, a doctor of medicine and professor of physic, and had never published a historical work. As a Norfolk royalist, he had suffered a period of exile after the second Civil War, and seems to have been brother to one Edmund Brady who was hanged at Norwich, after an abortive royalist conspiracy, in 1650. The Norwich royalists had been condemned by a High Court of Justice which, like the more famous tribunal at Westminster, could justify its proceedings by appeal either to the ultimate sovereignty of the people, or else to the concept of an ancient constitution in defence of which any action was legitimate—two arguments often confused or used in combination. In so far as the High Courts of Justice and their apologists made use of the latter argument, their claim to jurisdiction had in fact rested on a perversion of history, and Robert Brady could have had his brother, as well as his sovereign, in mind when he declared in his letter of 1675:

Some brave men and such as have done [the crown] and their country eminent service have perished by fragments and partial story (picked out of mouldy parchments and obscure authors which perhaps they never knew of), improved by the artifice of cunning abettors of popular envy, malice, fury or mistake.

[1] *Cal. S.P.D.*, 3 April 1675. For more detailed references, including the manuscript version of this letter, see the present writer's article, 'Robert Brady, 1627–1700. A Cambridge Historian of the Restoration', in the *Cambridge Historical Journal*, vol. x, no. 2 (1951), pp. 186–204, in which an attempt was made to collect all the known facts about Brady's life and writings. It can be consulted for amplification of all that is here said of him. It may be mentioned here that, in the Preface to his *Jus Anglorum ab Antiquo* (1681), Atwood quotes from a letter allegedly written by Brady to Shaftesbury, in which an offer is made to defend the hereditary rights of the House of Lords. If such a letter was ever written, it may have belonged to the year 1675 and the controversies attending the case of *Shirley* v. *Fagg*. Brady was not a man to be approaching Shaftesbury in 1679 or 1680.

He may also have been thinking of Strafford and Laud, for the same historical doctrines had served to substantiate the charges of treason 'against the fundamental laws' on which these ministers had been condemned. The common-law interpretation of history was a powerful and deadly political weapon, and Brady's energies as a historical scholar were to be spent in the struggle against it on behalf of the crown. For the present, however, his letter to William-son bore no fruit, and it was only the publication of *The Antient Right of the Commons* and *Jani Anglorum Facies Nova* which brought him on the battlefield. He served, therefore, as a combatant on the historical wing of the Filmerian controversy. His auspices now were those of Archbishop Sancroft, who put him in touch with Dugdale; it must have been agreed that Brady's reply to Petyt should be published—it appeared in early 1681, with an appendix attacking Atwood, entitled *A Full and Clear Answer to a Book written by William Petit, Esq.*—while that which Dugdale had prepared should be with-held.[1] The latter survives in manuscript,[2] however, and may be compared with Brady's as a means to estimating the difference in historical mentality between the two men.

Both had now reached the point in the development of royalist thought where it seemed desirable to assert that there had been a Conquest—or rather to deny the traditional assertion that there had not, for neither seems to draw any positive political conclusions from the claim they make. But they set about proving it in signifi-cantly diverse ways. Dugdale accumulated instances of William's high-handedness, his violence, cruelty and treacherous dealings, and pointed out that this was not the behaviour of a monarch who felt himself responsible to law. When he dealt with the question of William's seizure of the land and redistribution of it in feudal tenure—which he did at some length, for his knowledge of the evi-dence was unparalleled—he went no further than to assert that this too was proof that William was bound by no law. It is noteworthy, too, that in this manuscript Dugdale continued his argument

[1] Bodleian Library, Tanner MSS. 37, fols. 22, 70; two letters from Brady dated 11 May and 17 June 1680. Mr Laslett (p. 36) thinks it conceivable that Sancroft was concerned in the republication of Filmer, and it is interesting to find him taking a hand in the ensuing debate.

[2] Bodleian Library Ashmole MSS.; Dugdale MSS. 10, fols. 94 ff.

that the tenants in chief were representative of their sub-tenants. In short, he was still failing to think of the law as altered in its foundations and its structure by the introduction of feudal tenures; and consequently, he thought of William not as the man who introduced new law or changed the society which the law was framed to govern, but as the man whose will was superior to the old law—a law which might not, for all Dugdale indicated, be so very different from the common law of 1681. He continued to think of the Conqueror in terms more juridical than historical.

Brady's treatment marks a radically new departure. Superficially, there is a likeness, and at the outset it may be desirable to emphasize that nearly all Brady's writings are those of a violent, ribald and abusive partisan. He derided his enemies as absurd[1] and hated them as seditious; and in tearing and trampling them, 'baffling and banging them and chasing them like squirrels from tree to tree', as an admirer once expressed it,[2] he not infrequently descended to argument on their own level, so that his essential historical views have to be disentangled from a mass of inessential debating points. Petyt and Atwood had denied that William was a conqueror; very well, it should be asserted in every possible way that he was in every possible sense; and consequently, there is much in the *Full and Clear Answer* that asserts the fact of conquest with no more perceptiveness than Dugdale displayed. But the guiding and connecting thread is of very different stuff. For Dugdale, William's feudalization of the land exhibited his indifference to the law; for Brady, William was the man who introduced feudal tenures and thereby a new kind of law, by altering the pattern of things of which the law must take account. This fact he treats with underlying consistency—whatever the cut and thrust of debate induced him to say on the surface—as of far greater moment than the fact that William ruled by right of conquest:

the Bulk and Maine of our Laws were brought hither from *Normandy*, by the CONQUEROR. For from whence we received our TENURES, and the

---

[1] Cf. *Introduction*, p. 6: '...he cites *Bede's Ecclesiastick History*, lib. 1. for the Report of this League and Union, where, if he finds it, he hath better luck than I have.'

[2] Fabian Philipps in a letter, 2 August 1684; Caius College MSS. 607, fol. 5.

Manner of holding our Estates in every respect, from thence also we received the CUSTOMS incident to those *Estates*. And likewise the quality of them, being most of them *Feudal*, and enjoyed under several MILITARY CONDITIONS, and SERVICES, and of necessary consequence from thence, we must receive the Laws also by which these TENURES, and the CUSTOMS incident to them were regulated, and by which every mans right in such Estates was secur'd according to the nature of them. But from *Normandy* (and brought in by the *Conqueror*) we received most, if not all our ancien *Tenures*, and manner of holding and enjoying our *Lands* and *Estates*, will appear by comparing our *Ancient Tenures* with theirs.[1]

In asserting so unequivocally that the old law was land law and that consequently a change in the manner of holding land must bring about a general change in the law, Brady was in the forefront of the historical thought of his age; and he could not have risen to such a height of perception if he had not been deeply versed in the kind of thinking of which Spelman had so far been almost the only representative in England. Except William Somner's *Treatise of Gavelkind* (written in 1647 and published in 1662) there had been no work since Spelman's time of his own stature, and Somner's study, excellent as it was on the Kentish tenures, made no application of feudal knowledge to legal or constitutional history in general—subjects with which it did not deal. But Brady followed Spelman—and in certain directions, as was proper, exceeded him— in his willingness to treat feudal tenure as the fundamental reality of Norman and Angevin England and to generalize from it about the nature of law, parliament and the duties of the subject in the whole of that epoch. This was to be his weapon in the Filmerian controversy; it enabled him to upset the notion of the ancient constitution by reconstructing the law and parliament of the past on the basis of an institution which had vanished from English life. It is still largely the business of English medievalists to pursue the line of

---

[1] *Introduction to the Old English History*, p. 14. The *Full and Clear Answer* is much more accessible as reprinted in this volume of 1684 (see below, p. 203) than in the rather uncommon separate edition of 1681, and references are therefore to the former except where it is desired to compare the two texts. In all quotations from Brady, capital letters are employed to convey some of the effect of the black-letter type that appealed to Brady or his printer (Thomas Newcomb, for Samuel Lowndes).

thought which Brady pioneered, and though they pursue it through modifications and refinements of which he cannot have dreamed, no alternative to feudalism as the starting-point of all thought about Anglo-Norman society seems yet to have been put forward; and the whole argument of the present book has been that there was no other method of curing the ills from which English historical thought suffered in the seventeenth century. The discovery of this method by Spelman and its revival by Brady must therefore be jointly reckoned as one of the most important occurrences in the history of our historiography. For the rest of his active life Brady was occupied in working out the consequences of his fundamental idea and applying them to the intellectual and practical problems of the age he lived in, and it is to this that we now turn.

Brady had to assert that, in consequence of the introduction of feudal tenures, not only was England after the Conquest governed by a feudal law, but this law was determined by the existence of a new class of feudal tenants who were the main governing and governed class; this in his view was the essence of the Conquest. Logically, he should have begun by proving that feudal tenure had not obtained before the Normans came, but though he knew Cujas, Hotman and Craig, he was handicapped by lack of Spelman's *Treatise of Feuds and Tenures* and could do little more than declare that the Saxons had had no military tenures as the Normans understood them.[1] But it was of far greater importance to meet Petyt's assertion that freeholders—men holding neither of the king nor of a lord, and by the same title as in King Edward's time—had survived the Conquest, for the gist of Petyt's argument had become that the freeholder and his rights were immemorial. Here Brady plunged into the thickets of Domesday Book, and his adversaries, notably Atwood, boldly pursued him. Brady sought to prove the single sweeping thesis that there was no land held by an Englishman that was not held of a Norman who held in chief of the crown; his enemies sought to pick holes in this generalization and use them as presumptive evidence that there had existed a class of non-feudal

[1] See the article 'Feudum' (which begins without title, telescoped with the preceding article on 'Election'), pp. 39 and 40 of the glossary appended to the *Introduction* and paginated separately.

freeholders who must be further presumed to have enjoyed parliamentary rights. There are well-known difficulties in the way of expounding a purely feudal interpretation of Domesday Book, and if Brady escaped the worst of them, this was because he was not primarily concerned with the manorial aspect of feudal society, or with the nature of rustic or unfree tenures, but with making the assertion that England had been ruled exclusively by and through a class of military tenants and that these alone had performed public services at the level of the shire courts and above. He was establishing the generalization that Norman England was a feudal state and that the relations implicit in military tenure governed and explained the whole conduct of its public proceedings. If it has been necessary for subsequent generations to modify this principle—if his contemporary opponents succeeded in finding anomalies, in Domesday or elsewhere, that could not be fitted into this generalization—we must bear in mind that the Whigs were endeavouring to deny it any validity at all and to maintain that the medieval history of England was intelligible, not on the presumption that feudal relationships had determined political organization, but on the presumption that the law and parliament of the seventeenth century were immemorial. The history of English medieval historiography in and since Brady's time would appear to bear out the thesis that the feudal generalization had to be established first and modified after, and that so long as it was denied or ignored there could be no progress in that branch of historical studies.

He proceeded to establish the feudal character of the Anglo-Norman governing class. In Brady's opinion, Petyt had habitually assumed that wherever he encountered the words *libere tenentes*, *liberi homines*, *legales homines*, and so forth, he was in the presence of the freeholder in a sense little different from that of 1681; and he had even tried, following Lambarde and for that matter Dugdale, to smuggle that concept into the term *baronagium*. This habit was characteristic of common-law historiography, but Brady had realized that by systematic use of the feudal generalization it could be set right, and this he now set out to do, reducing the *libere tenentes* to the feudal context in which alone they were intelligible. The freemen of the kingdom, named in the alleged laws of William I, were to perform their Military Services, with Horse and Arms, according to their Fees and Tenures. Therefore they were Tenents in *Military Service*, (which in these times *were the only great Free-men*, and that *Service the only free Service*) which were meant in this *Law*. And how different they were from our ordinary Free-holders at this day...I leave to the Judgment of every ingenuous Reader.[1]

Proceeding with his demonstration that the modern freeholder had not existed in the society governed by the *feudum*, Brady turned next to the shire court. This was the theatre in which the freeholder appeared at his most characteristic, and elected his representatives in parliament; and it was of great importance to Brady to show that its Anglo-Norman constitution must be understood on feudal lines. These, he says of the *libere tenentes*,

were the Men, the only LEGAL MEN that named, and chose *Juries*, and served on *Juries* themselves, both in the *County* and *Hundred Courts*, and dispatched all Country business under the great Officers....The judgment they were to give, and the justice they were to do...(besides that in their own Courts and Jurisdictions) was principally as they were Jurors or Recognitors upon Assizes, *etc.* (though some of the greatest of their *Milites* were often Sheriffs, Hundredaries, and other under Judges, and ministerial Officers of Justice in the several Counties)....This of being Suitors to the County and Hundred Courts, *etc.* was a Service incident to their Tenures: Before them, many times anciently in the County, and Hundred Courts, and not privately in a Chamber, were executed *Deeds*, *Grants*, and *Donations* of Lands contained in very small pieces of Parchment, Witnessed by *Thomas* of such a Town, *John* of another, *Richard* of a third, *etc.* which were KNIGHTS, *and* LIBERE *Tenentes in Military Service* in those Towns of considerable Estates, and *not the Lower sort of the People*: And this execution of Sales, and Assurances in open Court, was as publick, and notorious, and as secure, as if at that time, there had been a *publick Register* for them.[2]

Here we can see that Brady overreached himself in the feudalization of the past. Not all *legales homines* were knights, and as for the suggestion that the knight acting as juror in a shire court was performing a service incident to his tenure, even the simplified bookfeudalism from which Brady was working should have warned him that the only court service a vassal could perform as part of his

---

[1] *Introduction*, p. 18.   [2] *Introduction*, pp. 18–19.

duty as a vassal was service in the court of his lord. Brady certainly
did not think that the shire court had been feudalized to that extent,
but he did not understand the process by which the knights had
settled down as landowners and attended the shire court as local
notabilities. But if he was wrong on the technical issue, he was
right in his main contention that the early knights of the shire had
to be understood as part of a class of military tenants, their actions
governed by the requirements of a world of feudal relationships.

The shire court, however, possessed a more critical importance to
his thesis. He was proposing to argue that if the first knights representing the county in parliament had been elected in the shire
court, they had been elected by just such men as described above.
Here he was following Spelman's original contention that the
knights of the shire in parliament had originated among the lesser
military tenants; but Spelman, arguing from Magna Carta, had
supposed that there was in and after 1215 a representation of the lesser
tenants *in capite*, which had by degrees evolved into a representation
of the freeholders generally, and his failure to make full use of the
shire court had inhibited his attempt to explain how this transition
had been accomplished. Brady had begun with the shire court,
emphasizing its feudal and military aspects and proposing to treat
it as the body which had, at a later date, elected knights to parliament. It was therefore important that he should make clear from
the start whether he supposed the *libere tenentes* of the shire court to
have been confined to the lesser tenants *in capite*, of whom Magna
Carta and Spelman had spoken, or to have included military sub-
tenants on a more general basis; for the Spelman theory implied
the existence of a considerable number of knights holding in chief
of the king and receiving in 1215 a general summons to great
councils. The problem was complicated by contemporary ideas on
the nature of the knight's fee. Spelman had followed Coke in
thinking of it as the land which the knight held and in respect of
which he owed military service to the crown. It is easy to see how
this interpretation might tend to obscure the true nature of knight-
service and tempt seventeenth-century scholars to think, as on the
whole they appear to have done, that a large number of knights
had held direct of the crown and formed a class of lesser tenants *in*

capite.[1] But as Professor Douglas has pointed out,[2] the *Posthuma* of Sir Robert Cotton (published 1657) contain an interpretation of the knight's fee exactly in line with that of Round; and Selden in his *Titles of Honour* seems to be moving in the same direction. When it was understood that the knight's fee was primarily the unit in which was reckoned the amount of military service which the tenant *in capite* owed the crown, and the number of knights he enfeoffed with land his own concern, it would be evident that the men who held by a knight's fee, or some fraction thereof, and ranked as knights and appeared in the shire court, would normally be sub-tenants rather than tenants of the crown. Brady's view of the knight's fee seems on the whole to have corresponded with that of Spelman;[3] but since he was following Spelman's thesis that the council had been constituted on a basis of tenure *in capite* until freeholders who were not the crown's tenants had appeared in what was now a parliament, it was necessary that he should decide whether the first knights sent by the shire to parliament had been tenants *in capite* or not. If we now compare what he wrote in the *Full and Clear Answer* with a revised account given some three years later, we shall see that his ideas were changing in favour of allowing an increased role to the sub-tenants. In 1681 he had this to say:

These [the military tenants] in all probability were the Men, that at first *Elected* two *Knights* in every *County*, out of their own number, and only they were *Electors*, when at first the Body of them began to be this way represented. [*In marg.*]—For it cannot be thought but that these blustering men that had the only pretence (as will appear afterward) to be present in the great Councils, would entirely preserve it amongst their own order, and not part with it to people at that time of no interest. Such were the other inferiour sort of people.

---

[1] Coke, *First Institutes*, lib. 2, c. 3, sect. 95 (7th ed., fol. 69), and elsewhere; Spelman, 1626 *Archaeologus*, p. 259. It is true that in 'Of Parliaments', possibly a late work, Spelman had suggested (*Reliquiae*, p. 64) that the number of lesser tenants in chief had never been very great, and that this would account for there being only two knights for each shire; but his words show that he thought of them as a class of at least sufficient weight to explain the original appearance of a lower estate of parliament.

[2] Douglas, *The Norman Conquest and British Historians* (see above, p. 135).

[3] *Introduction*, Glossary, pp. 42–4.

This points pretty exclusively to the lesser tenants *in capite*; but in 1684 he revised the whole work for inclusion in a larger book, called *An Introduction to the Old English History*, and the corresponding passage now ran:

These with the *Military* Tenents, from whom they derived their Titles, in all probability were the Men, that at first *Elected* two *Knights* in every County, out of the *Tenents* in *Capite*, and only they as Suitors to the *County Court* were *Electors*, when...[while the marginal comment disappeared altogether].[1]

Beyond this opinion, a very partial modification of Spelman's thesis, still suggesting the existence of a large class of knights holding *in capite*, Brady's views did not develop; but the point is not quite vital to the main structure of his argument. It was his task to prove beyond doubt the still-contested thesis that before Edward I the king's council had been primarily an assembly of tenants in chief, and it was more important that he should do this than that he should settle the difficult problem of *omnes alios qui de nobis tenent in capite*. To demonstrate his thesis Brady devoted by far the greater part of his controversial writings, working with the unflagging energy and unpolished style characteristic of his age through every recorded council of the eleventh to thirteenth centuries, and arguing that they were normally composed of bishops, earls and barons, who were the king's greater tenants in chief, and that when it was necessary to suppose the presence of others besides these, it could be proved in a sufficient number of cases that the additional attendance was that of lesser tenants in chief. Assemblies of this kind made up the *communitas regni*, and Brady was one of the earliest English historians to discuss this elusive term. Petyt, in typical common-law fashion, had simply assumed that it meant 'commonalty of the realm', ergo 'House of Commons'; but Brady, true to the underlying principle of his work, busied himself to prove that it must in the thirteenth century be understood first of all in a feudal sense, as a *communitas militum* comprising both greater and lesser tenants in chief.[2] Whether at any time before Edward I's reign the *communitas*

---

[1] *Introduction*, p. 19; and the parallel passage in the 1681 *Full and Clear Answer*, p. 42.

[2] *Introduction*, pp. 73–6, 80–1, 84 and *passim*.

regni included knights of shires who did not hold in chief, Brady is not absolutely clear; he deleted from the 1684 edition a passage which suggests that they rather unwillingly made part of the *communitas* which wrote to the pope in 1258,[1] and there are many passages in which he dogmatically says that the term was confined to greater and lesser tenants in chief, the latter not being of much account. On the other hand, in the article on 'Communitas' which forms part of the glossary appended to the 1684 volume,[2] there are certain phrases which suggest that Brady was beginning to doubt whether military sub-tenants should not on occasion be reckoned with the *communitas*,[3] and this would fall into line with the change which we have seen was taking place in his views on the first elections of knights of the shire to parliament. The truth seems to be that Brady's ideas on the knightly class were still undetermined: his old-fashioned theory of the knight's fee perhaps predisposed him to believe in a large class of knights holding direct of the crown, but his studies of the shire court seem to have opened his eyes to the importance of knights who held of other military tenants. But, in common with Spelman, he had perceived, however dimly, that the key to the future lay in the emergence of the latter class and the consequent decline of military tenure as a determinant of rights and duties. On how this came about, however, he had little to say, beyond the not very helpful suggestion that the fragmentation of the knight's fee ultimately compelled the legislation of Henry VI which confined the parliamentary franchise to those having freehold to the value of forty shillings.[4]

On the origin of the House of Commons itself Brady is a leader of his century; he gives a more thorough and perceptive account of the events, in and after 49 H. 3, leading to the regular summons of knights and burgesses, than any historian before, or indeed many after him. He traces in some detail the events culminating in the summons of a parliament after Lewes,[5] quotes the crucial writ to the sheriffs for the sending of two legal and discreet knights, and

---

[1] *Full and Clear Answer*, p. 127; compare *Introduction*, p. 81.
[2] *Introduction*, Glossary, pp. 26–35.
[3] *Ibid.* pp. 32, 33; these references are to events in 30 and 34 Edw. I.
[4] *Introduction*, pp. 19–20.   [5] *Introduction*, pp. 130–6.

emphasizes first, that it was not stated how these knights were to be chosen, secondly, that there is no record of what this parliament did or what part they played in it.[1] Resuming the narrative after the restoration of normal procedures, he observes that the king for some time after summoned only those barons whom he could trust— there is a hint that it was at this time that the writ of summons began to undermine the purely tenurial composition of the baronage[2]—and that the attendance of knights and burgesses was not at this time continued. Indeed, he argues forcibly that they are not to be found in those parliaments which passed the principal statutes of Edward I. The first knights are encountered in the eighteenth, and the first burgesses in the twenty-third year of that king; and while the knights began now to be elected—presumably according to the procedure described above—it remained with the king to decide how many from each shire were needed to do his business for him.[3] There are writs in which the king dismisses the knights and burgesses, or all such as are not of his council and have not special business to transact;[4] the knights often displayed reluctance to accept the burden of attendance, and arrangements were made to pay them their expenses.[5] As far back as 1258—Brady mentions in an earlier context[6]—there is record of an inquisition to be conducted by four knights in each county, who are to make their reports in person to the king's council in parliament.

Thus the year 49 H. 3 loses much of its prominence, and the picture given by Brady is essentially one in accordance with much later scholarship: improvisation, the shire court being brought gradually and at the king's intermittent will into the transaction of business by the parliament of the realm. There is no revolution; nobody is deliberately founding the House of Commons or altering the balance of forces in parliament by the introduction of a new estate of the realm. Though Brady lacked the information to carry the story into the fourteenth century or investigate the stages by which the knights and burgesses became a single house and rose to prime importance in the constitution, he refrained from antedating

[1] Introduction, pp. 140–3.   [2] Introduction, p. 145.
[3] Introduction, pp. 149–51.   [4] Introduction, p. 154.
[5] Introduction, pp. 151, 154.   [6] Introduction, p. 141.

these things with admirable self-discipline. Though he did not follow the tenurial council past the time of its first decline—his principal concern being simply to establish the fact of its existence— he left his successors what could have been used as a secure foundation for study of the next phase.

While he worked out (always in the course of a brutal controversy, usually in the negative form of refuting his opponents' allegations) his new interpretation of parliamentary history, Brady was evolving a further idea of considerable importance. He had observed how Petyt constantly assumed that *libere tenentes* meant 'freeholders', that *communitas regni* meant 'commonalty of the realm'; and in the course of showing that these words could only be understood by reference to the feudal society of which they formed part, he began to see that the intellectual fallacy at the root of nearly all argument designed to prove the extreme antiquity of familiar institutions was the habit of interpreting words out of their contexts —a practice which could only end in identifying them with their usages at the present day. To us this is a commonplace; to Brady and his generation it was a discovery. Since the first stirrings of philological science a century earlier it had been known in a general way that the form and meaning of words changed with the generations; but not till now—at least in the study of English law—had the tools been available for the systematic reduction of words to a particular institutional context. As Brady composed his arguments and his glossary, it became evident to him that the whole cult of immemorial law was bound up with the fallacy of anachronism. He was now in a position, as hardly any scholar had been since Spelman, to distinguish the feudal law both from that which had preceded and from that which had followed it. He therefore began to see both that there was a cult of immemorial law and how it might be destroyed; and he even turned his thoughts to the question of how it had grown up.

It was clear beyond argument that the law under which the Anglo-Norman military tenants had lived had been a feudal law; yet there were constant contemporary accounts of how the Conqueror had confirmed the Confessor's law, and constant contemporary demands and undertakings that it be confirmed again.

Brady did not know that several of the relevant documents were unauthentic—he believed in 'Ingulf of Croyland' and in the *leges Edwardi Confessoris*—but it was not of the first importance that he did so. For he pointed out, even more emphatically than Spelman, that most of these documents, purporting to give the law of pre-Conquest England, made use of Norman terminology and described feudal institutions which could not have been in use before William I's reign; and these were the grounds on which later scholars resolved to reject the documents concerned or treat them as quasi-imaginative. Brady believed that there had been a known 'law of the Confessor' and that the Conqueror had confirmed it after amendment, but he insisted that the amendments had been feudal in character and so far-reaching as to convert the old law into Norman feudal law. From this he drew a further conclusion. The Norman kings had claimed to rule by the Confessor's law and in every crisis from 1100 to 1215 or later there had been calls for its confirmation as guarantee of the 'ancient liberties' for which the baronage were fighting. Yet it was obvious that in 1100

Edward the CONFESSOR'S LAWS here desired, were those LAWS WHICH WILLIAM THE CONQUEROR HAD AMENDED; they being very pleasing and acceptable to the *Normans* (who set up *Henry*) having thereby their RELIEFS MADE CERTAIN, THEIR MILITARY FEES HEREDITARY, and FREED FROM ALL EXTRAORDINARY TAXES....[1]

While in 1215,

at this great Solemnity for asserting the *Common Liberties*, which they claimed...the far greatest part of MAGNA CHARTA, concerned *Tenents in Military Service* only, and the LIBERTIES, which our Ancient Historians tell were so mightily contended for, if seriously considered, were mainly the LIBERTIES of *Holy Church*, by which, in most things, she pretended to be free from *Subjection* to a *Temporal Prince*; and the Relaxation of the *Original Rigor* upon which *Knights*, or *Military Fees* were first given by the *Lords*, and accepted by the *Tenents*.[2]

When the baronage demanded the Confessor's laws, they were in fact demanding confirmations of their feudal privileges, or relaxations in their feudal services, in the guise of a pre-feudal 'ancient

[1] *Introduction*, p. 29. [2] *Introduction*, p. 76.

law'; and when the common lawyers of Brady's century called for the restitution of Magna Carta, they were demanding concessions to a parliament of freeholders in the guise of what was in fact a feudal document. Once it could be shown that the laws and liberties of a feudal society were neither those of Anglo-Saxon nor those of post-feudal England, it followed that there had been a double falsification of history, first in the thirteenth and then in the seventeenth century. In explaining the first of these misrepresentations, Brady's Stuart Erastianism came to the fore. He was convinced that the aim of the thirteenth-century insurgents had been as much to win privileges for the church—and, he suspected, to introduce canonist sophistications into the original simplicity of feudal law—as to obtain concessions to the tenants *in capite*; and (perhaps remembering the production of Henry I's charter by Stephen Langton in 1213) he believed that erroneous notions concerning the nature of the Conquest, the ancient liberties, and the right of resistance had first been put about by the medieval clergy and from them had descended to the common lawyers and parliamentarians.[1] Behind it all lay the fallacy of anachronism. In prefacing the *Introduction* of 1684 Brady summed up matters thus:

The old *Romish Clergy* at first, in whose Management were all the Affairs of the Nation, out of Design, to *Bowe* the *Secular Government*, and make it *Truckle* under *Holy Church*, and by that means under themselves, published many Popular Notions concerning Ecclesiastick and Secular Liberty in those Antient Times, and raised up thereby the *Barons* and *Military Men*, to break the King's Power, and lessen his Authority, that by their Assistance they might obtain Dominion over him. These *Popular Notions* have ever since been kept up according to the sound of the Words they were first delivered in, by such as *Succeeded* those *Clergy-Men* in their *Places* and *Offices*. Though many of the Things then contended for, were either for ever sufficiently secured; and others not long after irrevocably vanished; and were all of such a Nature, or so Established, as afterward there could be no Controversie about them, yet the *Words* having been retained, and used, and interpreted according to vulgar Acceptation, 'tis scarce credible what *Mischiefs* and *Bloodshed* they have occasioned in *Successive* Ages, even to our own Days.

Brady was the first to treat the 'Whig interpretation of history' (in its earliest form) as itself an active force in the making of English

[1] *Introduction*, p. 20.

history, and the first to indicate how its fallacies might be set right. Waging the first open struggle against the concept of the ancient constitution, and himself extremely conscious of its explosive political possibilities, he declared that the belief in immemorial rights—the outcome of which must be an elective crown and an omnipotent parliament—could be corrected and nullified by the systematic reduction of the older English laws to their proper historical context. His own work was the elaborate, yet urgently practical reinterpretation of a key period in constitutional history in the feudal terms which alone could render it intelligible. He prefaced the collected edition of his controversial tracts in words which may be taken, together with the passage last quoted, as giving the full measure and character of his historical thought.

I have Intituled these several Discourses, *An Introduction to History*; for indeed so they are, if we observe the Things themselves, and not the Method. *Introductions* I know are Written after another manner; but as to the Matter here treated of, whoever reads our Old Historians and hath not a true Understanding and Apprehension of it, neither can he truly, and as he ought, understand them, nor will he ever be able to *arrive* at the Knowledge of our *Ancient Government*, or of what Import and Signification the Men were that lived under it according to their Several Denominations; of what Power, and Interest they were, what they did, and how they behaved themselves; nor who, nor what they were, that *contended* with our Ancient Kings about *Liberty*, and Relaxation of the Government, nor indeed what truly the Liberties were they contended for.[1]

There is a sense in which these words represent the high-water mark of Spelmanist historiography: the greatest degree of historical insight to which those who wrote as Spelman's immediate disciples ever attained. Having said so much, we must next consider the character and the limitations of the movement which these disciples conducted.

III

From one point of view, it might seem as though the effects of Brady's reinterpretation of medieval politics should have been similar to those which attended the revolution carried out in the

---

[1] *Introduction*, 'Epistle to the Candid Reader'.

study of Roman law by the sixteenth-century humanists. There should have been a growing realization that the affairs of the eleventh to thirteenth centuries were the affairs of a remote period with a social structure all its own, and could be understood only by constant reference to the main principles of that structure, which now belonged to the past and corresponded to nothing in Stuart England. No one could have put that point with greater clarity than had Brady himself in the passage just quoted; but we should expect to find him, or another soon after him, drawing the conclusion that medieval politics were irrelevant to those of the present day and worth the attention only of those who were interested in studying them for their own sake. We might even—following the analogy of the French sixteenth century—expect to come upon a movement of protest against the uselessness of this study, and hear of men attempting to discover what principles or what political lessons were common to the feudal politics of the thirteenth century and the parliamentary politics of the seventeenth. We might expect to hear admissions that if the main effect of the Norman Conquest had been to introduce a system based upon feudal tenures, then it could not directly determine the rights and liberties of Englishmen who no longer lived in such a system; and even, that if the authority of the monarch had once been primarily that of a feudal lord over his vassals, then this too was the case in England no longer, and that the prime duty of the historian was to discover by what means the monarchy had survived into the post-feudal age and on what foundations its authority now rested. To take the former of these two steps would have been to solve the problem which had been too much for Hale; to take the latter, to bring the systematic scholarship descended from Spelman into line with the conclusions more intuitively arrived at by Harrington. To take both would have imported the historical method into English constitutional thought to a degree never before known. Scholars would first have asserted antiquity's right to be considered independently of the present, and then have passed to investigating the precise nature of the connexion between the two.

None of this happened, however; and there are two principal reasons. In the first place, Brady, and the group of collaborators that grew up around him, were committed to using their new historical conclusions in support of the Filmerian thesis that the laws and liberties of England had come into being at the will of a sovereign king; though, as we shall see, it is disputable how far the new doctrines would support such an interpretation, and even how diligently Brady and his friends tried to make them do so. In the second place, they were at least so far successful in involving the new historiography in the battle between parties that when the cause for which they fought was rejected for ever in 1688, their attitude to history was rejected with it and prevented from exerting its full influence on the course of English thought. To conclude the story of Spelmanist historiography it is necessary to explain more fully the points which have just been made, and to begin with an account of the role which Brady and his friends played in the polemical writings of the 1680's.

By 1684, when Brady revised his *Answer* to Petyt and published it with the other treatises in the *Introduction to the Old English History*, he was no longer immediately engaged in exchanging pamphlets with the Exclusionist opposition. Petyt's only reply to him had been a small and universally ignored pamphlet called *The Pillars of Parliament Struck at by the Hands of a Cambridge Doctor*,[1] and though Atwood in two more works—*Jus Anglorum ab Antiquo* and *The Lord Holles his Remains*[2]—had attempted to sustain the distinction between *barones regis* and *barones regni*, Brady took no notice of them. After 1682, indeed, his adversaries published nothing further —warned, perhaps, by the fate of Algernon Sidney—and Brady's

[1] There seems no reference whatever to this work in the writings of Petyt's friends or his enemies, and its existence is known only through the learning of bibliographers. There is a copy in the Bodleian and another in the Advocates' Library, Edinburgh.

[2] Published 1681 and 1682. The latter is a work of some miscellaneous interest. Atwood published a posthumous tract by Holles on the question of the bishops' right of judgment in capital cases in the House of Lords, and added attacks of his own on Thomas Hunt, who had written in support of the bishops, and on a work called *Antidotum Britannicum*, which had been written against Nevile's *Plato Redivivus*. He improved the occasion by making further onslaughts on Brady, and questions of parliamentary history and the Norman Conquest occur sporadically throughout all the works connected by the *Remains*.

larger works appeared on the high tide of royalist reaction that fills the years between Exclusion and Revolution. The *Introduction* is a collection of his controversial writings—the replies to Petyt and Atwood, a demolishing attack on a minor Whig tract called *Argumentum Antinormannicum*[1] and a reprint of a tract on the succession he had written during 1681[2]—designed to supply the reader with a full statement of the feudal interpretation and clear his mind of traditional errors before he went on to read the first volume of the *Complete History of England*, which appeared in 1685 and in which we may perhaps see the realization of the plan Brady had advanced to Williamson ten years earlier. (This volume extends as far as the death of Henry III; a second, reaching the deposition of Richard II, was not published until 1700.) The relation of the *Introduction* to the *Complete History* admirably illustrates that it was through his polemical writings that Brady hammered out his basic interpretation of the medieval past, and these also accounted for his unobtrusive but notable position in the England of James II.[3] By 1685 Brady was a court physician and a man trusted by the government; in July of next year he was awarded the salary usually paid to the keeper of the records in the Tower; and about this time we must note the publication of a group of books by other scholars, all of which reveal his influence and can be shown by correspondence or internal evidence to have been written in his support.[4] Dugdale's last book, *A Perfect Copy of all Summons of the Nobility to Parliament...since*

[1] This is now attributed to one Edward Cook, but Brady thought it to be by Petyt or Atwood. He was right in suspecting it to be associated with them in some way, for a copy in the present writer's possession bears the inscription: 'Silv. Petyt. Ex dono Authoris'. Silvester Petyt was William's brother. It is entertainingly discussed by Professor Douglas, *English Scholars*, pp. 152-3.

[2] *A True and Exact History of the Succession.*

[3] For details of Brady's career during these years, the reader is again referred to the *Cambridge Historical Journal* for 1951.

[4] Dugdale's letters to Brady may be found in Hamper, *Life and Writings of Sir William Dugdale*, and the Preface to *A Perfect Copy of All Summons* is obviously aimed at Petyt and Atwood. Johnston's correspondence with Brady (Johnston MSS., Magdalen College, Oxford) belongs to a later time, the aftermath of the Magdalen College affair, when Johnston was preparing a work called *The King's Visitatorial Power Asserted*; but his earlier book abounds with references to Brady. Philipps's letter to Brady is in Caius College MS. 607, fol. 5.

the XLIX of Henry III, appeared in 1685; Dr Nathaniel Johnston, Yorkshire physician and antiquary, published his *The Excellency of Monarchical Government* in 1686; and the eccentric and quixotic Fabian Philipps his last and largest book, *Investigatio Jurium Antiquorum* (sometimes known as *The Established Government of England*) about the end of the same year. This concerted effort by royalist scholars to express a high-Tory theory of the rights of the crown, by arguments based in different ways upon the feudal interpretation of medieval England, is a noteworthy part of the intellectual reaction of the 1680's, and it also brings to an end the first great phase in the relations of the ancient constitution and the feudal law.

Now if we except Dugdale—whose last book contains few statements of theory or general principle—on the grounds that he never quite shook off a belief in the immemorial, all these scholars wrote under the influence of the republished works of Filmer. That is to say, to prove that parliament and the common law were not immemorial seemed in the context of Filmerian theory virtually identical with proving that these things, and with them all the liberties of Englishmen, owed their being to the will of the king, from which it followed that Charles II might revoke any of them as having been granted by one of his predecessors, no matter how remote. This was the view of the work of the royalist historians adopted by all their adversaries and, in the years when the borough charters were being revised on grounds of *quo warranto*, it seemed evident that Charles was in fact doing precisely what a Filmerian historiography claimed that he might do. We shall see presently that both Johnston and, to a lesser extent, Brady wrote as if the purpose of their historical studies was to present a version of constitutional history in which all was descended and derived from the will or permission of the king. But in actual fact, the Spelmanist technique of reinterpreting medieval history must logically lead, as we have seen, to conclusions of a different sort: if law and parliament had once been feudal in character, then by the same criteria the same must be true of the royal authority, and the problems would arise of determining how the monarchy had become what it now was, and of deciding whether conclusions could be drawn, from its authority in so unfamiliar a past, about its authority in the present.

There were therefore two far from consistent tendencies at work in the thought of the royalist historians, and the problem in interpreting their writings is to ascertain whether one of these tendencies predominated over the other, and with what results.

Johnston's *Excellency of Monarchical Government* is based in approximately equal parts upon Brady and Filmer, and may be taken as expressing the purely Filmerian interpretation which the royalist intellectual in the 1680's placed upon the feudal theory of history. He adopts (at last) the argument which the Whigs had feared for so long: that William I acquired absolute power by his conquest and that consequently all the laws and liberties of England exist as the result of concessions made by sovereign kings. He denies that the effect of his doctrine would be to return the people to the bondage they were in after the Conquest, and asserts that the kings are bound by the laws to which they have consented; but since it is only their consent which binds them, and not the law, he has obviously provided no safeguard against the king's withdrawing his consent at pleasure—nor, in view of his political record, is it likely that he intended to. He uses the fact that the king was feudal suzerain in the age when the great charters were granted as proof that these were no more than unilateral concessions by a sovereign monarch, and proceeds to press Filmer's arguments for the king's sole authorship of all legislation. He employs Brady's feudal interpretation of the period from the Conquest to Edward I to show that the House of Commons, being of late origin and created gradually by a series of royal summonses to men below the rank of tenant in chief, owes its existence to the king's will and must accept the place in the constitution—that of an adjunct to the king's council, a petitioner and assentient in legislation—which the *Freeholder's Inquest* had allowed it.[1] In all this Johnston does not quote or refer to Filmer, whose influence is none the less apparent, but he incessantly cites, quotes and transcribes Brady, with whom he corresponded and who, he does not seem to doubt, held views identical with his. Before we consider whether he was absolutely right in this assumption, there is another aspect of the feudal and Filmerian approach to history which merits attention, and something

[1] See generally Johnston's Introduction and his 22nd to 29th chapters.

should be said of that strangest of figures in contemporary legal erudition, Fabian Philipps.

Craig, and long after him Hobbes—the latter anticipating each main point of the royalist argument of the 1680's—had observed that in a feudal monarchy the king enjoyed the advantage that every proprietor of land owed him the special and personal allegiance of the vassal; and they had supposed that every feudal society was in fact of this sort, a pyramid of dependence upon a sovereign king. This authoritarian interpretation of feudalism was due in part to the impression created by reading the *Libri Feudorum*, the product of a fairly centralized society, which gave scholars the idea that feudalism was a legal system imposed from above; but it also arose from contemplating feudalism through the medium of the English courts of common law, which enforced the principle that all land was held of the king and took the whole system of feudal relations under the king's direct protection. Philipps (born in 1601) had in the first part of his life been an official of the Court of Wards and had there seen the conception that the king was universal seigneur in action. From 1660 to his death in 1690 he devoted himself to pleading on every occasion that the abolition of the feudal tenures had been a disastrous mistake, as they were necessary to the security of the throne.[1] Philipps believed—and it is said that Lord Keeper Guilford was inclined to agree with him[2]—that it was essential that every proprietor of land should have the direct personal relation with the king which tenures *in capite* alone provided; he called them the nerves, sinews and ligaments of society and felt that in any commonwealth where they were absent there was nothing to ensure the obedience of the subject. A freeholding society in Philipps's view was rather like a contractual society as envisaged by Filmer: nothing ensured the subject's obedience except his own will to obey, which he might withdraw at any moment. And just as Filmer endeavoured to represent the royal authority as having the inescapable physical quality of paternity, Philipps emphasized that the vassal's heirs for ever were bound to render the lord's heirs for ever the same un-

---

[1] The best account of Philipps is that of Professor Douglas, *English Scholars*, pp. 160–4.

[2] Roger North, *Lives of the Norths* (1890), vol. 1, p. 31.

conditional and fervent loyalty as was implied in the original act of homage.[1] He saw feudal society as one in which each proprietor, by the mere fact that he inherited land, was the king's man, with all that this implied; and he thought that the relationship of homage was the only secure social tie—a fabulous vision but not without a certain nobility.

Feudalism, to Philipps, meant patriarchal monarchy. But if he was Filmerian in his interpretation of the social relationships which feudal tenure implied, he was far enough removed from either Filmer or Spelman in his attitude to feudalism's place in history. The disadvantage of having learnt his feudalism as part of the living English law was that he had not passed through the complex adventure of the mind by which Spelman and Brady had discovered it in the past and, conversely, had discovered a past which could only be explained on its principles. Not only, therefore, did he believe that the state of things which he idealized had lasted down to the Civil War and could even now be restored; he was also, at least in his earlier writings, capable of describing the tenures as:

those ornaments in peace and strength in time of war, which have been for so many ages and Centuries since King *Ina*'s time, which was in an. 721 now above 940 years agoe (and may have been long before that) ever accompted to be harmlesse and unblameable, and in King *Edgar*'s Time, by a Charter made by him unto *Oswald* Bishop of Worcester, said to be *constitutione antiquorum temporum*, of antient time before the date of that Charter....[2]

Philipps, in short, had a lawyer's belief in the ancient constitution, with the sole difference that he held the essence of that constitution to be tenure *in capite*. It is true that his last book, the *Investigatio*, written when he was about eighty-five, bears marked traces of the Spelman-Brady influence and shows historical perceptiveness well in advance of the above paragraph; for example, he stresses the gradual and unforeseen nature of the changes which brought the freeholders to predominant power in parliament.[3] Nevertheless,

---

[1] *Tenenda non tollenda* (1660), p. 13. This (as the date suggests) was the first of Philipps's works upon this subject, and remains his best statement of the case for idealized feudalism.   [2] *Tenenda non tollenda*, p. 25.

[3] *Investigatio jurium antiquorum*, pp. 66–98, 110–13, 116–17, 296–9.

his exceptional background—rather than the eccentricity of his ideas—causes him to stand somewhat apart from Johnston and Brady, showing neither Filmer's desire to prove the whole constitution of the king's making, nor Spelman's interest in reconstructing feudalism as a state of society existing in the past, to such an extent as the Master of Caius, to whom, as the key figure of the royalist school, we must now return.

Viewing Brady's writings as a whole, we see in them the end of that period in which royalists would accept the doctrine of an immemorial constitution and justify the king's prerogatives on the grounds that they were the essence of this constitution and themselves immemorial. There were still royalist writers who clung to this argument,[1] but Brady served notice that he considered it dead when he attacked the whole concept of pre-Conquest ancient law as a heresy of the common lawyers and included the name of at least one eminent royalist among those whom he criticized for upholding it.

What I have here delivered upon this subject [the feudalization of English law at the Conquest] may probably meet with great prejudice, from such especially who have, or may read Sir *Edward Coke*'s Prefaces to his third, sixth, eighth and ninth parts of his Reports, his reading upon the Statute of Fines, or other parts of his Works: Sir *John Davis* his Preface to his *Irish* Reports; Mr *Nathan. Bacon*'s *Semper Idem*. The late learned Lord Chancellor's Survey of *Hobbs* his *Leviathan*, p. 109, 110. And many other works of eminent Persons of the long Robe, or indeed any of our *English* Historians, and therefore I am necessitated to dwell the longer upon it.... And beyond them all Sir *Edward Coke* concurs in opinion with Sir *John Fortescue*....[2]

Brady rejected the Clarendon tradition of common-law royalism at least partly because of Filmer's influence; and this raises the problem of the political moral which he expected to be drawn from his historical writings. It would not be difficult to draw up an array of quotations to prove that he meant to teach the same lesson as Johnston: that, as Bémont wrote of him, 'royaliste déclaré...[il]

[1] E.g., the author of *Antidotum Britannicum* (1681; see p. 149 n. 2, above).
[2] *Complete History of England*, vol. 1, p. 182. 'Semper Idem' is the sub-title of Nathaniel Bacon's *Historical Discourse of the Uniformity of the Government of England* (1647).

s'efforça de prouver que toutes les libertés dont jouissait le peuple anglais étaient un pur don de la royauté'.[1] For example, in the 'Preface to the Reader' of the *Complete History of England* (1685), he claims that from the book as a whole

> there is a clear Demonstration, that all the *Liberties* and *Priviledges* the People can pretend to, were the *Grants* and *Concessions* of the Kings of this Nation, and Derived from the Crown;

and there are other remarks to the same effect. For all this, however, Brady does not tell us how this conclusion is to be demonstrated; he rather leaves it to be inferred, and it never becomes very clear in what sense he supposes it to be true. In those sections of the *Complete History* which are critically written—only a small proportion of the book, as we shall see—he paints the portrait of a feudal monarchy which he supposes to have been centralized, authoritarian and even patriarchal in a very high degree. Since the feudal king was supreme lord of every piece of land, Brady imagines him to have been virtual sovereign; the liberties which he granted were contained in charters of which, since he had granted them, he was sole interpreter; and—Brady intimates—if, as we are constantly assured, the liberties of the people are the same as those contained in the charters of John and Henry III, there can be no doubt that they derive from the concessions of a sovereign will.[2] If the feudal king was sovereign, then all our laws and liberties must be derived from him.

But if this was indeed Brady's case for the descent of liberty from royal concession, it was thin in character and juridical rather than historical. That is to say, he had not proved that the modern liberties —the rights of Englishmen before the common law and in a representative House of Commons—had, as a matter of actual traceable historical development, been created by the king or come into being as a direct result of royal actions; nor did he ever make any serious attempt to do so. The reasons why Brady could not do this are of interest, as they bring us at last into contact with the limitations of Spelmanist historiography. It will be recalled that Spelman was able to reconstruct the main institutions of English

---

[1] Bémont, *Chartes des libertés anglaises* (1892), pp. lv-lvi.
[2] *Complete History*, vol. I, 'General Preface', pp. xxx-xl.

feudalism by arguing from the character of the continental *feudum* to the known characteristics of English law, but could not show how this system of things had passed away—how feudal tenure had ceased to be a key institution in English society—and had contented himself with observing that the process of decay must have been slow and gradual. Brady shared this disability to the full; there is a passage in the *Complete History* on the decline of villeinage[1] which shows clearly that he did not really know what could have brought it to an end except 'time and desuetude' working 'by insensible degrees', and though he has less to say about the decline of military tenure, it would seem as if he regarded this process in a similar light.[2] Now a slow and gradual process of change is nothing if not impersonal; it cannot be thought to flow from the sovereign's will, though its effects in the legal and constitutional fields may indeed require to be legitimized by his permission; and therefore, when Brady was dealing with so essentially post-feudal a phenomenon as the rise of a representative House of Commons, he might argue that the king's permission and even the king's legislative initiative had been necessary to begin and continue the summoning of knights and burgesses, but he could not suggest that the king had been responsible for the position of importance which the commons later assumed in the social structure. He wrote in the *Introduction*, speaking of the first summonings of the commons by Edward I,

...it is most evident, that it was from the [? this] *Kings Authority* and *time* that the House of *Commons* came to be *fixed*, and *established* in the present constant form, it now is, and hath been in, for many Kings Reigns, and that the King in this Age was not altogether *confined* to any *certain number* of *Knights, Citizens,* or *Burgesses,* nor were several strict *forms* and *usages* now practised, ever then thought of....[3]

The Filmerian implication is plain enough, but Brady was well aware that the knights and burgesses of Edward I's time were not of the social importance they afterwards assumed, and he thought of the process by which they had become important as one of slow

[1] 'General Preface', pp. xxvi–xxviii.
[2] 'General Preface', p. liii, and *Introduction to the Old English History*, pp. 19–20.
[3] *Introduction*, p. 151.

and gradual change which owed nothing to the king's will except the legitimization of its effects; and there is a passage in Fabian Philipps's *Investigatio* which says plainly that when Edward I began to summon the commons he could not have foreseen the ultimate consequences of what he was doing, because he could not have foreseen the effects of such economic changes as the dissolution of the monasteries, which were to make the freeholders excessively powerful in the state.[1] The king was no demiurge in Spelmanist historiography; much happened that was not by his will, produced by social processes which he could not control; only his legal sovereignty was preserved intact. The royalist historians did not, as they might have done, produce a myth of the king as the wise and benevolent author of each change in the life of his people. Their sense of historical criticism was too strong for that.

But it was a serious limitation on Brady's power to write history that he could build up the picture of a strongly monarchical feudal society, but could not show how this society had declined, except by vague allusions to unspecified general processes. As we shall see, it robbed his *Complete History* of all character as a general narrative. He showed how the feudal monarchy had been created, quite suddenly and catastrophically, at the Conquest; he described its workings—but he could not show, at the same level of historical perception, what happened next. He could not show how the actions of kings, barons and knights, living within feudal society and grappling with the problems with which it confronted them, led to the setting up of institutions which formed no part of feudal society and were bound to transform its character. For him feudal society was something fixed and rigid, and only time which antiquates all things—only a process of gradual decay taking place in the forms of tenure which lay at its root—could account for its ultimate disappearance. His historical thought did not extend as far as the idea that the seeds of change might have been present in feudal society from the beginning; there is no dialectic in history as he conceives it. It is probable that his royalism was partly to blame here. He desired to show that the monarch in a feudal society had been unchallenged sovereign and found it easy to do so by em-

[1] *Investigatio jurium antiquorum*, p. 299.

phasizing the purely feudal nature of that monarch's authority, as
recipient of every freeholder's homage for the lands that he held.
It did not occur to Brady that there were elements of weakness as
well as strength in the feudal monarch's position, or that the ruler
might evolve institutions designed to strengthen his control over
feudal society, but bound in the end to alter its nature. This is particularly evident in his treatment of the common law in the Middle
Ages. His remarks on this subject are scattered and speculative, but
they leave the impression that he was inclined to regard the common
law of the thirteenth century as the force hostile to monarchy which
it appeared to be in its own time. He criticizes the law of Bracton's
day as a mass of unnecessary subtleties, produced by the introduction
of canonist sophistications into the original purity of feudal custom;[1]
and it will be recalled that he suspected the churchmen who had
aided the baronial rebels of a design to bring about just this result.[2]
Notions of ancient liberty and the lawfulness of resistance, he considered, had come into England through the influence of clerics
like Langton, and as he clearly thought of common lawyers as the
standard-bearers of such ideas in his own age, he may well have
associated them with the cleric-dominated common law of the
thirteenth century. At all events, it is plain that he had no notion of
the historical importance which we should attach to the name of
Henry II;[3] there is no sign that he thought of the founding of the
common-law courts as a measure on the king's part to increase his
power, or of the substitution of the king's writ for private justice as
one of the foundations of royal authority. Brady's failure to grasp
the historical character and importance of the common law is one
of the principal reasons why he was never able to show that changes
went on within feudal society—changes which in the end transformed it—or that there were reasons for these changes occurring.

The name of Harrington should be enough to show that it is not
anachronistic to criticize Brady for failing to discover some sort of

[1] *Complete History*, vol. I, 'General Preface', p. lv.
[2] See above, p. 208.
[3] When dealing with that king in the main body of the book he deals with
the appointment of itinerant justices (pp. 308–10, 325, 333–4) and gives a translation of the Assizes of Clarendon (pp. 326–8) and the Assize of Arms
(pp. 337–8); but allows them to pass without any comment.

dialectic at work within feudal society. We might prefer to emphasize the strength of the medieval English kings, with Brady,
rather than their weakness, with Harrington—whom Brady
obviously surpassed in his technical knowledge of the *feudum* and its
workings—but that does not alter the fact that Harrington knew
there were deep-seated causes of tension between the king and his
magnates, and that the steps taken by either party to achieve its aims
might lead to radically new constitutional developments. And it is
not only Harrington, among writers of the later seventeenth century,
in whose works we can discover a sense of the medieval dialectic
in some ways surpassing Brady's. There is an unfinished study of
parliamentary history among the surviving papers of Francis North,
Lord Keeper Guilford.[1] Guilford was a Tory common lawyer
interested in the feudal interpretation; this essay, however, lays no
great emphasis on tenure or vassalage.[2] The point on which he
seized was that under that political system the kingdom contained
no means of binding a man to observe the oath which he had taken.
Accordingly it fell to the Church to punish oath-breakers and to bind
and loose the obligations contracted by oath, and in the thirteenth
century the aggressive popes made use of this power to obtain
increasing control over the realm. But this came to an end with
John's surrender of the kingdom to the pope.[3] Henceforward,
though he had no power to resist the pope, he could break his oath
to his subjects with impunity; but events proved that he had not so
much power that he could revoke customs or the grants of land or
privilege which he had made to them. His subjects, for their part,
found a means of self-protection in associating in *communitates* and
finally in the *communitas regni*, and being thus leagued together,
determined to obtain a comprehensive and irrevocable grant of
liberties, expressed in the charters of Henry III. Only the king's
oath guaranteed the charters, and at first the *communitas* stood ready

[1] It occurs (British Museum Add. MSS. 32, 518, fol. 157) among a
collection of transcripts of his surviving papers made by his brother Roger.
To judge from ch. 389 of his brother's *Life*, Guilford was active in records
research between 1675 and 1682, when he received the great seal. There is no
mention of his knowing or reading Brady. He died in 1685.

[2] Though he believed in a tenurial parliament (fol. 158).

[3] Fols. 159, 159b–160, 161b–162.

to maintain them by force. When the magnates were summoned to meet the king in *commune concilium*, they were in a stronger position than at any other time to state their wishes and form confederations to enforce them. But this fact was in itself convenient to the king, for he could free himself of his bondage to the pope by protesting that though he desired to do the latter's bidding, the community of his realm would not suffer it. Thus the assembly of the *commune concilium* was in the interest of king and barons alike and the idea of consent to legislation gained ground, not because there was any suggestion that the king could not act on his own authority, but because it strengthened his hand—especially *vis-à-vis* the pope—to have the assent of his barons. The king and the *communitas* accordingly reached an agreement, expressed in a grant under the great seal, that the council should meet regularly and have the right of consent in all great matters. The king was only bound to summon those who held of him and he did this by letters, not proclaiming a common council as a constituted body, but letting it be known that those who wished to give their assent should come and do so; it being clearly understood by all parties that the resolute constitutionalists 'would be sure to come, and would come so strong that the King should not be able to force them to anything they did not approve of '.[1]

Now whether or not this account bears any close resemblance to what actually occurred, it is clearly a remarkable piece of historical writing, holding a place in the late seventeenth century comparable to that occupied by Davies's *Discoverie* in the earlier. Guilford makes no attempt to describe feudal society as a single body of institutions (and thus face himself with the problem of accounting for its decline as a whole); he selects a single point in its system—the difficulty of enforcing an oath—and shows how king and barons, men divided by immediate conflicts yet having certain interests in common, were driven by the inconveniences which either inherited from this

---

[1] Fols. 162–4. Guilford held a sophisticated version of the 'Dugdale' thesis of the origin of the Commons; he saw their beginning in a revolt against the great men of 'the Comunalty which I suppose were 1st, the kings tenants, & afterwards the freeholders in generall', of which the first sign was the protest of the community of bachelors in support of the prince ('which I suppose were the gentlemen of the kingdom'). Fols. 166–167 b.

weakness to reach a solution of their differences which was at the same time a modification and a strengthening of the constitution. He shows how the weakness of one faction, where the other was strong, the measures taken by each to remedy its weakness, and the constant pressure exerted by a hostile third party, led by cause and effect to a readjustment of relations in a new system of politics. This is the logic of political development which Brady could not bring into his writings, and it may perhaps be characterized as a Trimmer view of history. Halifax and (as his notes reveal)[1] Guilford himself were interested in political parties, in their tendency to demand too much and in the possibility of bringing them to demand what would be acceptable to their opponents as well as themselves.[2] In the fragment just summarized, Guilford seems to be applying such a *tact des choses possibles* to the history of the thirteenth century and in so doing to move forward from the mere repetition of Spelman's interpretation. But Brady's ultra-Toryism prevented his attempting anything similar.

The main shortcoming of Brady's historical thought, then, was its lack of a pattern of development; and this is reflected in an interesting way in the structure of his *Complete History*. The 1685 volume of this work, which reaches the death of Henry III, is a bulky folio of about a thousand pages, but of this total only a small proportion consists of the kind of critical reconstruction of institutions which makes Brady a figure worth studying. This proportion is subdivided into a number of essays which the author calls Prefaces—the 'Preface to the Reader', the 'General Preface', the 'First Part of the Saxon History', the 'Preface to the Norman History'—and it is in these alone that Brady develops his thesis that Saxon institutions are to be studied on the basis of a pre-feudal form of Germanic land tenure and Norman institutions on the basis of feudal tenure; nor could it be said that these Prefaces, penetrating and instructive though they are, were written in a manner

---

[1] Other papers in the same volume of Add. MSS.

[2] The development of a Trimmer attitude to more recent history has been summarized by Professor Butterfield, *The Englishman and his History*, pp. 86–96. This is the only case known to the writer of its extension to medieval history.

either lucid or methodical. As for the many hundred pages which make up the rest of the volume, they consist almost exclusively of a conflation of the various medieval chronicles to which Brady had access, digested into a single narrative the scope of which naturally does not extend beyond the stories which the various chroniclers had to tell. Some attempt is made at certain points (notably the crises of John's and Henry III's reigns) to illustrate the story by means of records from the Tower; but in general it can be said that the narrative part of Brady's history does not concern itself with tenures, laws, councils or other institutions, and that these are dealt with only in the Prefaces. It was only in the reinterpretation of institutions on the basis of land tenure that Spelman and Brady had developed their critical method, and Brady at least knew of no means of combining this side of his work with the narrative of the doings of kings which he brought together, by strictly scissors-and-paste methods, from the chroniclers. He could not yet show how the conflicting actions of, say, king and magnates in the thirteenth century had led to the setting up of new institutions, or how these had affected the pattern of obligations which arose from tenure and so, in turn, had modified the place of tenure in society. Harrington and Guilford, we have seen, had gone somewhat further towards historical thinking of this kind, but Brady had scarcely begun; and the significance of this fact in the general history of historiography is worth dwelling on. Though he was prepared to reconstruct the whole received picture of medieval institutions on the basis of new principles, Brady had clearly no sense that he ought to apply similar critical techniques to the history of men's deeds. He actually congratulates himself on interpolating nothing of his own in his chronicle material, but on setting the whole of it down as nearly as possible in its authors' words.[1] In short, once he was away from his own field of feudal institutions, he shared the general opinion of his age that the historian's function was merely to repeat or report what his 'authorities' told him—the view which convinced Montaigne and Descartes and Locke and Dr Johnson that history was an altogether inferior branch of intellectual activity. In Brady we have followed to a high degree of development a particular technique of historical criticism

[1] *Complete History*, vol. I, 'Preface to the Reader', last two paragraphs.

that arose in the study of English law and produced in him vigorous and subtle historical insight; but we are compelled at the last to admit that he had no notion of how to combine the reconstruction of institutions with the narrative of men's deeds—how to combine legal antiquarianism with history as a literary art. To this extent, and viewing the matter from this standpoint, we are still in the prehistory, or in a primitive age, of modern historiography; though it is true that as historians we should do better to emphasize how much the scholars of Brady's generation had achieved, than how much they had still to do. But until some marriage between the two branches of study could take place—until some technique of critical reconstruction could be applied to the stories of men's deeds told by the chroniclers, and until laws and institutions could be shown as changing and developing in response to the actions of men, themselves motivated partly by the need to solve problems posed by the character of existing laws and institutions—there was little chance of history's becoming an autonomous science, an independent mode of approach to the structure of human society as a whole. Brady certainly did not envisage history as an independent science; it is significant that he described his essays in the reconstruction of past society not as history, but as introductions to history: 'an introduction to the old English history', 'the preface to the Norman history'. It seems likely that 'history' to him meant still the reporting of what the chroniclers had said, and his use of the definite article before the word suggests that he thought of it as something fixed and unalterable; you could not know more of the past than what the chroniclers had told you. Yet he knew that he had himself reconstructed the institutional and social context in which the Anglo-Norman chroniclers must be read if they were to be understood aright. It was the idea that there existed a science of rewriting the chronicles in the light of new general notions about the structure of medievàl society which was still beyond Brady, and which the thought of his generation was only beginning to grasp. Before it could be grasped and employed, the idea of the development of institutions must be explored more fully than Brady's limitations allowed him to do.

If he had failed to solve the problem, he had done much to pose it in the terms on which it must ultimately be solved. He and his friends, working along the same lines as Spelman's unpublished papers, had established that English society had passed through a feudal phase and had described that phase more fully and technically than had ever been done before. It was their description, or one more detailed and thorough still, which would have to be incorporated in future histories of the development of the English constitution. In such histories there might be room for the thought of Harrington or Hale, but it would be with Brady and his allies, and with Spelman, that historians would have to reckon—if, that is to say, the world of English learning was prepared to listen to Brady, and through him to Spelman. It was exactly this condition, however, which was not to be realized. Brady had written as a partisan of the two last Stuarts, and since it was so largely his royalist ardour which had led him to formulate his conclusions, this does him no discredit;[1] but he could not escape the consequences of political partisanship, which in his case included the consequences of defeat. With the downfall of the last king he served[2] came the rejection of his historical ideas. He was deprived of his post as acting keeper of the Tower records and the keys of the office were given to Petyt.[3] Before this occurred, Petyt had figured as one of the legal counsel who advised the Lords in the Convention debates of January 1689, and had had opportunity to associate the doctrine of the ancient constitution with the legitimization of the Revolution.[4]

Dugdale was dead and Philipps at a great age; Johnston, apparently as a Jacobite agent, lived for a time in penury and semi-hiding. Brady returned to his Cambridge mastership, and did not allow his

[1] Byron's verdict on Mitford, the anti-democratic historian of Greece, strikes the present writer as peculiarly applicable to Brady: 'Having named his sins, it is but fair to state his virtues—learning, labour, research, wrath and partiality. I call the latter virtues in a writer, because they make him write in earnest.' (Note on *Don Juan*, Canto XII, stanza xix.)

[2] He took part in a last-minute attempt, promoted by Bishop Turner of Ely, to dissuade James from his second flight. For details of Brady's closing years, the reader is once more referred to the *Cambridge Historical Journal* for 1951.

[3] The warrant is dated 12 March 1689; S.P. Dom. Warrant Book 34, p. 216 (in Public Records Office).

[4] See below, pp. 229-30.

views on hereditary succession to carry him into association with the non-jurors, where we might otherwise expect to find him; in October 1691 he certified that all Fellows of Caius had taken the oaths of allegiance. Non-juring tradition apparently bore him no ill will for this, but the step cut him off from the only cause on behalf of which he might have undertaken further historical writing. In 1690 he published a *Treatise of Boroughs*, a not very satisfactory inquiry into their early history which had probably been in preparation some years earlier, but in general the spate of writings which associated the Revolution with the classic Whig version of parliamentary history went unanswered by the chief of royalist historians. It is significant that the second volume of the *Complete History*, published in the year of his death, contains chronicle matter only; there are no 'Prefaces' or other interpretative comment. The only hint of its author's personal opinions is the bishop of Carlisle's protest against the deposition of Richard II, which, printed in full, closes the narrative part of the volume.[1] Such is Brady's rather unheroic last word to rebels and alterers of the succession. He died on 19 August 1700.

It could be said, then, adapting some well-known words from another context, that the heirs of Spelman 'died beaten and broken men, perishing among the spears of triumphant' Whiggery. With their defeat ended the first serious attempt to give feudalism its proper place in English history, and there was not another until the nineteenth century, when the task was successfully accomplished by historians whom we may feel to be still our own contemporaries. The failure of Brady to convince his countrymen undeniably marked a setback for the course of English historiography. At the same time, the historical thought of the age that followed his was far from being a mere prolongation of the thought of Coke and Petyt, and something more must be said on this subject. There is room for an epilogue in which a little may be done to place Spelman and Brady in perspective as part of the history of historiography.

[1] *Complete History*, vol. II (1700), pp. 438–43.

CHAPTER IX

Conclusion: 1688 in the History of Historiography

IT is possible to regard the fall of James II as a triumph, on the plane of historical thought, for the concept of the ancient constitution. As we have already seen, in the microcosm of the Tower records office the Revolution meant the fall of Brady and the substitution of Petyt, who reigned there as a respected scholar to the end of his days; and he had opportunity to assist the House of Lords in their efforts to define what had happened in 1688 by laying his doctrines of English history before them. There is some record of this occasion, and the circumstances are of interest. The House had reached the point, in debating the resolution sent up to them by the Commons, where they were asked to agree that James had broken the original contract between king and people. They had recourse to the legal counsel appointed to advise them and inquired what this original contract might be, 'and whether there be any such or not'. The greater part of this body of counsel—the six judges, Atkyns, Montagu, Dolben, Levinz, Nevill, Holt—were all of the opinion that the contract might be a most liberal and rational concept, but they could not find it in the laws of England. Two of the three additional counsel, Bradbury and Whitelocke, spoke in favour of the contract, but in vague and inconclusive language. Then came Petyt's turn. We have some notes of what he said.[1]

The original of government came from Germany. When they came they settled a heptarchy, and that settled in one. Spelman. Kings should be elected *per sacerdotitium et populum*. There you have laws made by what we call a Parliament, as well the laity as the clergy. All the kings acted and transacted by what we call a Parliament. In Selden's *Titles of Honour* you had the oath before any did homage. The King took the oath to maintain

---

[1] *Historical Manuscripts Commission, XIIth Report*, Appendix VI, pp. 14 ff.

the Church, to do right between man and man and do justice. The disputes about the crown were treated there thus till William I. Edward Confessor was chosen in a Parliament. D. Normandy comes to be crowned at London; the Archbishop of Canterbury demands of the English, will you be pleased to have this King? They said 'Yes', with one voice, as inspired. Rufus, Henry I, Stephen, Henry II, Henry III, all these claim no right but by Parliament. Two Acts to be read. There was always an agreement in the Saxons' times, and so it continues. 25 Ed. III, that settles (?) the right of the crown. He is bound by his oath to make remedy and law to his people in removing mischiefs.

The part which the ancient constitution might play in the ideology of the Revolution is here made very clear. Petyt is making out a case for the people's right of deposing and, apparently, electing their kings; but he does not ground it upon the original contract as defined in works of political theory, partly no doubt for the reason already given by the judges—the concept cannot be found in English law—but also, we may suspect, because it cannot be cleansed from the suggestion of popular sovereignty, which it was no part of the Whigs' intention to allow lest they should return to the days of the Commonwealth. We can understand Petyt's speech, made in January 1689, better if we bear in mind the efforts of contemporary extremist pamphleteers to suggest that by the deed of James the constitution was dissolved and all power returned into the hands of the people.[1] That could not happen if the constitution were as Petyt describes it. The people indeed recognize the king on hearing him swear to maintain law; they may evidently depose him if he breaks his oath; but there is no suggestion that the law itself is of their making and every reason, having regard to Petyt's earlier writings, to suppose that he meant it to be ancient and immemorial. The remark that 'the original of government came from Germany' is not absolutely compatible with this interpretation; it was easy, in the context of 'Gothic' ideas, to imagine a tribe assembling at the dawn of their history to draw up their fundamental constitution. But the Gothic idea does not appear significantly in Petyt's *Antient Right of the Commons*, where parliament is rather presented as

[1] E.g. John Wildman, *A Letter to a Friend Advising in this Extraordinary Juncture How to Free the Nation from Slavery Forever*. There are other traces of this argument to be found in vol. x of the Somers Tracts.

immemorial within Britain.[1] To all appearances, then, we have here what Petyt had defended against Brady: an immemorial constitution, one (we may gloss) which guarantees the people's rights, of which they are the guardians, but which they cannot lightly change. The 'original contract' is not 'the original of government'; it is identified with the coronation oath, an oath to observe the ancient constitution—which, it seems probable, binds the people as well as the king.

To this, then, had the ancient constitution come: a conservative and legalist version of the contract, a sanction—as Brady had pointed out[2]—by which the doctrines of election and deposition might be justified. But, in however attenuated a form, it is significant that it should have been retained in the Whig ideology of the eighteenth century. Perhaps the notion of fundamental and unalterable law ceased to be of any serious importance in that age, but to the end of their *grand siècle* the Whigs—and all Englishmen who took their stand on the principles of 1688—clung to the habit of appealing to a supposedly actual English past not less and perhaps more than to abstract principles of government. There is a doctrine in Bolingbroke, to be found also in men less elaborately sceptical of historical knowledge of remote ages, which well illustrates this point. He says that whatever the rights of parliament and the subject may have been in times past, the Revolution has settled the point beyond doubt and there is no need to look further back than 1688 for the foundation of our liberties. Nevertheless, for the satisfaction of

[1] There is reference to a supposed British parliament called the Cyfr-y-then, and phrases like 'hath ever been' and '*a crepusculo temporis*' frequently occur.

[2] *Introduction to the Old English History*, 'The Epistle to the Reader': 'Two sorts of *Turbulent Men* there are in the World, who under *plausible Pretences* have appeared for the *Liberty* of the People, or indeed the *Change* of the Government....One of these sort of Men preach to the *People*, *That the Origin of all Power and Government is from them; That Kings or Magistrates derive their Authority from them*...*and may be Tryed, Sentenced, Deposed, or put to Death by them*....The other sort are such as hold forth to the People, *Ancient Rights* and *Privileges*...and that this was an *Elective* Kingdom, which as often as they have opportunity they cunningly insinuate, though they do not plainly *assert* it in terms....Any Man that shall observe, what the last Men craftily drive at, and *compare* it diligently with what the former assert, will not find much *Difference* in their *Principles* and *Designs*.'

such as still desire to feel that Revolution principles are in accord with the remoter precedents of English history—here follows a reasonably orthodox 'common-law' account of history, relating the Revolution to the survival of parliament and limited monarchy from pre-Conquest times.[1] It was still perfectly possible to see the Revolution in terms of the 'myth of the confirmations', ranking 1688 with 1066, 1215 and 1628 in the list of dates on which the ancient and fundamental law had been solemnly reasserted by the nation. The common-law version of history survived, and it survived essentially in the form in which it had been stated by Petyt. There were variations of emphasis and implication from writer to writer and from moment to moment; but in general it remained common ground that law and parliament, having originated in a way usually not specified, could be discovered early in Saxon times and had survived the Conquest, and that certain principles of liberty, deriving from the Saxon forefathers, had animated the English in their resistance to absolute monarchy alike in the thirteenth century and in the seventeenth. The Whiggish idea of the constitution and of liberty continued to rest in part on this version of history, and those who attacked it in the eighteenth century because their idea of the constitution differed from that of the Whigs did not attempt to substitute Brady's feudal interpretation for it. Cartwright and Paine, with their followers and competitors, fought over again the battle waged by Lilburne and Overton; they looked back to a Saxon golden age in which the people had been more than their representatives; they declared that the origins of parliament were in Norman tyranny, and the origins of most governments in conquest and usurpation; and they went on from this last principle to reject history altogether and aver that the criterion by which any government must be judged was not its antiquity, but its rationality. The similarity between their arguments and those of the Levellers is itself evidence of how little the Whig version of history had changed in the intervening century and a half.[2]

[1] *Dissertation on Parties*, 7th ed. (London, 1749); cf. pp. 124–5 and 132–3.
[2] Christopher Hill's essay 'The Norman Yoke' (cited above, p. 54) discusses some changes in emphasis that occurred within the Whig myth

Nevertheless the concept of the ancient constitution, considered in the setting of eighteenth-century ways of thought, had plainly lost much of its original character. Politically, it had ceased to be principally—perhaps at all—an appeal to the binding force of ancient custom; historically, it had ceased to be essentially a conviction that the law and constitution were immemorial, based upon a too exclusive knowledge of the common law with its dogma that the law was custom and custom immemorial. The reasons why this should have been so are many and various, but we can gain an idea of their character by recapitulating some of the themes of this book.

In Sir Edward Coke's time the concept of the ancient constitution had meant essentially that the whole body of English law—including the customs of the high court of parliament—could be represented as immemorial in the sense that custom was immemorial. Coke had shown himself ready to apply this doctrine to history with a high degree of literalness and actually discover law and parliament in an age before the first written records, on the grounds that they were ancient custom. This delusion had been rooted in the presuppositions of common-law thought, and in a period when the study of the common law did much to determine the character of English thought and learning, it had been accepted and believed by a great many Englishmen of the politically minded classes. But if law and parliament could be represented as immemorial, so too by the same arguments could the prerogatives of the king, and men like Hyde repaired to the standard of Charles I in the belief that by fighting for the crown they were fighting for the immemorial laws of England. There was nothing antimonarchical in a belief in immemorial custom; politically, it represents the medieval concept of an impersonal, unmade and immanent law which defined the just rights of every organ of the community. But when James I was thought to be claiming too wide and undefined a power—and was known to hold, as a point in political theory, that all laws,

during the eighteenth century. Perhaps the most interesting is that Alfred replaced Edward the Confessor as patron saint of the Saxon constitution, apparently because he was supposed to have founded the shire system.

customs and privileges were derived ultimately from his will—it became possible to argue that these things were rooted in ancient custom and consequently were not derived from his will, which came to be thought of as a power divorced from custom and standing over against it. Once that which was immemorial and that which was willed were set in sharp contrast to one another, an ideological gap was opened which could not be easily bridged, and the concept of the ancient constitution became alternative to and incompatible with the sovereignty of the king. The idea that it belonged to parliament to define the content of the ancient constitution, and that all actions undertaken in its defence were legitimate, obviously led to the revolutionary sovereignty of that body; yet it is paradoxically significant that parliament should have clung as long as it could to the doctrine that its acts were justified by fundamental law—by a body of ancient custom which it repudiated all claim to have made. The concept of an ancient law which defined the scope of parliament and prerogative alike died hard, and when Prynne denied that the House of Commons was immemorial, his aim was to subordinate it to a law which was. But during his lifetime Filmer and later Hobbes, working from assumptions perhaps incompatible with one another, had seen that the position of parliament could be attacked in a much deadlier way. It was now parliament, rather than the law as a whole, which was being presented as immemorial; and the claim to be immemorial had been virtually identified with the claim to be sovereign. Because parliament was supposed to owe its beginning to no man, it could claim to act as it thought fit in defence of the law; and if it was added that the law too was immemorial, this merely underlined parliament's right to interpret the law by its uncontrolled ordinances and resolutions. The whole concept of ancient custom had been narrowed down to this one assertion, that parliament was immemorial. If parliament was immemorial, parliament was sovereign: if parliament was not immemorial, then he who had made it was sovereign. The medieval concept of universal unmade law, which the notion of ancient custom had sought to express, had collapsed. Filmer and Hobbes each saw that it was possible to argue that every law originated in some man's will and that such a man must have possessed sovereignty and transmitted it to his heirs; and each began to argue that it was possible to prove from history that the House of Commons was not immemorial but the work of the king. When next it was claimed that parliament was sovereign and immemorial, the works of Filmer were re-published; and we have already seen how these revitalized the ideas of Spelman, who had attacked parliament's historical claim from a new angle.

It is plain, then, that the development of parliamentary thought on the ancient constitution had been such as to sap the notion of custom, on which the idea of the immemorial ultimately rested. We saw how law as custom could mean either law in perpetual adjustment or law as unchanging and immemorial, and how the latter idea always tended to predominate, until we could contrast Hale, whose concept of custom as a perpetual process had real profundity, with Petyt and Atwood, in whom the ancient constitution had come to mean nothing but a crude dogma that there had always been a parliament. The conflict between two claims to sovereignty accounts for the degeneration of Cokean thought in the hands of the Exclusionist writers. If Hale had answered Filmer, he might—unless the problem of conquest had proved too much of a stumbling block—have anticipated much of the thought of Burke, but Petyt and Atwood were concerned only to deny the king's sovereignty and smuggle in that of parliament under a thin disguise, and consequently they expressed the problem in the simplest possible terms. If parliament has a known beginning, it must be in someone's will and therefore the king will be sovereign; but parliament is immemorial (and therefore it is sovereign). This formulation underlies all their writing and reduces the concept of the ancient constitution to the point of logical absurdity. Put like this, the argument was one which, even without the battering which they suffered from the Spelmanist historians, the Whigs could hardly help losing. We may now see why a new way out of the dilemma, in non-historical or anti-historical terms, was sought and found in the work of Locke.

Locke answered the patriarchal, not the constitutional arguments of Filmer; or, put another way, he answered him on the plane of sacred, not national history. His concern, however, was to remove the debate from the plane of history altogether. Filmer had cornered the Whigs with the argument that every law must originate in some man's command; since sovereignty was inalienable, that man's heir must have inherited it. Locke, by means of arguments too well known to need repeating, sought to show that law was not derived from the will of any sovereign, whether patriarchal or popular, but from the natural rights of every individual and from his will, as a rational and sociable being, to set up machinery to secure them. Hence it did not matter if law could be traced back to the will of some patriarch or some conqueror; his will had no power to rivet sovereignty on the men of his own generation, still less on their heirs. They retained possession of their rights and these must be the foundation of any government, no matter how it had been instituted. The whole chain of consequences, extending to all eternity, which Filmer and Petyt, and in moments of weakness even Hale, had supposed to follow the introduction of a sovereign into history, seemed by this argument to be dissolved.

Hale's concept of custom had almost led him to the conclusion that no sovereign could impose his power on succeeding generations; only the thought of conquest had been too much for him, and since that was an argument which the royalists could never wholeheartedly accept, we may allow that a reply to Filmer could have been constructed in Hale's pre-Burkean terms. It would have differed greatly from Locke's, for it would have presented custom, the gradual process by which men adjusted their institutions to their needs, as the origin of all law and the ultimate reason why laws could not be derived from the sovereign's will. History would have been turned against the sovereign. But in Locke the ultimate guarantee against sovereign will is located in principles of nature and reason which lie outside history and do not change with its changes: a fact which was to influence the English attitude to the past. Locke's whole cast of mind led him towards a non-historical theory of politics, and there were profound tendencies in contemporary thought pointing the same way. But Hale's ideas, no less than Locke's, are part of the history of their era, and some part in the genesis of Locke's *Treatises of Civil Government* and their reception must be allowed to the fact that the reply to Filmer's version of

English history was made in Petyt's terms and not in Hale's. Since Petyt's attempt to deny that parliament had been created by the king by asserting that it had been created by nobody at all had manifestly failed, it was the more significant that the *Treatises*, when they appeared, should have shifted the argument to a sphere in which the whole appeal to history seemed irrelevant. The popularity of Locke's theory owes something to the inanition of common-law thought.

This does not make it altogether unremarkable that Locke should have omitted all mention of English history from his writings on politics, or that, so far as can be learnt, the surviving records of his intellectual life contain no sign that the subject of this book had the smallest interest for him. If one thing is certain, it is that the attempt to understand English politics through the history of English law was an all but universal pursuit of educated men in the seventeenth century, so much so that to discover a man who did not engage in it is to discover something of a rarity. Yet Locke appears to be such an exception, perhaps the only one among the important political writers of the age. He seems to have taken no interest whatever in the historical aspect of the controversy about Filmer's works—it is true that he owned Atwood's books written against Brady,[1] but he nowhere mentions him—and his chapter on conquest in the *Second Treatise*, though it is full of discernible allusions to the juridical problems which his contemporaries feared would arise had the Normans conquered England, makes only the most cursory attempt to prove that this did not happen. Locke does not so much deny that William conquered England as assert that it is absurd to suppose the question of any importance; even if it were true, he says, 'as by history it appears otherwise', a conqueror can acquire only the most limited rights, which cease to be valid within a generation, for reasons which he proceeds to expound at length and which are rational, not historical, in their character. Once again, Locke is removing the debate out of the field in which history appears relevant, and this may well seem a sufficient explanation of his refusal to discuss it. But he was not the only man of these years to attempt a non-historical theory of politics, and most of those who

[1] I owe this information to Mr Peter Laslett.

did ended by drifting back to English history by way of some such parenthesis as Locke's 'as by history it appears otherwise', magnified to much greater length. Algernon Sidney, for example, having unequivocally stated that what mattered was whether a government was good or evil, not whether it was old, instantly added:

But if that liberty in which God created man, can receive any strength from continuance, and the rights of Englishmen can be rendered any more unquestionable by prescription, I say, that the nations, whose rights we inherit, have ever enjoyed the liberties we claim, and always exercised them in governing themselves popularly, or by such representatives as have been instituted by themselves, from the time they were first known in the world.[1]

He then, in many pages, set forth the familiar version of early English history (emphasizing the idea of a common 'Gothic' origin to a degree beyond most of the writers of whom we have been treating). The appeal to ancient liberty was hard to abandon. Even Tyrrell and Molyneux, men who knew Locke well at different times, based their writings on Petyt's as well as on his and acknowledged the former as their master in a degree second only to Locke. It may be that Locke was more clear-headed than these lesser figures and refused to drag history back into an argument from which it had just been eliminated; or he may have thought that the appeal to the past was losing its hold on the public—though it is doubtful if it was; but as likely an explanation is that Edward the Confessor and Magna Carta and the rest of it simply did not interest him.[2] After all, for

[1] *Discourses concerning Government*, 3rd ed. (1751), p. 380; see generally pp. 375–98.
[2] Dr von Leyden remarks (John Locke, *Essays on the Law of Nature*, ed. W. von Leyden, Oxford, 1954, p. 37 and elsewhere) that Locke's view of natural law differed from those of Grotius and Selden in being 'chiefly epistemological, [while] theirs was mainly legal or historical'. He dwells on Locke's denials that that natural law can be known from tradition or the general consent of men. Mr E. A. Olssen of the University of Otago has suggested to me that Locke's 'chiefly epistemological' attitude may account for his lack of interest in custom, precedent or prescription. I find this suggestion illuminating; yet it probably does not altogether explain why Locke should have been uninterested in seeing his principles reflected in the positive law of England. Tyrrell shared Locke's views on natural law and tradition (von Leyden, p. 86), yet wrote copiously on the ancient constitution.

those capable of taking an interest in history, when one has proved that a certain mode of government is the most conformable to reason and abstract justice, there is at least an illustrative value in showing that this constitution has been normally observed in time past— even in time immemorial.

'Our constitution is rational', it might now be said; 'that substantially the same constitution existed among our Saxon ancestors proves both that the principles of reason on which it is founded are eternal, and that our ancestors in their unpolished way were rational beings too, as all free men should be.' Something like this must have been the thought underlying many of the appeals to the ancient constitution made in the age of political rationalism; and in so far as this was the character of eighteenth-century constitutional antiquarianism, it was clearly unlike that of the seventeenth century. The concept of immemorial custom, founded on the interpretation of the common law, was—let us repeat it—in decay. Ideas of sovereignty had undermined belief in an ancient custom binding on both king and community; the concept of custom itself had hardened into an obscurantist insistence that parliament must not be known to have had a beginning. In addition to all this, and for reasons many of which lie outside the scope of this book, the first decades of the new century witnessed a wave of historical scepticism—Bolingbroke is its best-known English exponent—in which both the possibility and the utility of knowing what had happened in remote ages were called in question.[1] In creating this mood of doubt it is possible that Spelmanist criticism played some part. Very shortly after Petyt had identified the original contract with the coronation oath, that oath itself was re-worded by the statute 1 W. & M. c. 6, and the traditional reference to the laws of Edward the Confessor removed,

forasmuch as the oath hath heretofore been framed in doubtful words and expressions, with relation to antient laws and constitutions at this time unknown.[2]

[1] See P. Hazard, *La Crise de la conscience européenne*, and for Bolingbroke, Douglas, *English Scholars*, ch. XIII, 'The End of an Age'.

[2] There is a discussion of this aspect of the oath in relation to the reign of James II in A. Taylor, *The Glory of Regality* (1820), pp. 335–42.

Conclusion: 1688 in the History of Historiography

'The rationalists of 1688', Professor H. M. Cam has called the instigators of this measure;[1] but are we in the presence of a rationalist indifference to the past, of a general scepticism as to the possibility of historical knowledge, of an uneasy awareness of the telling criticisms launched by Spelman and Brady, or of a mixture of all three? It is hard to tell, but we may note the words in which Evelyn denounced the legal and historical education dispensed by the Inns of Court: he declared that young lawyers and students of law were 'shamefully ignorant in the Feudal [Law] and our own', and that they must be taught 'whence our holding by Knight's service and Feudal Laws have been derived, whether from Saxon or Norman'.[2] Similarly Thomas Madox, the greatest medievalist of the next generation, permitted himself the remark:

> One may justly wonder that *Feudal* Learning (if I may so call it) should be so little known or regarded as it seems to be by the Students (I ask their pardon) of the Common Law of *England*.[3]

Evelyn and Madox were echoing Spelman's criticism of Coke, and it would appear that neglect of feudal history aroused dissatisfaction and furthered the decline in the intellectual reputation of the Inns of Court; but this is only one small aspect of that little-studied and important phenomenon, the way in which the Inns ceased to teach, ceased to be a third university for the gentlemen of England and ceased to exert a determining influence on English historical and political thought. Perhaps this development, more than even that decline in medieval scholarship which Professor Douglas detects about 1720,[4] may be taken to mark the end of the age of Coke and the transformation of the concept of the ancient constitution. In the days of Coke, of Prynne and Hale, even of Petyt and Atwood, the idea of immemorial law had sprung direct from the Inns of Court; it had been shaped by historical presuppositions implicit in the common law, and had been the ideology of a period in which

---

[1] *England before Elizabeth* (1950), p. 55.
[2] *Letters on Various Subjects to and from William Nicholson*, ed. John Nichols (1809), pp. 137 ff.
[3] Madox, *Formulare anglicanum* (1702), Preface, section VIII.
[4] *English Scholars*, ch. XIII.

that law exercised an influence on education, scholarship and political thought greater than it possessed at any other time in English history. In the age of the Inns' decline the presuppositions on which it was founded must have undergone radical change. The minds which believed in it now had not been formed by an exclusive study of the common law, and consequently must have believed in it for reasons differing from those analysed in this book.

Italian historians concerned with the political and historical thought of the *mezzogiorno*[1] speak of a process, which they date about the year 1700, whereby the kind of thinking which attempted to solve problems in political thought by reference to existing and ancient law (the 'tradizione giuridica') was largely replaced by political thought which they describe as Cartesian, and which brought about corresponding changes in the contemporary attitude to history. In so far as the period following 1688 witnessed a transference of emphasis from ancient custom and precedent to unhistorical reason, we may be in the presence of something similar in the history of English thought; and it is suggested that the concept of the ancient constitution was itself transformed, to a considerable extent, by being based on reason rather than custom. But the appeal to the Saxon and medieval past did not altogether lose its original significance when prolonged into the eighteenth century. As Burke was to point out, it was of no small importance that Englishmen of the great Whig epoch preferred, as often as not, to describe their liberty as an inheritance from their ancestors than as a thing rooted in abstract reason; and a foreign observer, de Lolme, remarked of the whole question that

there was a far greater probability of success, in raising among the people the notions (familiar to them) of legal claims and long-established customs, than in arguing with them from the no less rational, but less determinate, and somewhat dangerous doctrines, concerning the original rights of mankind, and the lawfulness of at all time opposing force to an oppressive government.[2]

[1] See the works of Romeo and Marini, cited in ch. I, pp. 16 n. and 18 n.
[2] *The Constitution of England* (ed. 1816), p. 8 n. It is interesting that this should be part of a comment on Spelman's remark that at the Conquest 'novus seclorum nascitur ordo'.

Conclusion: 1688 in the History of Historiography

De Lolme had seen the conservative and anti-theoretical character of the appeal to the past; but, true to his age, he supposed this to be the result of a shrewd calculation by those who had elected to use this argument rather than its alternative. The present book contends, however, that its use in the seventeenth century is better interpreted as arising from habits of thought deeply rooted and almost instinctive in the English mind; and there is reason to believe that its prolongation into the eighteenth century indicates, after all, some survival of these traditional habits. The great masters of common-law thought, when all is said, continued to be read and studied in the age that succeeded their own; so too did their opponents, Spelman and even Brady; and the ideas of Burke, which close the eighteenth century as an age in the history of English political thought, can be fully appreciated only if we realize, first, that he had studied the controversy between the partisans of the ancient constitution and those of the feudal law,[1] and come to the conclusion that this controversy was of importance in the history of English politics; secondly, that his own thinking was saturated in the ideas of Coke and Hale. Burke's essential ideas are that institutions are the products of history; that history consists in an unceasing and undying process, in which the generations are partners and in which men perpetually adapt themselves to new needs and new situations; that existing institutions are the fruits of this process and, whether because they represent the latest adjustment or because they have been retained through many adaptations, embody the wisdom of more men, in a higher state of refinement, than the individual intellect can hope to equal or exceed; and that political wisdom lies in participating in this process—which can be identified with order and nature—not in attempting to reconstruct institutions on *a priori* lines. In all this we cannot be mistaken in recognizing the voice of

[1] The evidence for this is to be found in his fragment 'An Essay towards an History of the Laws of England', *Works*, Bohn ed., vol. VI (1877), pp. 412–22. See also Butterfield, *Man on his Past* (Cambridge, 1955), pp. 18, 68–9, with a quotation from Acton. Acton was much impressed by Burke's sympathy for the Middle Ages, as compared with Bossuet and the eighteenth-century writers; but should he not have compared him rather with the English legal historians of the seventeenth century? Professor Butterfield remarks that Acton's knowledge of these writers seems deficient (pp. 65–6).

the great tradition of common-law thought, and in particular of those men who had conceived the law of England as custom and custom as perpetual adaptation. Every one of Burke's cardinal points, as just enumerated, can be found in Hale rebuking Hobbes, in Coke rebuking James I, or in Davies rebuking the partisans of written law; and in Hale we have seen an adumbration of Burke's philosophy developed to a high pitch of subtlety. It is as if the concept of custom, and of English institutions as founded on custom, ran underground about the time of Hale's death, to burst into sunlight again in Burke's letters and speeches. From what sources Burke derived it, and with what elements of eighteenth-century thought and his own genius he enriched it, are questions for the specialist; but that Burke's philosophy is in great measure a revitalization of the concept of custom and the common-law tradition may be safely asserted as part of the present study's contentions.

By the time of Burke, however, the historical outlook of Englishmen was very different from what it had been in the time of Hale or Brady. In order to understand this difference, we must first consider whether the feudal interpretations founded by Spelman played any part in the historical thinking of the eighteenth century. The full investigation of this question remains a task for future researchers; but it would appear that, while after 1688 there was general determination not to allow the presence of feudal elements in English medieval history to upset the dogma that parliamentary liberty was pre-Conquest in character, the existence of those elements as a field of possible study may have been neglected but was not actually denied. Whig bishops of the Revolution settlement—Gibson, White Kennett and Nicholson—completed the editing of Spelman's unpublished works and commented learnedly on his feudal investigations; all through the century he was acknowledged and quoted as one of the greatest of authorities, and even Brady's writings did not go unread. Eminent writers on the common law were in time able to admit the importance of Spelman's doctrines: Wright and Blackstone, Gilbert and Sullivan expounded the derivation of English law from a feudal origin, while in Scotland Kames and Dalrymple carried on the tradition of Sir Thomas

Craig.[1] But the writings of these sound and conservative scholars leave one wondering (though the point requires further investigation) whether anything important had been added to the knowledge of feudalism since the early seventeenth century. Dalrymple, for example—still considered a writer worth reading on Scottish feudal tenures[2]—had not advanced beyond deriving feudalism from a Lombard origin and, though there are clear signs in some writers of the influence of Montesquieu on this topic, it does not seem that eighteenth-century British scholarship had entirely reached the point of treating feudalism as a plant of Frankish and Carolingian growth.[3] Compared with the times of Spelman, Brady or Madox (d. 1727), the high eighteenth century appears to have seen the exploration of feudal society at a standstill. For this there are various reasons; the unpopularity of the subject in an age still wedded to the ancient constitution was one of them. Blackstone, for instance, though his whole account of the origins of common law presupposes a knowledge of feudal society, is bent on treating Norman feudalism as a mere intrusion on English constitutional history. For him the driving force of thirteenth-century politics is still the desire of 'the nation' to recover its ancient liberty, which the Conquest had submerged. Many writers of his age, having apparently given all due weight to the importance of the Norman introduction of feudal tenure, then undermined their own writings by insisting on treating feudalism as a mere interruption of the true course of the national life, and the habit of presenting 'feudalism' and 'the nation' as opposite and antagonistic concepts coloured much of

[1] Sir Martin Wright, *An Introduction to the Law of Tenures* (1729); Sir Geoffrey Gilbert (d. 1726), *Treatise of Tenures* (1754); Blackstone, *Commentaries on the Laws of England* (published 1765–9); F. S. Sullivan, *An Historical Treatise on the Feudal Law* (1772); Henry Home (later Lord Kames), *Essays upon Several Subjects concerning British Antiquities* (1746); John Dalrymple, *An Essay towards a General History of Feudal Property in Great Britain* (1757).

[2] H. M. Cam, *Liberties and Communities in Medieval England* (Cambridge, 1944), p. 220, n. 4.

[3] But cf. Robertson's *History of Scotland* (*Works*, collected ed., London, 1824, vol. 1, p. 35 n.), which does not, however, clearly state that feudal tenure originated in Frankish society. See also Hume, *History of England* (1762), vol. 1, p. 263.

the historical thought of the nineteenth century, in a way no longer thought illuminating. It seems that we must look to the age of Kemble and Palgrave for signs of fresh life in this branch of thought.

But there is another way in which this apparent slowing-up of feudal studies is important. It would seem as if feudal society was not being investigated as part of a live movement of research, based on the recovery, editing and interpreting of charters and other forms of evidence; as if, in short—and this seems the general opinion among scholars—the great movement of seventeenth-century antiquarianism had come to an end. We have seen how the concept of custom and the intellectual ascendancy of the common law both lost importance at the end of the Stuart period, which may help to explain the general decline. It is as if the security of the Whig state and Church after 1714 loosened the ties which bound England to her past. The foundations were felt to be solidly established and fairly recent, and what had happened in remoter ages, while it remained in doubt, could no longer so vitally affect the present. If this generalization can be maintained, we may say that we draw to an end of the first great age of modern historiography: that in which the structure of society is authoritatively determined by the laws and sacred books of the past; in which means exist of interpreting these authorities by canons which are those of modern historical criticism, and so of reconstructing the past of which they formed part; but in which the structure of the present is still thought to be vitally affected by the reconstruction which is made of the past. In such a period the writing of history is inevitably partisan, but may not be much the worse for that; there is an intimate and passionate concern with the details of the past, and the organic unity of past and present is vigorously asserted. But in so far as the eighteenth century was an 'age of reason', in so far as it supposed itself to be securely based on principles independent of history— neither generalization is of course absolutely true—its whole attitude to the past must have been very different; and in this alteration there was both loss and gain.

The past tended to lose its immediate and controversial relevance to the present, so that there was some slackening of partisan zeal

among English medievalists; but on the other hand we observe
not only a tendency to lose interest in the whole subject, but the
rise of a new and unfamiliar problem. Of great stretches of past
time it could now be said that the way in which they were interpreted could not make any difference to the lives of men in the
present. What then was the point of studying them at all, and what
was the attitude which the modern intellect should adopt towards
them? It is the same problem, though differently arrived at, as that
which had been more remotely discerned by the critics of Cujas.
Bolingbroke's *Letters on the Study of History* attempt to answer such
questions as these, but by universal consent the solution they propose
is an unsatisfactory one. Bolingbroke cannot imagine any cultivated
man studying the remoter and less sympathetic periods of history
with the idea of finding out what they were like or how they
worked. For him the function of historical study is not to discover
how men have lived—thinking nothing human alien to its inquiries
—but to inculcate the moral and practical lessons of statecraft, and
the man of affairs need concern himself only with those periods
likely to contain examples relevant to his own situation, a definition
which ends by ruling out the greater part of recorded history. This
is certainly a deplorable attitude, and there is something peculiarly
unpleasing about the spectacle of Bolingbroke blotting out vast
tracts of human experience as unworthy of serious attention. But
he had called attention to a real problem: if it was no longer thought
that the form of the modern state was directly determined by what
had happened in the eleventh century, why should that period be
studied at all, except by dry-as-dusts cut off from their own age
and incomprehensibly interested in the past for its own sake?
Concepts of custom and sovereignty, of the origins and ultimate
authority of law, had once bound the present to the past; if these
were abandoned, what was called for was virtually a new conception of the unity of history—with the disappearance of historical
study as an alternative. It was the achievement of the eighteenth
century—of Vico and Voltaire, of the Göttingen and Edinburgh
professors—to formulate general ideas and construct schemes of
universal history; and if their work points in some respects to the
intellectual disasters which befell and are befalling the human race

with the advent of historicism, this does not alter the fact that, in replacing the intense but limited concern with the past that characterized the antiquarians with a set of general ideas that made it possible (however inadequately) to see the present state of mankind as emerging from the whole of its past experience, they were doing what had to be done if historiography was to survive. There is a certain case to be made for Bolingbroke against the antiquarians who surpassed him in scholarship and whose scholarship he said he despised. He was detached from the past as they could never be, and though his detachment made him often superficial and obtuse, it also gave him the power to reflect on the historical process and on the problem of a man's defining his own place in it; and here he often displayed a subtlety of perception which was beyond better scholars. He knew that historical situations did not exactly recur, so that we must beware of applying too rigidly any generalizations we formed from past experience;[1] and he had a sense of historical relativism—he liked to observe that arguments about the nature of the constitution had been used in the seventeenth century which it would not be appropriate to use in the circumstances of his own day.[2] Bolingbroke could appreciate ideas of this kind because he had an awareness, beyond anything possessed by Spelman, Harrington or Hale, of living in a generalized historical process. His generalizations were often unsound and superficial; but generalizations, and perhaps even superficiality, were what the age needed. They were necessary to the construction of schemes of universal history which alone could give an 'age of reason' a sense of oneness with its past.

Even in Bolingbroke's most cocksure judgments about those periods of history in which a polite statesman will, or will not, find anything deserving his attention, we catch a hint of that aspect of eighteenth-century historical thought which was, for good and ill, to be of greatest importance for the future. This is the habit of generalizing about the periods of history, of supposing each of them

[1] This point is discussed in Professor Butterfield's *The Statecraft of Machiavelli* (London, reprinted 1955), ch. IV, where Bolingbroke's debt to Guicciardini in this matter is emphasized.

[2] *Dissertation on Parties*, 7th ed., pp. 124–31.

to have been governed by certain general characteristics, so that it could be further supposed that there was a certain logic about the way in which one period succeeded another, and that the dominant characteristics of one period might help to explain how it had been transformed into another or replaced. Thought of this kind—which certainly belongs to the eighteenth century, whatever used to be said to the contrary—points the way to historicism and to the idea that the entire process of history can be abstracted and turned into a single set of laws, and as such we may deplore it; but we ought also to admit that such a habit of generalization provided a solution to the problem which had been too much for Brady. He had been able to reconstruct the institutions of a past time, but he had not been able to show how these institutions had evolved into something different, to combine a narrative of the evolution of institutions with a narrative of the deeds of men, or to apply the techniques he used upon legal and governmental records to the study and interpretation of chronicles; and consequently he had apparently not conceived of history as a single unified discipline. His limitations were, it seems probable, those general in his age. But eighteenth-century historians—Vico, Voltaire, Montesquieu, Millar, Schlözer[1] —were able, each in his way, to observe that in a period supposedly governed by certain characteristics it was natural that certain social institutions, certain habits of thought and forms of art should exist in conformity with the dominant characteristics, and that they should fall and be replaced by others as the character of the period changed. It remained only to show how the actions of men might contribute to altering the whole pattern of the age, and the problem was solved. In comparison with their predecessors of the seventeenth century, the difference between Voltaire's 'rationalism' and Vico's 'historicism' loses some of its importance. The writers of the eighteenth century converted history into a

[1] The present writer derives virtually all his knowledge of the Edinburgh school from a series of articles by Mr Duncan Forbes in the *Cambridge Journal* ('*Historismus* in England', April 1951; 'James Mill and India', October 1951; 'The Rationalism of Sir Walter Scott', October 1953; and 'Scientific Whiggism: Adam Smith and John Millar', August 1954), and of the Göttingen school and Schlözer from Professor Butterfield's *Man on his Past*.

unified science, capable (at least in theory) of looking at the whole of human life from a standpoint distinctively its own. It had not been in that condition when they found it.[1]

They carried out this great change in ideas partly because they were willing to engage in sweeping generalizations, many of which were naturally unsound. Craig and Spelman may have been too ready to deduce all the phenomena of feudal tenure from a single Lombard origin, but in spite of Maitland's famous remark, Spelman did not speak of a 'feudal system', a phrase which seems to belong to eighteenth-century terminology; it was Robertson, writing between 1753 and 1759, perhaps under Montesquieu's influence, who could say 'the genius of the feudal government, uniform in all its operations, produced the same effects in small, as in great societies'.[2] If the English and Scottish writers of this age did little new research on feudalism, it was because they were making an 'ism' of it; they were reflecting on its essence and nature and endeavouring to fit it into a pattern of general ideas. In so doing they committed and perpetuated many great fallacies; they transmitted some of the mistakes of their predecessors and did not always profit by their best work. It is true that the best in the older tradition did not altogether die out. The thought of Burke, it is suggested here, owed far more to the common-law concept of custom than to the system-building historicism of the eighteenth century; and, in our own times, is it too fantastic to suggest that the contrast between Fisher ('one emergency following another') and Toynbee represents a continuing conflict between the two traditions? It is not yet certain that when feudal studies came to be revived in the nineteenth century, Spelman, who was still read, was altogether without his influence. However all this may be, it is nevertheless fairly certain that the eighteenth-century historians failed to continue, to appreciate as they should, or to learn as they might from the work of the seventeenth-century legal historians; and it is irritating to find Bolingbroke's facile contempt for the antiquary occasionally

---

[1] It may be worth mentioning that 'the eighteenth century' is here, as always, an elastic term. It could well be extended to cover the period of Hazard's 'crise de la conscience européenne', beginning about 1680.

[2] *Works*, vol. I, p. 62.

repeated by Robertson and Gibbon.[1] But it is hard to shake off the feeling that their superficiality was perhaps an essential part of their real achievement, which was to generalize history and make it universal. Generalizations are necessary and must be permitted some inaccuracy.

The commonest approach to the history of historiography is one more likely to do injustice to Coke and Hale, Spelman and Brady, than to the great men of the next age. In Robertson's hands history was its modern self, capable of attempting to narrate the whole evolution of a human society;[2] in Brady's it was not, and there is an obvious and natural temptation to begin the history of historiography at the point where it became a unified and independent science and treat all who lived before that time as forerunners, collectors of material for others to use, voices crying in the wilderness. But this seems a fallacy, of the same order as that committed when the history of the subject was taken to begin only with the rise of German *Historismus* and the men of the eighteenth century were relegated to a sort of prehistory—the view still prevalent in most general histories. Mr Duncan Forbes and Professor Butterfield have both reminded us that *vixere fortes ante Germanos* and encouraged us to look for concepts of universal history and subtleties of historical perception in the eighteenth century; the present study simply seeks to extend the subject a stage further back. Mr Forbes in particular warns us against the danger of a 'Whig interpretation' in this field; he suggests that we ought not to look merely for the precursors of the fully fledged German romantic concept of history.[3] Similarly, it may be sug-

[1] Professor Momigliano (*op. cit.*) sees Gibbon as carrying out a great synthesis of philosophical history and antiquarian erudition in the field of ancient history. It was as well for Europe, then, that he abandoned his idea of writing on the English barons' wars, for no such synthesis was likely to be achieved there.

[2] This is not to deny that there was much of an unhistorical character still surviving in eighteenth-century practice, or that the German historical movement carried out a vast deepening of perspectives. But eighteenth-century historiography proposed to itself the object of treating the evolution of society as a whole and, whatever its defects, it had not been thought before that this could be done.

[3] In '*Historismus* in England', cited above, pp. 389–90.

gested that the moment when history became a distinct and self-conscious way of looking at things is indeed of the greatest importance, but that there was historical thought which we must take seriously long before that date. The history of historiography is not only the history of the rise and perfection of a particular manner of thought—tremendous subject though this is—it is the history of all the ways in which men have felt committed to their past and bound to find out what it was and how they are related to it, and all the attempts they have made to deal seriously with the problems in which this inquiry involves them. The men who form the subject of this book felt bound to their past by the law under which they lived, and their interpretation of the law and their interpretation of the past depended upon and influenced one another. Through their law, historically interpreted, they could learn much about their past; but to think of their law historically was rendered difficult by the character of that law itself and by many ideas about the present, to some of which it had given rise; and to succeed in this aim would alter their attitude to both the law and the present. That was the problem with which they were faced by their sense of being bound to the past. That they thought about it seriously, and often fruitfully, is the justification for treating them as a chapter in the history of historiography. At last the age in which law was supremely important in determining men's thought about the past was succeeded by another in which that importance had been lost.

BIBLIOGRAPHY

A. MANUSCRIPT SOURCES AND CALENDARS

Bodleian Library (Ashmole MSS.) Dugdale MS. 10.

Bodleian Library Tanner MS. 37.

British Museum Additional MS. 32, 518.

Caius College (Cambridge)ʳ MS. 607.

Inner Temple MSS.; Petyt MS. 583 (17).

Johnston MSS., Magdalen College, Oxford.

Calendar of State Papers (Domestic).

Historical Manuscripts Commission, VIth Report.

Historical Manuscripts Commission, XIIth Report.

B. ORIGINAL PRINTED WORKS

Atwood, William:· *Jani Anglorum Facies Nova.* London, 1680.

———: *Jus Anglorum ab Antiquo.* London, 1681.

———: (ed.) *The Lord Holles his Remains.* London, 1682.

Aubrey, John: *Brief Lives* (ed. Oliver Lawson Dick). London: Secker and Warburg, 1949.

———: *Brief Lives and other selected writings* (ed. Anthony Powell). London: Cresset Press, 1949.

Bacon, Nathaniel: *A Historical Discourse of the Uniformity of the Government of England.* London, 1647–51.

Baudouin, Francois: *De institutione historiae universae et ejus cum jurisprudentia conjunctione prolegomenon* (1561). An edition was published at Halle in 1726.

Blackstone, Sir William: *Commentaries on the Laws of England,* 19th ed. London, 1836.

Bodin, Jean: *Methodus ad facilem historiarum cognitionem* (1566), in Pierre Mesnard, ed., *Oeuvres Philosophiques de Jean Bodin,* vol. I. Paris: Presses Universitaires de France, 1951.

Bolingbroke, Henry St. John (Viscount): *A Dissertation on Parties,* 7th ed. London, 1749.

———: *Letters on the Study and Use of History,* in *The Works of Lord Bolingbroke,* vol. II. London, 1754.

Brady, Robert: *A Full and Clear Answer to a Book Written by William Petit, Esq.* London, 1681.

———: *A True and Exact History of the Succession to the Crown of England.* London, 1681.

———: *An Introduction to the Old English History.* London, 1684.

———: *The Complete History of England,* vol. I. London, 1685.

———: *A Treatise of Boroughs.* London, 1690.

———: *The Complete History of England,* vol. II. London, 1700.

Bibliography

Burke, Edmund: "An Essay Towards a History of the Laws of England," in *Works* (Bohn edition), vol. VI. London, 1877.

Burnet, Gilbert (Bishop): *History of the Reformation.* London, 1865.

Camden Society: *An Italian Relation of England about the year 1500.* London: Camden Society Publications, first series, no. 37, 1847.

Clarendon, Edward Hyde, 1st Earl of: *A Brief View and Survey of the Dangerous and Pernicious Errors in Church and State in Mr. Hobbes's Book Entitled Leviathan.* London, 1676.

Coke, Sir Edward: *First Part of the Institutes of the Laws of England,* 8th ed. London, 1670.

_____: *Second Part of the Institutes of the Laws of England,* 4th ed. London, 1671.

_____: *Reports* (eds. J. H. Thomas and J. F. Fraser). London, 1826.

Cook, Edward: *Argumentum Anti-Normannicum.* London, 1680.

Cowell, John: *Institutiones juris anglicani ad methodum et seriem institutionum imperialium compositae et digestae.* London, 1605.

_____: *The Interpreter or Booke containing the significance of words.* London, 1607.

Craig, Sir Thomas: *Jus Feudale tribus libris comprehensum* (1603). James Baillie, ed. Edinburgh, 1732.

Cujas, Jacques: *Iacobi Cuiacii operum quae de jure fecit.* Paris, 1637.

Dalrymple, John: *An Essay towards a General History of Feudal Property in Great Britain.* London, 1757.

Davies, Sir John: *Les Reports des Cases & Matters en Ley, Resolves & Adjudges en les Courts del Roy en Ireland. Collect & digest per Sir John Davis Chivaler, Atturney Generall del Roy en cest Realm* (1612). London, 1674.

_____: *A Discoverie of the True Causes why Ireland was never entirely subdued, nor brought under Obedience of the Crowne of England, untill the Beginning of His Maiesies Happie Raigne* (1612). London, 1747.

_____: *Historical Tracts.* London, 1786.

De Lolme, J. L.: *The Constitution of England.* London, 1816.

Dugdale, Sir William (ed.): *Glossarium Archaiologium* (by Sir Henry Spelman). London, 1664.

_____: *Origines Juridiciales.* London, 1666.

_____: *The Baronage of England,* vol. I. London, 1675.

_____: *A Perfect Copy of All Summons of the Nobility to Parliament . . . since the XLIX of Henry III.* London, 1685.

Ellis, Sir Henry (ed.): *Letters of Eminent Literary Men.* London: Camden Society Publications, first series, no. 23, 1843.

Filmer, Sir Robert: *Patriarcha and Other Political Works* (ed. P. Laslett). Oxford: Basil Blackwell, 1949.

Fortescue, Sir John: *De Laudibus Legum Anglie* (ed. S. B. Chrimes). Cambridge University Press, 1942.

Fulbecke, William: *A Parallel or Conference of the Civil Law, the Canon Law and the Common Law of this Realm of England.* London, 1601.

Bibliography

Gilbert, Sir Geoffrey: *A Treatise of Tenures*. London, 1754.

Hale, Sir Matthew: *The History of the Common Law of England,* 2nd ed. London, 1716.

————: Unpublished reply to Hobbes, in vol. V of W. S. Holdsworth, *History of English Law.* London: Methuen, 1903–38.

Hamper, William (ed.): *The Life and Writings of Sir William Dugdale.* London, 1827.

Harrington, James: *The Oceana and Other Works of James Harrington* (ed. John Toland), 3rd London ed. London, 1771.

————: *Oceana* (ed. S. B. Liljegren). Lund and Heidelberg: Skrifter utgivna av Vetenskapssocieteten i Lund, 1924.

Hobbes, Thomas: *Leviathan* (ed. M. Oakeshott). Oxford: Basil Blackwell, undated.

————: *Behemoth* and *Dialogue of the Common Laws,* in vol. VI of *English Works* (ed. Sir William Molesworth). London, 1839–45.

Holles, Denzil, 1st Baron: *The Case Stated Concerning the Judicature of the House of Peers in the Point of Appeals.* London, 1675.

————: *The Case Stated Concerning the Judicature of the House of Peers in the Point of Impostures.* London, 1676.

————: *The Lord Holles his Remains* (ed. William Atwood). London, 1682.

Home, Henry (later Lord Kames): *Essays upon Several Subjects concerning British Antiquities,* 2nd ed. London, 1749.

Hotman, François: *De Feudis commentatio tripetita.* Lyons, 1573.

————: *Anti-Tribonian* (1567). Paris, 1603.

————: *Francogallia* (1573). Eng. trans. by Robert, Viscount Molesworth, 2nd ed. London, 1721.

Hume, David: *History of England.* London, 1752.

Hunt, Thomas: *An Argument for the Bishops' Right in Judging in Capital Causes in Parliament.* London, 1682.

James I: *Political Works* (ed. C. H. McIlwain). Cambridge, Mass.: Harvard University Press, 1918.

Johnston, Nathaniel: *The Excellency of Monarchical Government.* London, 1686.

————: *The King's Visitatorial Power Asserted.* London, 1688.

Lambarde, William: *Archaionomia.* London, 1568.

Locke, John: *Essays on the Law of Nature* (ed. W. von Leyden). Oxford: Clarendon Press, 1954.

————: *Two Treatises of Civil Government* (ed. P. Laslett). Cambridge University Press, 1960.

Madox, Thomas: *Formulare Anglicanum.* London, 1702.

Molyneux, William: *The Case of Ireland's Being Bound by Acts of Parliament in England Truly Stated.* Dublin, 1698.

Neville (or Nevile), Henry: *Plato Redivivus.* London, 1682.

Nichols, John (ed.): *Letters on Various Subjects to and from William Nicholson.* London, 1809.

North, Roger: *Lives of the Norths.* London, 1890.

Bibliography

Petyt, William: *The Antient Right of the Commons of England Asserted.* London, 1680.

_____: *Miscellanea Parliamentaria.* London, 1680.

_____: *The Pillars of Parliament Struck At by the Hands of a Cambridge Doctor.* London, 1681.

Philipps, Fabian: *Tenenda non Tollenda.* London, 1660.

_____: *Investigatio Jurium Antiquorum.* London, 1687.

Prynne, William: *A Plea for the Lords.* London, 1648.

_____: *The First Part of a Historical Collection Concerning the Ancient Parliaments of England.* London, 1649.

_____: *A Preface to the Abridgment of the Records in the Tower.* London, 1657.

_____: *The First Part of a Brief Register of Parliamentary Writs.* London, 1658–59.

_____: *The Second Part of a Brief Register of Parliamentary Writs.* London, 1660.

_____: *The Third Part of a Brief Register of Parliamentary Writs.* London, 1662.

_____: *The Fourth Part of a Brief Register of Parliamentary Writs.* London, 1664.

_____: *Animadversions on Sir Edward Coke's Fourth Institutes.* London, 1669.

Robertson, William: *The History of Scotland,* in *The Works of William Robertson,* vol. I. London, 1824.

Selden, John: *Titles of Honour.* London, 1614; enlarged ed., 1631.

_____: *Dissertatio Ad Fletam* (ed. D. Ogg). Cambridge University Press, 1925.

Sidney, Algernon: *Discourses on Government,* 3rd ed. London, 1751.

Smith, Sir Thomas: *De Republica Anglorum* (ed. L. Alston). Cambridge University Press, 1906.

Somner, William: *A Treatise of Gavelkind.* London, 1662.

Spelman, Sir Henry: *Archaeologus.* London, 1626.

_____: *Glossarium Archaiologium* (ed. Sir William Dugdale). London, 1664.

_____: *The History of Sacrilege* (ed. White Kennett). London, 1698.

_____: *Reliquiae Spelmannianae* (ed. Edmund Gibson). London, 1698.

_____: *Codex Legum Veterum,* in David Wilkins, *Leges Anglo-Saxonicae,* London, 1721.

State Tracts in the Reign of Charles II. London, 1693.

Sullivan, F. S.: *An Historical Treatise on the Feudal Law.* Dublin, 1772.

Taylor, A.: *The Glory of Regality.* London, 1820.

Twysden, Sir Roger: *Certain Considerations upon the Government of England.* London: Camden Society Publications, first series, no. 45, 1849.

Tyrrell, James: *Patriarcha non Monarcha.* London, 1681.

_____: *Bibliotheca Politica.* London, 1694.

Bibliography

W. W.: *Antidotum Britannicum*. London, 1681.

Wildman, John: *A Letter to a Friend Advising in this Extraordinary Juncture How to Free the Nation from Slavery Forever*, in *A Collection of Scarce and Valuable Tracts* . . . ("Somers Tracts"), vol. I. London, 1729.

Zouche, Richard: *Elements iurisprudentiae . . . quibus accessit Descriptio iuris et iudicii temporalis secundum consuetudines feudales et normannicas*. Oxford, 1636.

C. SECONDARY WORKS

Acton, Lord: *Historical Essays and Studies*. London, 1908.

Allen, J. W.: *English Political Thought, 1603–42*. London: Methuen, 1951.

————: *Political Thought in the Sixteenth Century*, 3rd ed. London: Methuen, 1951.

Barzun, Jacques: *The French Race*. New York: Columbia University Press, 1932.

Bémont, Charles: *Chartes des libertés anglaises, 1100–1305*. Paris: A. Picard, 1892.

Blocaille, E.: *Etude sur François Hotman*. Dijon, 1902.

Bloch, Marc: *Métier d'Historien*. Paris: A. Colin, 1964. (Eng. trans.: *The Historian's Craft*. New York: A. Knopf, 1953.)

Bolgar, R. R.: *The Classical Heritage and Its Beneficiaries*. Cambridge University Press, 1954.

Butterfield, Herbert: *The Englishman and His History*. Cambridge University Press, 1944.

————: *George III, Lord North and the People*. London: G. Bell, 1949.

————: *Man on His Past*. Cambridge University Press, 1955.

————: *The Statecraft of Machiavelli*. London: G. Bell, 1960.

Cam, Helen M.: *Liberties and Communities in Medieval England*. Cambridge University Press, 1944.

————: *England Before Elizabeth*. London: Hutchinson's University Library, 1950.

Church, W. F.: *Constitutional Thought in Sixteenth-Century France*. Cambridge, Mass.: Harvard University Press, 1941.

Cooper, Lord: *The Dark Age of Scottish Legal History*. Glasgow University Press, 1952.

Dareste, R.: *Essai sur François Hotman*. Paris, 1850.

Declareuil, J.: *Histoire générale du droit français*. Paris, 1925.

Delaruelle, L.: *Guillaume Budé (1468–1540): les origines, les débuts, les idées maîtresses*. Paris: Bibliothèque de l'Ecole des Hautes Etudes, 1907.

Douglas, D. C.: *English Scholars*. London: Eyre and Spottiswoode, 1951.

————: *The Norman Conquest and British Historians*. Glasgow University Press, 1946.

Fink, Z. S.: *The Classical Republicans*. Evanston: Northwestern University Press, 1945.

Bibliography

Forbes, Duncan: *"Historismus* in England," *Cambridge Journal,* vol. IV, no. 7 (1951).

_____: "James Mill and India," *Cambridge Journal,* vol. V, no. 1 (1951).

_____: "The Rationalism of Sir Walter Scott," *Cambridge Journal,* vol. VII, no. 1 (1953).

_____: "Scientific Whiggism: Adam Smith and John Millar," *Cambridge Journal,* vol. VII, no. 11 (1954).

Ford, Franklin L.: *Robe and Sword: The Regrouping of the French Aristocracy after Louis XIV.* Cambridge, Mass.: Harvard University Press, 1953.

Forster, Leonard: *The Temper of Seventeenth-Century German Literature.* London: Athlone Press, 1951.

Frank, J.: *The Levellers.* Cambridge, Mass.: Harvard University Press, 1955.

Ganshof, F. L.: *Feudalism* (ed. P. Grierson). London: Longmans, 1952.

Gilmore, Myron P.: *Argument from Roman Law in Political Thought, 1200–1600.* Cambridge, Mass.: Harvard University Press, 1941.

Gough, J. W.: *Fundamental Law in English Constitutional History.* Oxford: Clarendon Press, 1955.

Haller, William: *Tracts on Liberty in the Puritan Revolution.* New York: Columbia University Press, 1934.

Hay, Denys: *Polydore Vergil.* Oxford: Clarendon Press, 1952.

Hazard, Paul: *La crise de la conscience européene, 1680–1715.* Paris: Boivin, 1935. (Eng. trans.: *The European Mind.* London: Hollis and Carter, 1953.)

Hazeltine, H. D.: "The Renaissance," in *Cambridge Legal Essays* (eds. Winfield and McNair). Cambridge University Press, 1926.

Hill, Christopher: *Puritanism and Revolution.* London: Secker and Warburg, 1958.

Holdsworth, Sir William: *A History of English Law.* London: Methuen, 1903–38.

Huizinga, J. H.: *Sobre el estado actual de la ciencia histórica.* Madrid: *Revista de occidente,* 12 (1934).

Inderwick, F. A.: *Calendar of the Inner Temple Records.* London, 1896.

Kern, Fritz: *Kingship and Law in the Middle Ages* (ed. S. B. Chrimes). Cambridge University Press, 1939.

Kliger, S. L.: *The Goths in England.* Cambridge, Mass.: Harvard University Press, 1952.

Ku Chieh-kang: *The Autobiography of a Chinese Historian* (trans. A. W. Hummel). Leiden, 1931.

Laird, J.: *Hobbes.* London: E. Benn, 1934.

Lemaire, André: *Les lois fondamentales de la monarchie française d'après les théoriciens de l'ancien régime.* Paris, 1907.

Maitland, F. W.: *English Law and the Renaissance.* Cambridge University Press, 1901.

Bibliography

————: *Constitutional History of England*. Cambridge University Press, 1908.

————: *Collected Papers*. Cambridge University Press, 1911.

Marini, L.: *Pietro Giannone e il Giannonismo a Napoli nel Settecento*. Bari: Laterza, 1950.

Mesnard, P.: *L'essor de la philosophie politique au XVIme siècle*. Paris: J. Vrin, 1951.

Momigliano, A.: *Contributo alla storia degli studi classici*. Rome, 1955.

Neale, Sir John: *Elizabeth I and Her Parliaments, 1558–81*. London: Jonathan Cape, 1953.

Pocock, J. G. A.: "Robert Brady, 1627–1700. A Cambridge Historian of the Restoration," in *Cambridge Historical Journal*, vol. X, no. 2 (1951).

Powicke, Sir Maurice: "Sir Henry Spelman and the Concilia," in *Proceedings of the British Academy*, vol. XVI. London, 1930.

Ranke, Leopold von: *History of England in the Seventeenth Century*. Oxford, 1875.

Robertson, D. B.: *The Religious Foundations of Leveller Democracy*. New York: Columbia University Press, 1951.

Romeo, Rosario: *Il Risorgimento in Sicilia*. Bari: Laterza, 1950.

Sabine, George H.: *A History of Political Thought*. New York: Holt, 1950.

Tawney, R. H.: "Harrington's Interpretation of His Age," in *Proceedings of the British Academy*, vol. XXVII. London, 1941.

Templeman, Geoffrey: "Edward I and the Historians," in *Cambridge Historical Journal*, vol. X, no. 1 (1950).

Thompson, Faith: *Magna Carta: Its Role in the Making of the English Constitution, 1300–1629*. Minneapolis: University of Minnesota Press, 1948.

Trevor-Roper, H. R.: "The Gentry, 1540–1640," in *Economic History Review Supplements*, no. 1. Cambridge University Press, 1954.

Van Norden, Linda: "Peiresc and the English Scholars," in *Huntington Library Quarterly*, vol. XII, no. 4 (1948–9).

————: "Sir Henry Spelman on the Chronology of the English Society of Antiquaries," *Huntington Library Quarterly*, vol. XIII, no. 2 (1949–50).

Viard, P. E.: *André Alciat*. Paris, 1926.

Woodhouse, A. S. P.: *Puritanism and Liberty*. London: Dent, 1938.

Wright, H. G.: *The Life and Writings of Arthur Hall of Grantham*. Manchester University Press, 1919.

Zagorin, Perez: *A History of Political Thought During the English Revolution*. London: Routledge and Kegan Paul, 1954.

A SELECTION OF BOOKS AND ARTICLES ON RELATED TOPICS, CHIEFLY SUBSEQUENT TO THE FIRST EDITION.

Bailyn, Bernard (ed.): *Pamphlets of the American Revolution*, vol. 1. Cambridge, Mass.: Harvard University Press, 1965.

Bibliography

Baron, Hans: *The Crisis of the Early Italian Renaissance,* rev. ed. Princeton University Press, 1966.

Bennett, G. V.: *White Kennett, 1660–1728: Bishop of Peterborough.* London: S.P.C.K., 1957.

Colbourn, H. Trevor: *The Lamp of Experience: Whig History and the Intellectual Origins of the American Revolution.* Chapel Hill: University of North Carolina Press, 1966.

De Caprariis, Vittorio: *Propaganda e Pensiero Politico in Francia durante le Guerre di Religione, 1559–1572.* Naples: E.S.I., 1959.

Ferguson, Arthur B.: *The Articulate Citizen and the English Renaissance.* Durham, N.C.: Duke University Press, 1965.

_____: "Reginald Pecock and the Renaissance Sense of History," in *Studies in the Renaissance,* vol. XIII (1966).

Forbes, Duncan (ed.): *Adam Ferguson: An Essay on the History of Civil Society.* Edinburgh University Press, 1966.

Franklin, Julian H.: *Jean Bodin and the Sixteenth-Century Revolution in the Methodology of Law and History.* New York: Columbia University Press, 1963.

Furley, O. W.: "The Whig Exclusionists: Pamphlet Literature in the Exclusion Campaign, 1679–81," in *Cambridge Historical Journal,* vol. XIII, no. 1 (1957).

Fussner, F. Smith: *The Historical Revolution, 1580–1640.* London: Routledge and Kegan Paul, 1962.

Giarrizzo, Giuseppe: *Hume politico e storico.* Turin: Einaudi, 1962.

Gilbert, Felix: *Machiavelli and Guicciardini: Politics and History in Sixteenth-Century Florence.* Princeton University Press, 1965.

Greenleaf, W. H.: *Order, Empiricism and Politics: Two Traditions of English Political Thought, 1500–1700.* London: Oxford University Press, 1962.

_____: "Filmer's Patriarchal History," in *The Historical Journal,* vol. IX, no. 2 (1966).

Haller, William: *Foxe's Book of Martyrs and the Elect Nation.* London: Jonathan Cape, 1963.

Hill, Christopher: *Intellectual Origins of the English Revolution.* Oxford: Clarendon Press, 1965.

Huppert, George: "The Renaissance Background of Historicism," in *History and Theory,* vol. V, no. 1 (1966).

Kelley, Donald R.: "Historia Integra: Francois Baudouin and His Conception of History," in *Journal of the History of Ideas,* vol. XXV, no. 1 (1964).

_____: "Legal Humanism and the Sense of History," in *Studies in the Renaissance,* vol. XIII (1966).

Lamont, William M.: *Marginal Prynne.* London: Routledge and Kegan Paul, 1963.

Laslett, Peter (ed.): *John Locke: Two Treatises on Government.* Cambridge University Press, 1960.

Lucas, Paul: "On Edmund Burke's Doctrine of Prescription: or, An Appeal

Bibliography

from the New to the Old Lawyers," paper delivered to the 1965 convention of the American Historical Association.

Macpherson, C. B.: *The Political Theory of Possessive Individualism: Hobbes to Locke.* Oxford: Clarendon Press, 1962.

Maffei, D.: *Gli Inizi dell' umanesimo giuridico.* Milan: Giuffre, 1956.

Piano Mortari, V.: *Diritto Romano e diritto nazionale in Francia nel secolo XVI.* Milan: Giuffre, 1962.

Pocock, J. G. A.: "Burke and the Ancient Constitution: A Problem in the History of Ideas," in *The Historical Journal,* vol. III, no. 2 (1960).

—————: "The Origins of Study of the Past: A Comparative Approach," in *Comparative Studies in Society and History,* vol. IV, no. 2 (1962).

—————: "The History of Political Thought: A Methodological Approach," in *Philosophy, Politics and Society: Second Series* (eds. Peter Laslett and W. G. Runciman). Oxford: Basil Blackwell, 1963.

—————: "Machiavelli, Harrington and English Political Ideologies in the Eighteenth Century," in *The William and Mary Quarterly,* 3rd series, vol. XXII, no. 4 (1965).

—————: "The Onely Politician: Machiavelli, Harrington and Felix Raab," in *Historical Studies: Australia and New Zealand,* vol. 12, no. 46 (1966).

Pole, J. R.: *Political Representation in England and the Origins of the American Republic.* New York: St. Martin's Press, 1966.

Raab, Felix: *The English Face of Machiavelli: A Changing Interpretation, 1500–1700.* London: Routledge and Kegan Paul; Toronto: University of Toronto Press, 1964.

Robbins, Caroline: *The Eighteenth-Century Commonwealthman.* Cambridge, Mass.: Harvard University Press, 1959.

Salmon, J. H. M.: *The French Religious Wars and English Political Thought.* Oxford: Clarendon Press, 1959.

Skinner, Quentin: "History and Ideology in the English Revolution," in *The Historical Journal,* vol. VIII, no. 2 (1965).

Snow, Vernon F.: "The Concept of Revolution in Seventeenth-Century England," in *The Historical Journal,* vol. V, no. 2 (1962).

Stewart, John B.: *The Moral and Political Philosophy of David Hume.* New York: Columbia University Press, 1963.

Trevor-Roper, H. R.: Review essay: "Christopher Hill, *The Intellectual Origins of the English Revolution,*" in *History and Theory,* vol. V, no. 1 (1966).

Vann, Richard T.: "The Free Anglo-Saxons: A Historical Myth," in *Journal of the History of Ideas,* vol. XIX, no. 2 (1958).

Weston, Corinne C.: *The House of Lords in English Constitutional Theory.* London: Routledge and Kegan Paul, 1965.

Wormald, B. H. G.: *Clarendon: Politics, History and Religion, 1640–61.* Cambridge University Press, 1951.

INDEX

Index

Index

Index

Index

Index

Index

Index

THE NORTON LIBRARY HISTORY OF ENGLAND

General Editors

CHRISTOPHER BROOKE
Professor of Mediaeval History
University of Liverpool

and

DENIS MACK SMITH
Fellow of All Souls College, Oxford

ROMAN BRITAIN AND EARLY ENGLAND, 55 B.C.–A.D 871
Peter Hunter Blair

FROM ALFRED TO HENRY III, 871–1272
Christopher Brooke

THE LATER MIDDLE AGES, 1272–1485
George Holmes

THE TUDOR AGE, 1485–1603
Margaret Bowker

THE CENTURY OF REVOLUTION, 1603–1714
Christopher Hill

THE EIGHTEENTH CENTURY, 1714–1815
John B. Owen

FROM CASTLEREAGH TO GLADSTONE, 1815–1885
Derek Beales

MODERN BRITAIN, 1885–1955
Henry Pelling